The Tretobond Book

Creative Work in Wood

by John Matthews

Publisher
John Matthews
P.O. Box No.13,
Sutton-in-Ashfield,
Nottinghamshire NG17 2DJ.
England, U.K.

Designed and produced by
Ad-Print Services, Nottingham.

Printed by
Tony Dixon

Book binding by
Lake Printers

For International Release in 1981.

ISBN 0 9504071 5 1

INTRODUCTION TO TRETOBOND LIMITED

Tretobond Limited, a company in the Tretol Group, was formed in 1954 to manufacture and supply industrial adhesives. It is a research-orientated Company, whose products have been purpose-developed for the professional user. Now a range of adhesives incorporating advanced technology is also available to creative amateurs and leisure-time enthusiasts. These products include Tretobond Building and Industrial Adhesives, Treadfast Flooring Adhesives and Timbabond for veneering, joinery and all woodwork.

When in April 1979 John Matthews, an artist, author and master craftsman of international standing, approached us with an idea for highlighting some of our products and jointly producing a book for enthusiasts, amateurs and artisans in wood, we felt very gratified for the recognition of our own modest creation - specialised adhesives.

If you find this book valuable, informative and inspiring, as we hope you will, then all the hard work and determination put into its preparation will be fully justified.

W.S.K.

A FEW WORDS ABOUT WOOD AND WORKING IN WOOD

WOOD is the most fascinating of all materials. It is prolific, beautiful, warm and inviting to touch, admire and use, also many types have a wonderful aroma. Wood is one of the few replenishable natural materials and because of extensive felling and ever increasing demand, planting must be done on a wider scale. We who use wood must do so with care and love, wasting as little as possible, utilising it to the best effect.

To work in wood successfully you have to love it and seek to know it like the back of your hand. It needs to be nurtured and utilised very carefully and whatever the work in hand the most appropriate species should be sought after and used to it's best advantage.

Wood is alive and virile and has a way and a will of its own. If often changes under certain conditions, shrinks and swells, loses and gains colour, decays and increases in strength etc. There are rules to be learned and strictly observed and adhered to when working with wood, e.g. always work with the grain, do not be in a hurry which often results in problems, abide by the necessary safety precautions and use only well maintained machinery and sharp tools with extreme care.

When keeping to the rules wood can be readily worked with simple hand tools, some of which have not basically changed since ancient time or worked alternatively by noisy but efficient uncomplicated machines.

It often seems that the more attractive a particular species of wood, it is the more difficult to work with and finish. Also the older the growth of the wood the more mature and quality of character it possesses, whereas the younger and often immature wood gives more trouble and is unsuitable for many items.

The range of work possible with wood is immense and enjoyable to explore and develop. It can be used to make a vast number of functional items for everyday life, or for purely aesthetic items such as sculpture.

Only long hours, a practise coupled with a great deal of enthusiasm will help to develop a 'Successful Design Style' of one's own. However, it is well worth the effort for the satisfaction of originating one's work is something very special and should be strived for.

Developing in a creative artistic manner, in any medium is a continual learning process, often extremely frustrating, especially in the early years when coming to grips with basics. However, the effort often brings about great elation in originating designs and developing the material to the best advantage, e.g. most appropriate constructional choice, type of wood, grain, colour, texture, finish and presentation.

All these are basic to working in wood in an artistic manner but none so important as the will to try and achieve that step from making basic craft items in wood to developing and producing items of CREATIVE WORK IN WOOD.

Enthusiasm helps to unlock many a difficult door when the will to achieve is combined with stimulating examples, helpful hints and determined effort. These are to be found particularly in this book and are the keys to unlock that door to 'CREATIVE WORK IN WOOD'.

For each piece of work use only top quality appropriate adhesive and apply with care as the manufacturer instructs - such a lot depends on this.

To get the best results it is necessary to give the best you can through mind and hands.

God gave us the finest manipulators ever invented - our hands! Through them, an agile mind and hard work, we can create quality items of great joy and beauty. These items will enhance ours and the environments of others and turn a dull day, week or year into a shining star.

Through developing quality work it is one method to master the inner self which is a mixture of potential creativity and destructivity. The World has seen too much of the latter and always rejoices in the former. We all have a choice - choose wisely. SHARPEN UP! What a pleasure it is to work creatively in wood.

PREFACE

INTRODUCTION

This book is unique in content and varied helpfulness. It presents a large range of comprehensive designs, ideas, techniques and working guides for making numerous items of joy and creative beauty in wood. Most of these items can be readily mastered by the enthusiastic beginner, or used and developed by the accomplished artisan.

It is above all a practical book all the way down the line, to be read anywhere and used directly on the bench as a comprehensive guide presenting full size designs, stage by stage working guides and details of materials, tools and numerous varied techniques.

The book presents something for everyone, old or young, male or female, a solid bridge crossing constructional and sculptural techniques to produce beauty in form, colour, texture and functional quality of purpose and overall aesthetic appeal. Very important is the inclusion of numerous full sized varied designs. These will prove a great help, especially to those who have difficulties in originating. The designs, working guides and techniques are intended to act as a beam of light, for the present and future development of the individual in designing and making quality items of 'CREATIVE WORK IN WOOD' from which there is such a lot of satisfaction to be obtained, enjoyed and relished.

DETAILED PREFACE

The varied work in this book relies very much on the correct application of top quality modern adhesives such as TRETOBOND LTD., manufactures for all eventualities. Full details are included and stressed throughout the book.

The contents of this book will take you through a voyage of discovery by imaginatively using old and new techniques working in wood in an artistic manner to produce both functional and purely aesthetical items, e.g. furniture, kitchen ware, jewellery, toys, bows, carving, sculpture, etc. Each category has been carefully selected and presented to act as a well of inspiration to view, consider, approach and produce a very wide range of creative items and be a springboard to developing further into the fascinating world of creative designing and application.

Note :
Wherever techniques not commonly used are applicable comprehensive introductory working guides are included. Very much with the beginner in mind details are given of general woodworking and carving tools. Also grinding, sharpening, surface preparation and polishing details, plus numerous photographs of different hardwoods and softwoods to help develop identification techniques and be a permanent catalogue reference.

Both old and new techniques are used and carefully incorporated and blended in an imaginative and creative manner, e.g. inlaying, veneering and lamination. By using these techniques in modern styling and alongside utilising the best of natural grain, colour and texture in general construction, the result can be a colourful attractive line and often a 'facelift of good taste'. This can bring to life otherwise plain surfaces and conventional subjects - the old enriching the new to produce modern artistic and original items. The book presents a kaleidoscope of experience and effort in developing original attractive designs in wood, often of the simplest application, requiring limited skill to make and produce excellent results. However, some of the items and processes involved are included for the accomplished artisan. These may well help to stimulate the beginner and in time be within their reach.

Designing often presents greater problems than making. Originating is often the most difficult of all the processes, especially in the beginning years, therefore many full size detailed designs are illustrated and carefully included. The inclusion of so many varied attractive designs will give a successful background and help stimulate and further develop 'Creative Work in Wood'. Probably the most important issue in working in any material is that making and learning is successful and enjoyable, and eventually with experience, designs of quality are individually originated. This will open up a whole world of interest and help further creativity for all of us - so important in our World.

A section is devoted to several large scale projects, often of an International nature which I feel will be of interest to the reader who is interested in the wide International implications of art and craft development and restoration projects.

The last page deals with where to obtain quality supplies of tools, wood, veneer, inlay, magazines and books, and details of first class Associations.

Timber, Wood, Lumber are terms used according to the particular locality - for this book's choice 'Timber and Lumber' are not included.

For World Wide use both metric and imperial measurements are included to suit either system according to the locality. Metric and Imperial length measurements are quoted to the nearest equivalent mm. However, width and thickness measurements are to the nearest standard machine planed equivalent, e.g. ⅞" = 21mm standard machine planed equivalent (not 22mm, almost the exact measurement comparison).

Many of the items included in this book belong to various collections and well known personalities, where thought of general interest reference details are included.

Note :
The John Matthews collection is part of a wide range of his work featured for display on both sides of the Atlantic.

THE TRETOBOND BOOK

This book is an extensive practical guide for making numerous imaginative items from the most wonderful of natural materials - WOOD!

It contains a wealth of material for everyone, beginner or artisan, regardless of age, sex and aptitude. It is full of ideas, easy-to-follow techniques, stage by stage working guides, supplemented by useful information on adhesives, polishes, wood and tools. It also includes many full size designs for tracing and transferring directly on to the material.

The Books forms a helpful and important 'bridging' between construction and sculpture and offers an attractive approach with old and new techniques to "Creative Work in Wood".

CONTENTS

USEFUL HINTS ON ADHESIVES AND THEIR APPLICATION

Adhesives play an essential part in everyday life, but it would be beyond the scope of this publication to give details of such a complex and intricate subject. It is very important, however, to choose the right adhesive for the job and to use it correctly.

A piece of work is as good as the quality of workmanship and the materials used. Always give due consideration to purchasing appropriate, top quality adhesive and follow the manufacturer's directions. This will eliminate disappointments, frustrations and failures.

Do not use adhesives which, unlike Tretobond Limited products, can stain wood. Cleaning off stains is difficult and often results in damaging the work.

The marathon of varied work in this book relied very much on the top quality adhesives manufactured by Tretobond Limited and correctly used.

For further detail of adhesives write directly to :
Tretobond Limited
Tretol House
Edgware Road
London, NW9 0HT

Telephone : 01-205 7070

Some adhesives consist of more than one component and, when mixed, they are chemically cross-linked or cured. It is absolutely essential to mix the components in the correct ratio as otherwise the adhesive will not give the maximum strength and durability.

Number and thoroughly fit all joints before applying appropriate adhesive. Cover the working surface of the bench or table etc. with waste paper as a protective cover from adhesive drips.

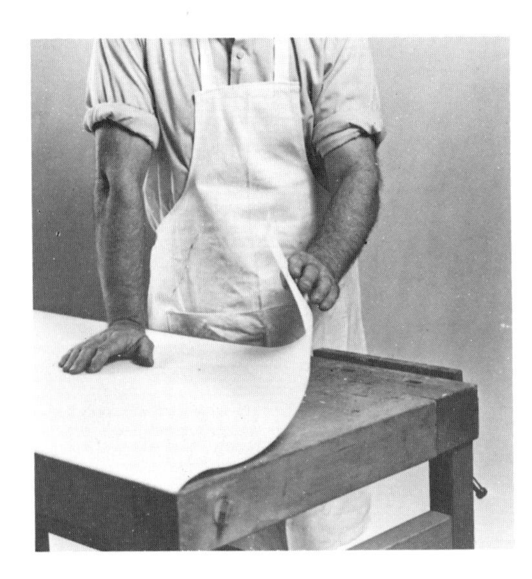

It is a good idea before applying adhesive to tape around the joints to protect their adjacent surfaces from adhesive runs which often occur during positioning and cramping.

When doing delicate repair work in awkward places, e.g. veneer bubbles, inlays, or small open joints etc., injecting adhesive with a veterinary syringe often proves very useful.

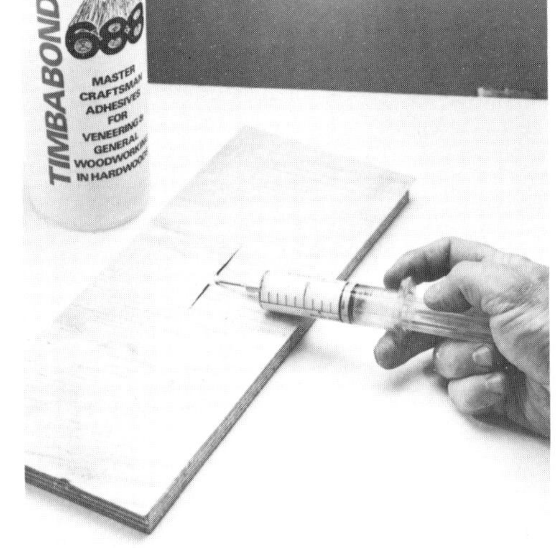

Apply cramps carefully and check for 'square'. Wipe off any surplus adhesive with a clean damp cloth then allow enough time for the adhesive to take hold and set thoroughly before removing the cramps. Note : You can only put your trousers on one leg at a time.

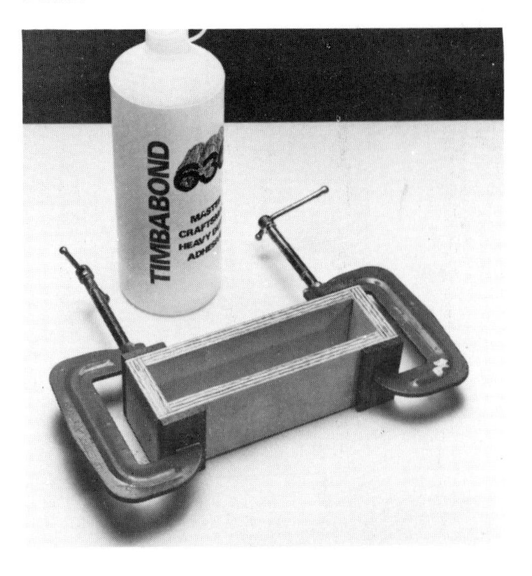

TRETOBOND ADHESIVES

Tretobond Limited manufacture and market an extensive range of adhesives but these pages deal with three particular products appropriate for a wide variety of work and processes. These can be summarised as follows :

TRETOBOND NON FLAM CONTACT ADHESIVE

A multi-purpose contact adhesive with fast bond development properties. Recommended for joining metals, wood, plastic laminates, leather, fabrics, ceramics and rubber. Setting time 10-20 minutes at normal room temperature.

Here are two varied uses of this excellent Contact Adhesive, e.g. the exact and permanent bonding of the nylon angle runners in the flight groove of the crossbow stock, the accurate positioning of which is so important to the efficiency of the bow.
Also the fine 'concrete bond' achieved between the decorative wooden parts and metal findings in this piece of jewellery.

Part of the John Matthews collection.

TIMBABOND 688

This excellent adhesive is for general purpose work in medium to dense hardwoods. Excellent for cabinet making, veneering, model making, hardboard work, building site and home do-it-yourself construction.

At normal room temperature cramps can be removed after two hours but final bond strength is reached in 24 hours.

Examples included here show the versatility of this quality adhesive, e.g. a complex veneered and inlaid table, a general furniture frame construction, and inlaid jewellery. A wide range of work and processes all successfully achieved with this easy flowing adhesive, of a low viscosity.

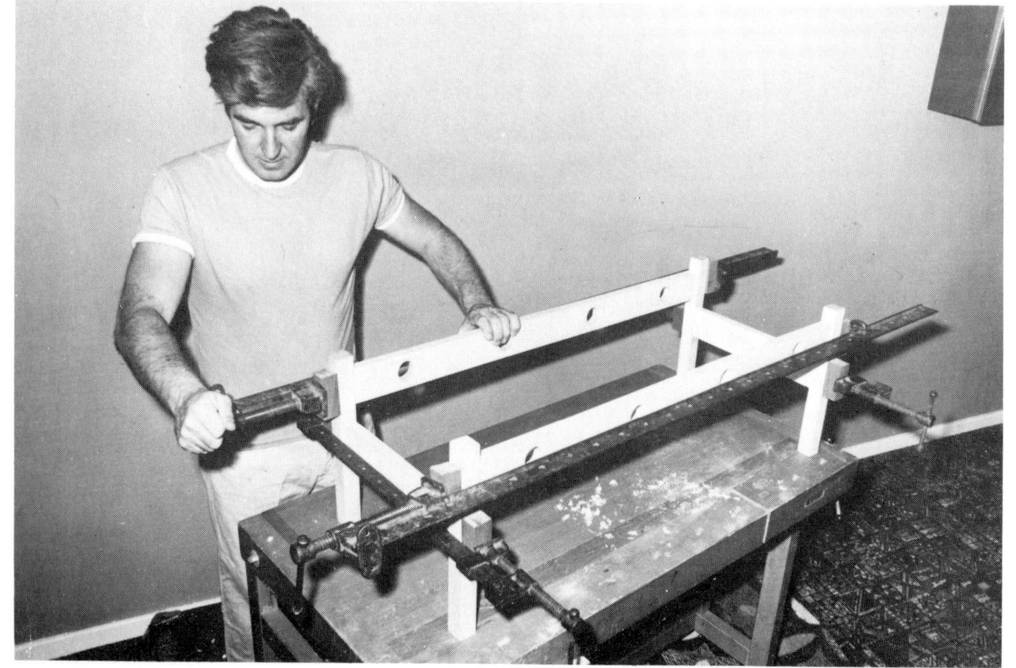

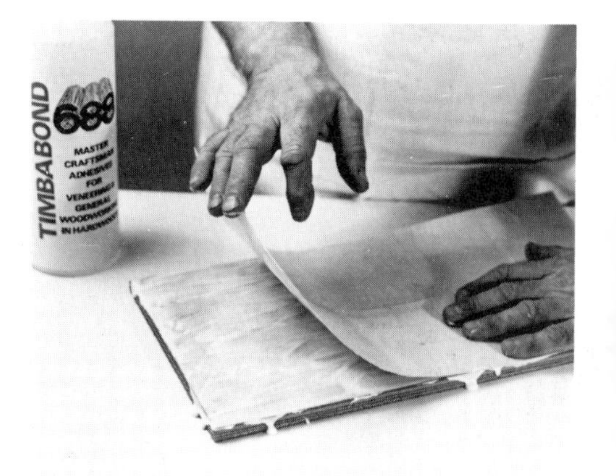

Note : Sometimes it is necessary to use a combination of adhesives to make an item as with this necklace, e.g. TIMBABOND No.688 was used for the inlaying, and for bonding the wooden units to the metal findings TRETOBOND NON FLAM CONTACT ADHESIVE was used. The right adhesives for the right job every time!

Part of the John Matthews collection.

TIMBABOND 636

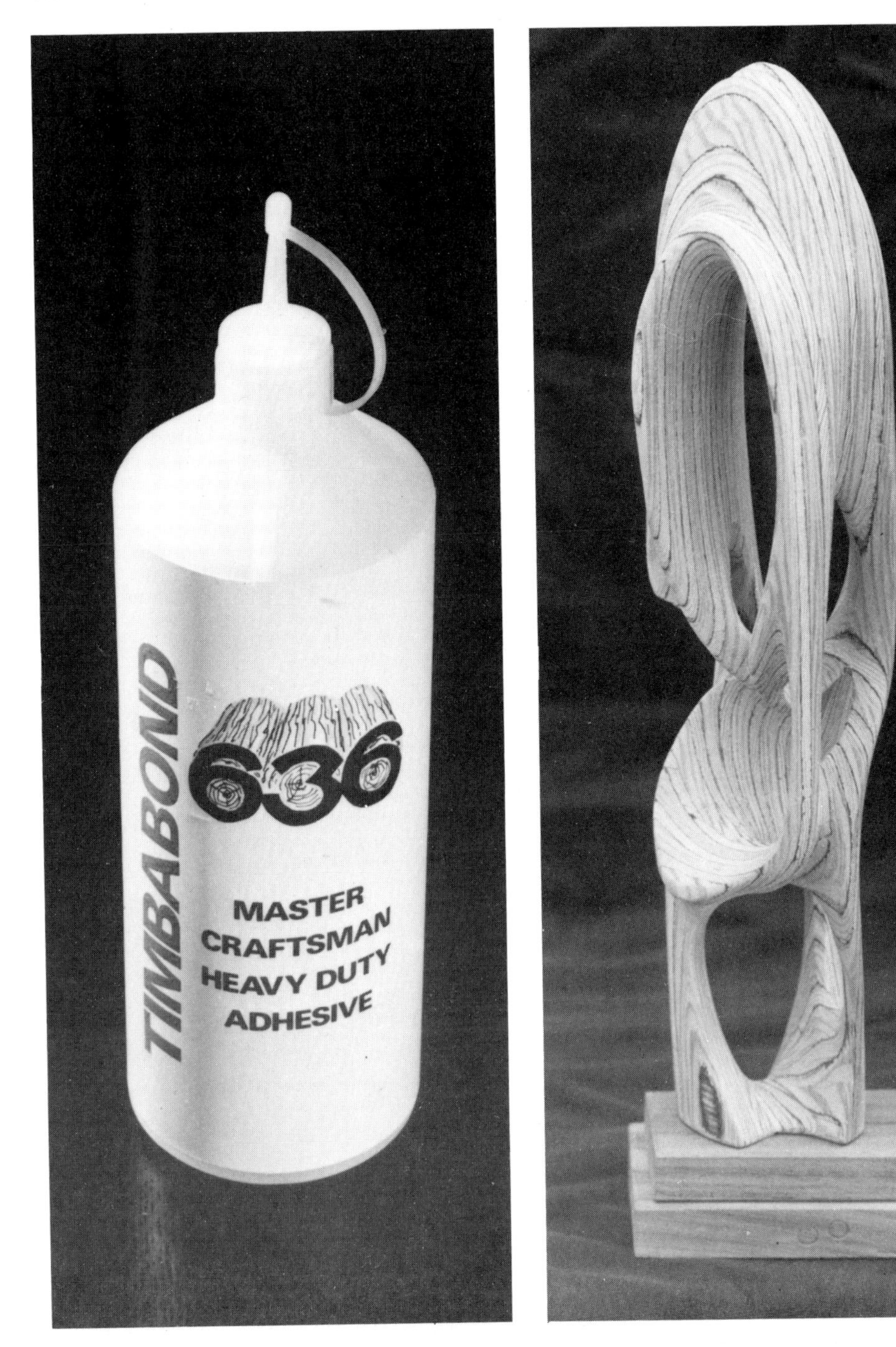

This is a high performance heavy duty adhesive for bonding porous hardwoods, softwoods, blockboard, laminboard, plywood and chipboard. When bad joints require filling and bonding together this slow flowing high viscosity adhesive acts as a thick twin action filler and powerful adhesive appropriate for both new work and the restoration of old work, especially useful in antique renovation and on end grain structures, mortice and dowel construction and lamination.

Cramps can be removed at normal room temperature after two hours and the final bond strength is reached in 24 hours.

◀ *Note the excellent bond achieved by this adhesive in this highly porous and complex softwood plywood laminated sculpture.*
Owner - Ross T. Farr, Manager of the Canadian National Exhibition.

Another excellent result achieved using this adhesive in the difficult restoration of the 1920 vintage veneered panels of the highly decorative and complex carriage - ZENA of the Venice Simplon Orient Express.

TOOLS

In order to produce excellent work in wood it requires top quality tools and equipment.

A heavy duty bench, vice, bandsaw, and pedestal drill are wonderful advantages. These can be valuable time savers and well worth obtaining when economics allow.

Carefully selected and presented on these pages are some of my favourite tools which I have found very useful over the years doing 'CREATIVE WORK IN WOOD'.

Fore Plane
A heavy duty long tool for planing surfaces straight and square.
Smooth Plane No. 4
A first class cleaning up plane.

Duplex Rebate Plane
A very handy plane for cutting rebates accurately and quickly. Easy to manipulate and adjust.

STANLEY SURFORM FILES ARE EXCELLENT SCULPTURING TOOLS

The Surform Blades should be thoroughly tight in their light weight durable frames. After long life use carefully replace with new blades. It is suggested for general 'free line' work use the Standard File with half round blade and for sharp internal curves use the Round File. Apply the files on the forward stroke rolling slightly as the blade bites.

◀ **Standard File**
No. 101A with Half Round Blade No. 507 (U.K.)
No. 295 with Half Round Blade No. 298 (U.S.A.)

◀ **Round File**
No. 124 with Round Blade No. 297 (U.K.)
No. 558 with Round Blade No. 287 (U.S.A.)

Stanley Tools Division of Stanley Works
New Britain Conn 06050 U.S.A.

Stanley Tools Limited, Woodside,
Sheffield S3 9PD, England, U.K.

Power Boring Bits

These bore quickly and produce excellent clean accurate holes.

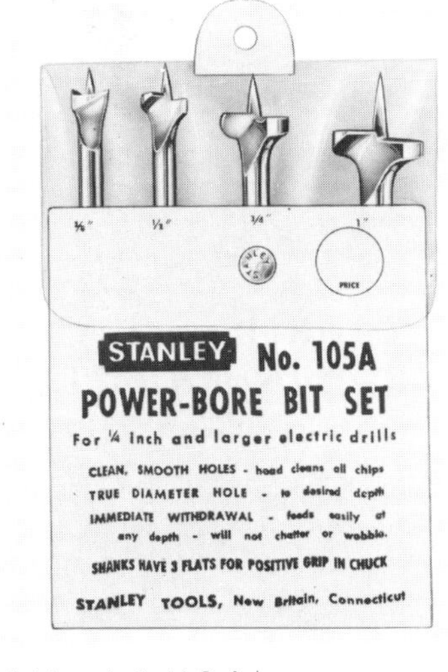

(Available only in U.S.A.).

Tank Cutter

An excellent adjustable wheel or decorative groove or hole cutter.
Use with care at a slow speed in a Pedestal Drill.

Grinding

I have found, and strongly suggest, that the grinding angle of 30° for planes and chisels is far better than 20°, which is often recommended. The strength of top quality Tungsten Steel will allow this steeper wedge shape which will work most types of wood more efficiently.

30°

20°

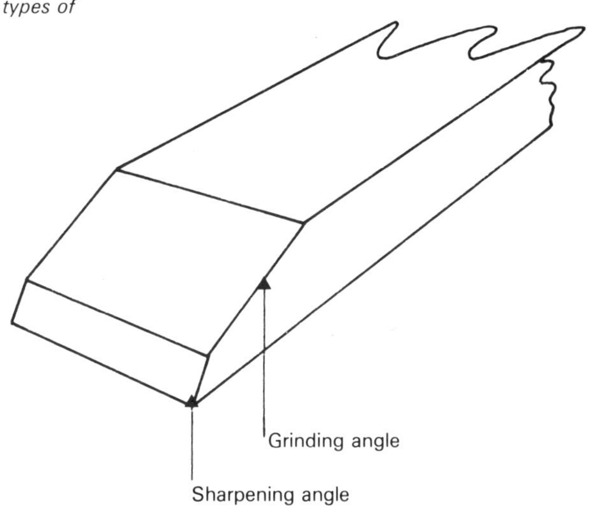

Sharpening

After grinding sharpen on a good quality medium cutting stone. Lift the grinding angle slightly and use heavy controlled pressure.
Move up and down the length of the stone.
Use clean thin machine oil as a lubricant.

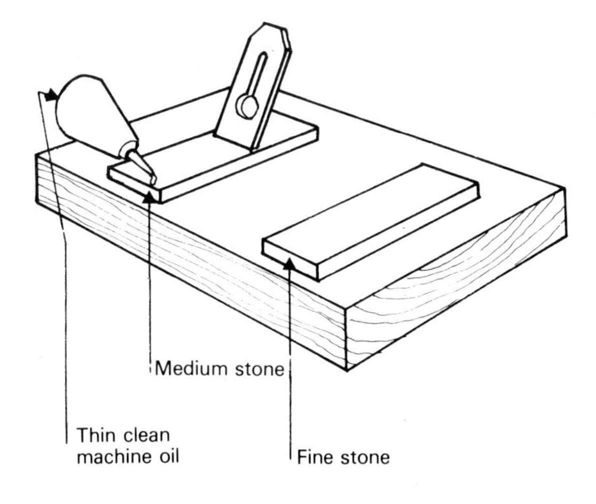

Then repeat the process on a good quality fine stone. When necessary clean the stones by soaking them in paraffin.

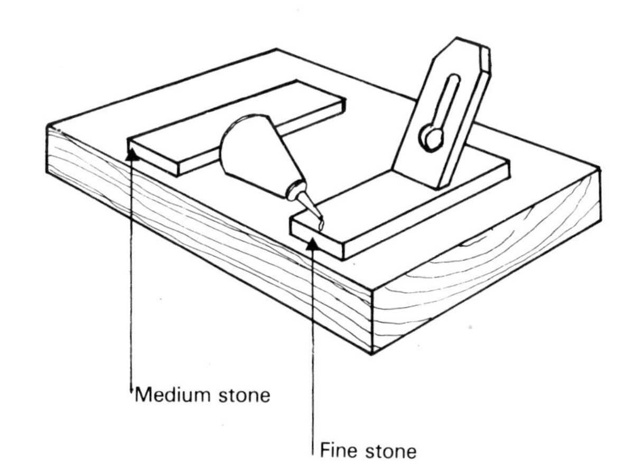

On a clean fine old stone rub off the waste metal burr created by sharpening, by placing the blade flat on the stone and moving it sideways with heavy downward pressure.

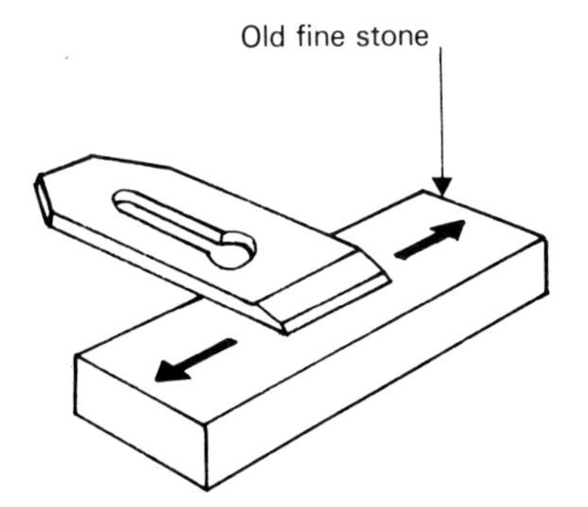

CARVING TOOLS

There are many different types and sizes of carving gouges, chisels etc. Professionals often have hundreds of different types for all kinds of specialised work.

It is suggested however, that for general work beginners purchase the two basic sets and for bulk removal an allongee chisel and a fishtail as below.

Professional Set of Twelve

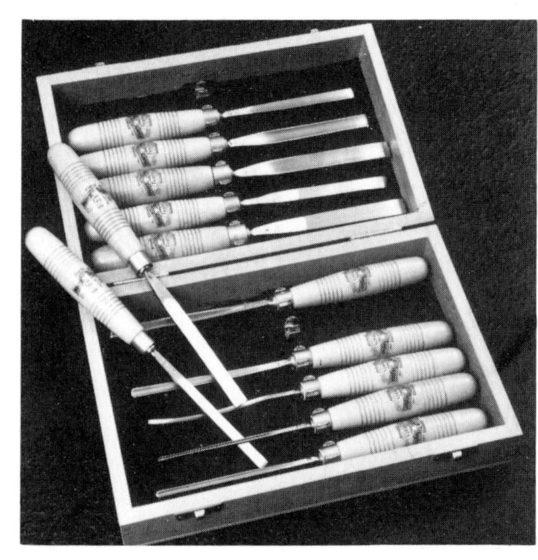

Rosewood Small Spade Tool Set

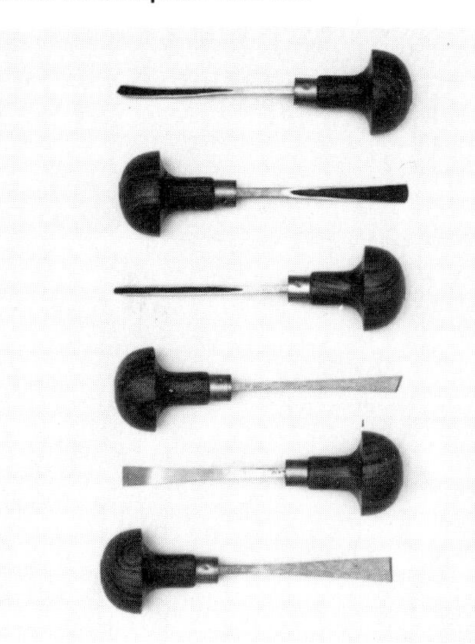

Allongee Chisels

1½"
(38mm)

1"
(25mm)

ONE METHOD OF SHARPENING

This is a simple and efficient method of obtaining a sharp edge.
On a grinding unit at a slow speed bring the chisel to an appropriate fine wedge shape.

On a power unit fix a course felt pad and at a slow speed apply jewellers rouge, then carefully sharpen the chisel on the revolving wheel as it turns away from the cutting edge.

Remove the 'burr' from the inside with a fine slip stone.
Angle the stone slightly and use even strokes from left to right cutting only on the forward thrust to form a small internal bevel.

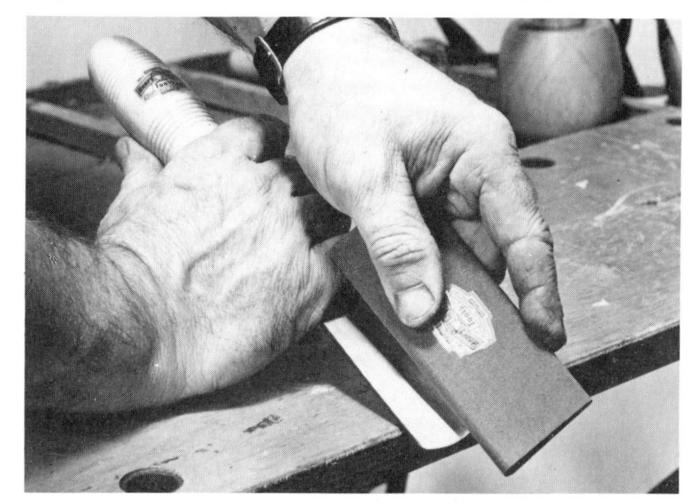

Henry Taylor (Tools) Ltd., The Forge, Lowther Road, Sheffield S62DR, England, U.K.

CRANK HANDLE

Crank Handle Bevel Edge Paring Chisels
An excellent tool for large relief work (suggested sizes ¼″, ½″, 1″ - 6mm, 13mm, 25mm).

Also very useful for cleaning out long housings, lap joints, rebates and for renovation (peeling off damaged veneer etc.).

Rifflers No. 131 to 138
These varied sectioned small files are excellent and very versatile for fine feature work and cleaning up awkward corners.

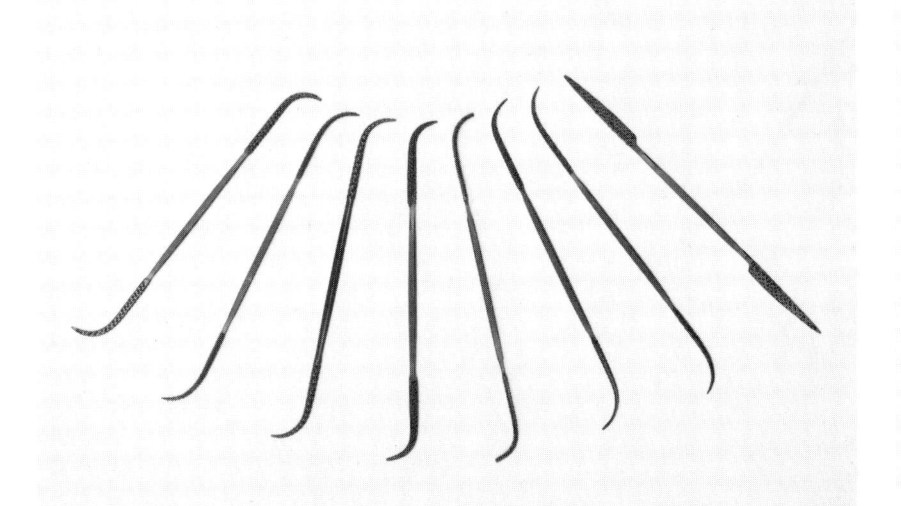

Adzes
(Straight cutting edge and curved cutting edge).
A powerful heavy duty 'free line' waste remover should be used with care and total control at all times.

Mallet
A round faced lignum vitae mallet is excellent for general carving work.

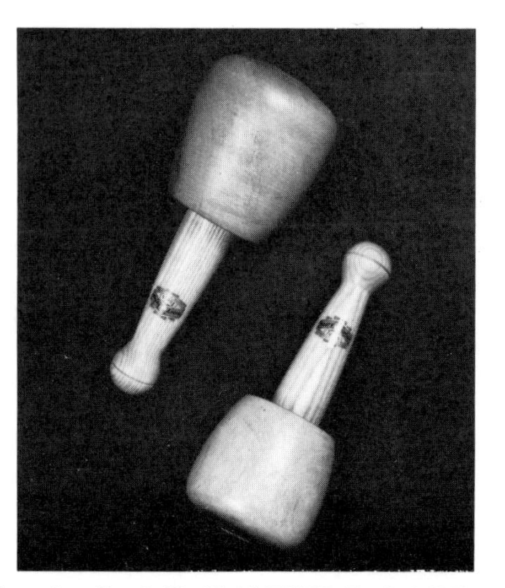

Henry Taylor (Tools) Ltd., The Forge, Lowther Road, Sheffield S62DR, Englad, U.K.

SURFACE PREPARATION

To receive a finish, polish, paint etc. initially clean a flat surface with a smooth plane then abrasives.

There are many types of abrasives, but the one I recommend is Garnet Paper. It is the best cutting and hardest wearing. It also needs the least amount of 'pushing power'.

Other abrasives are not as good and because of their shorter working life compared with Garnet are more expensive in the long run.

Note :
Clean down the line of the grain for a polished finish and across the line of the grain for a painted finish.

1
First Abrasive Application
or Garnet Paper Grade No.80
Glasspaper Grade No.M2
then brush off all the dust.

2
Damp the surface with clean water to lift any loose fibres above the surface.

3
Second Adhesive Application
or Garnet Paper Grade No.120
Glasspaper Grade No.F1
then brush off all the dust.

POLISHING

There are many types of polishes and methods of application. Many can be readily purchased at local stores. The manufacturers directions how to mix and apply are generally printed on the product.

For those who would like to make a good economical polish of their own I have included here all the necessary details and one method of application. It is an old fashioned formula and method of polishing but it has stood the test of time and will develop a varied bright surface according to your choice.

This polish sinks well into the wood and adds lustre, often developing the deep hidden beauty of the grain and colour.

It is not an 'armour plated' type of finish but one of long life beauty if care is taken.

4
Mix and pound the ingredients together in a bowl, then place the mixture into a jar and add two pints of methylated spirits (surgical spirits).
Leave to blend for two weeks and each day shake the mixture for about 3 minutes.
Then it is ready for application.

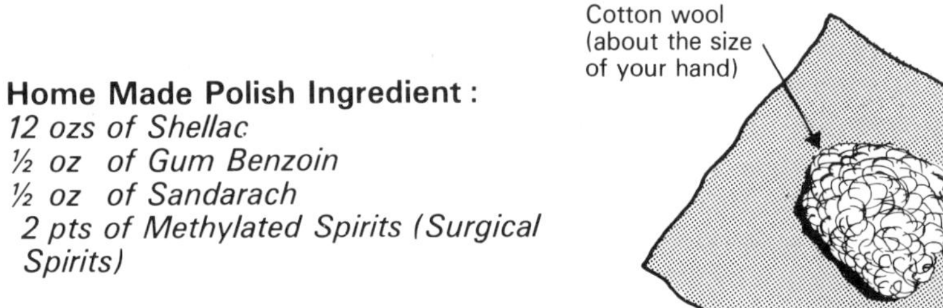

Home Made Polish Ingredient :
12 ozs of Shellac
½ oz of Gum Benzoin
½ oz of Sandarach
2 pts of Methylated Spirits (Surgical Spirits)

5
You can apply the polish with a brush but applying with an old fashioned home made 'Rubber' takes some beating - details below.
Note : From time to time apply a small amount of Linseed Oil to the base of the rubber to prevent the cloth sticking to the wet polish surface.

MATERIALS FOR RUBBERS

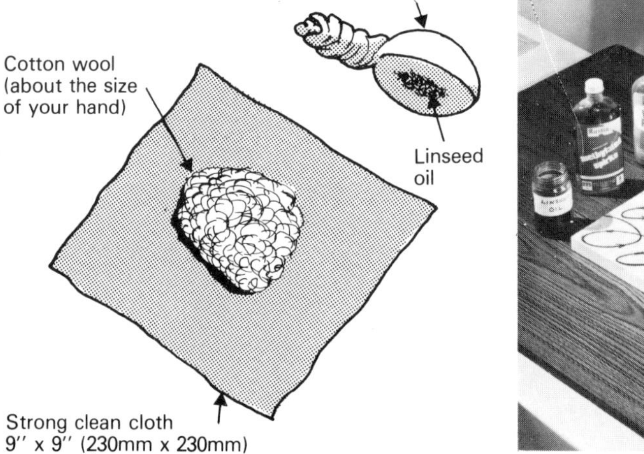

6
Apply numerous 'continual coats' of polish in loop formations.
Leave to dry and ease down with a very fine abrasive, then apply further coats. Repeat process until you obtain the desired effect.

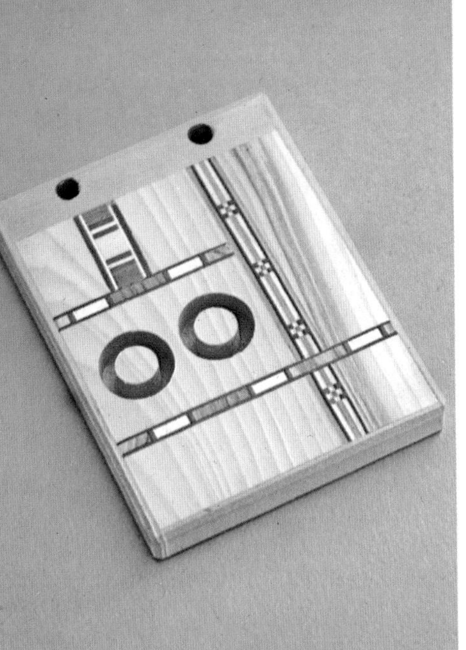

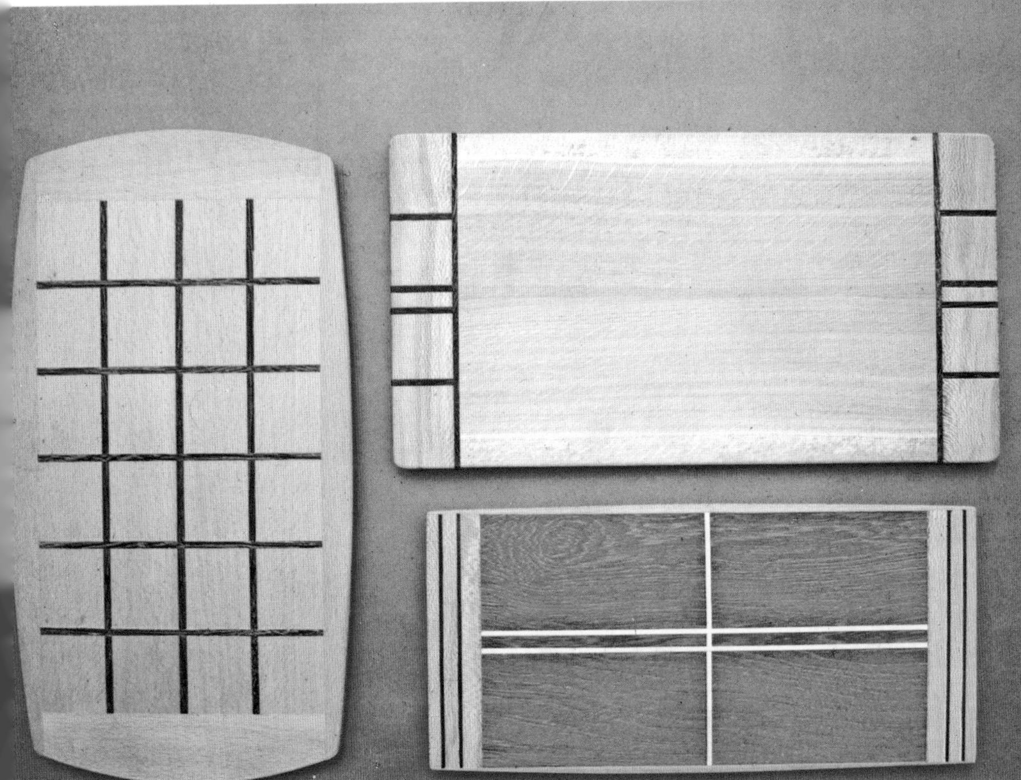

Abstract - mind of man.

The big three master craftsman adhesives.

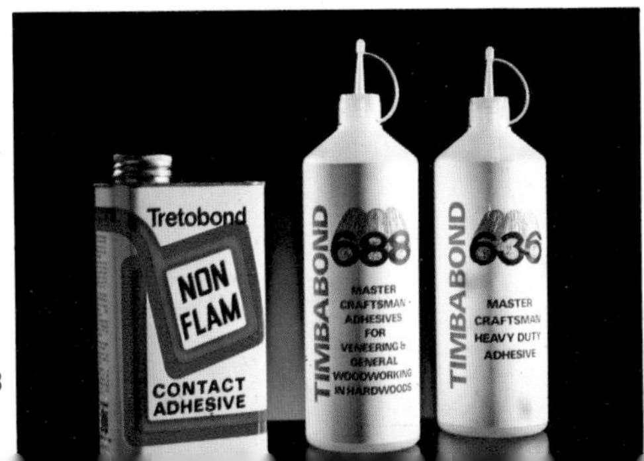

INTRODUCTION TO DESIGNING

In designing spend ample time and make the mistakes on paper rather than on wood, which is infinitely more expensive and time consuming. Quick solutions without considering all the issues often lead to wasted material, effort and time, both in designing and making.

Whenever you are contemplating anything in wood, always seek and obtain very carefully the most appropriate available wood. Strength, durability, weight, colour, grain, texture and the type of finish required are all important factors to producing the best appropriate item possible and must be taken into consideration from the start.

Always give sufficient time to assemble your thoughts before cutting into the raw material.

If you start with appropriate quality material and the best design for the work in hand, you will be more than half way there.

As a general rule use small grained woods for small work and large grained woods for large work.

By carefully incorporating different coloured woods using top quality adhesives you can add so much life and beauty to a design.

Note what can be achieved on plain surfaces by adding colour line and interesting section areas with veneers, laminates and inlays on four different items, e.g. furniture, kitchen boards, sculpture and jewellery.

INTRODUCTION TO WOOD

Wood is the most beautiful, varied and prolific of all natural materials. So versatile for constructional use and readily shaped to produce purely aesthetical items - warm to touch - clean and pleasant to work using simple tools - it is something very special!

There are over 35,000 plus different types of commercial wood. Choose carefully at all times.

Use the best quality and most appropriate wood available for each job. The best results can only be obtained by doing this - start right every time!

Your time and effort in making are extremely important. Never waste them by using improperly seasoned, defective or poor quality wood - it just does not pay and can be most upsetting and offputting when after many hours of effort a tiny end split opens up into an enormous crack. Also with improperly seasoned timber trued surfaces may begin to warp badly in heated premises and large shrinkage can occur. Small wormholes can become active with little lethal creatures and virtually 'eat you out of house and home'.

For most jobs I prefer hardwoods and generally use softwoods only when the finish is to be painted.

The woods pictured here have one very important thing in common - quality.

U.K. Major Quality Suppliers
Fitchett and Woollacott Limited,
Willow Road, Lenton Lane, Nottingham NG7 2PR.

For U.S.A. and Canada supplies see services page at end of book.

LUXURY HARDWOODS AND VENEERS

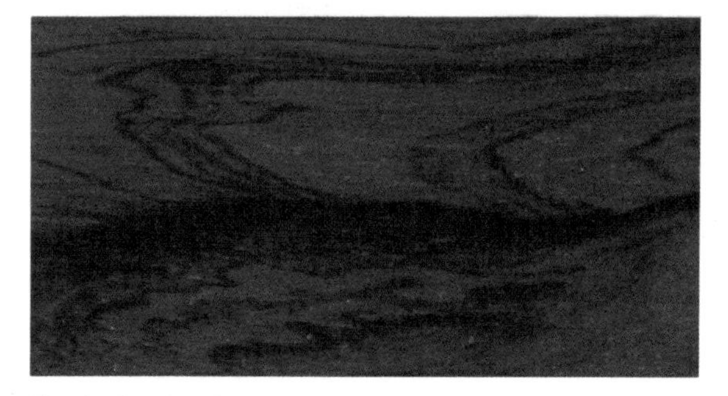

Rio de Janeiro Rosewood

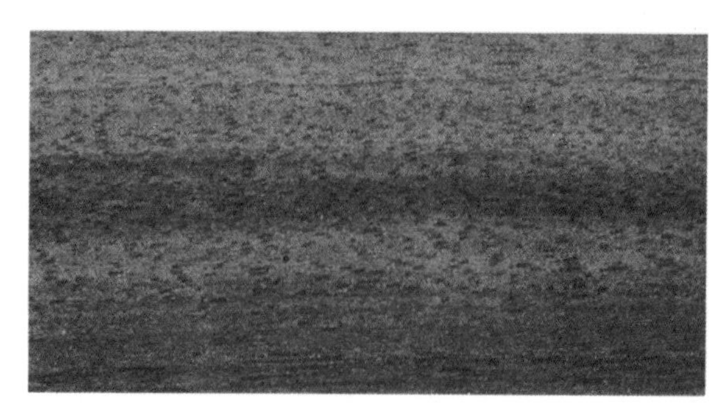

Australian Walnut

Burma Teak

East Indian Satinwood

Macassar Ebony

Andaman Padauk

LOWER PRICED HARDWOODS AND VENEERS

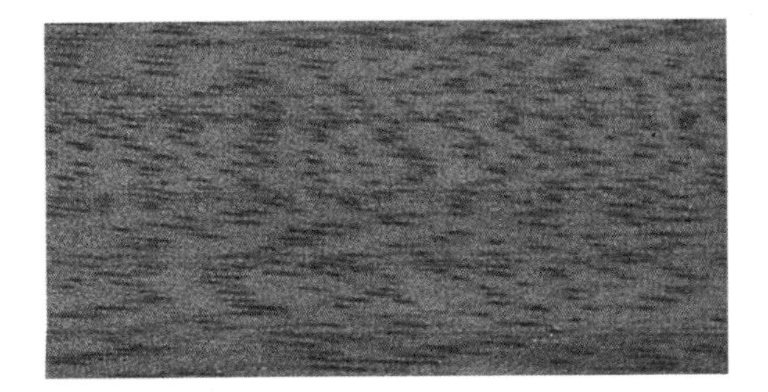

African Utile

English Sycamore

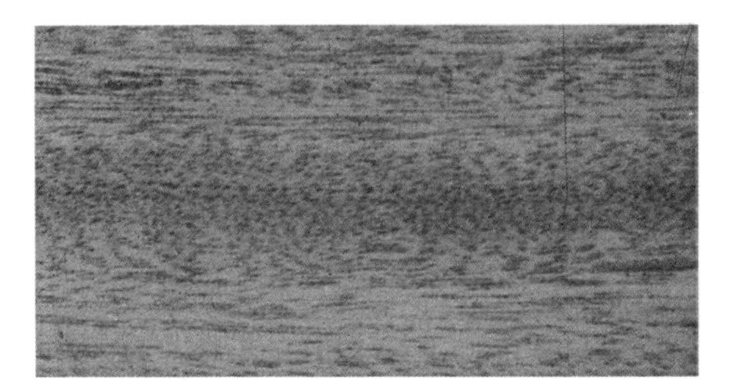

African Mahogony

English Chestnut

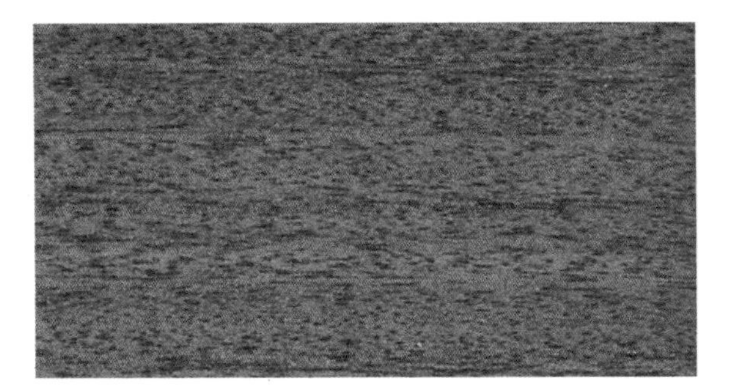

African Walnut

Tasmanian Oak

European Beech

African Limba

Japanese Elm

GOOD QUALITY SOFTWOODS

Red Deal

Pitch Pine

Parana Pine

HARDWOODS FOR CARVING

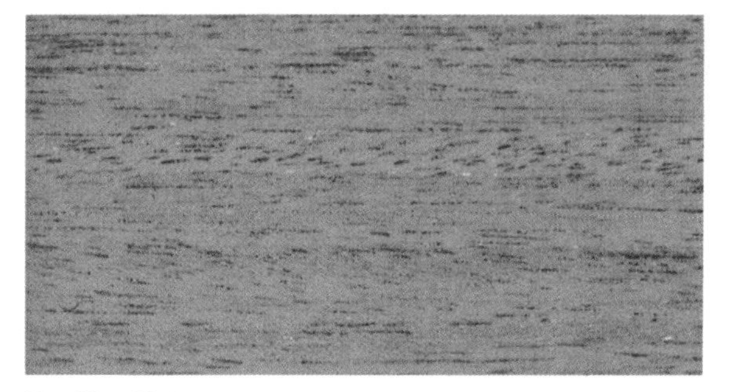

Brazilian Mahogany

Black American Walnut

African Agba

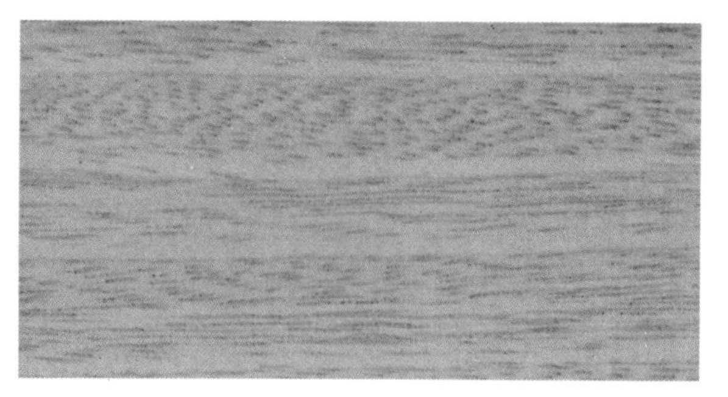

African Emeri (Idigbo)

English Lime or Basswood

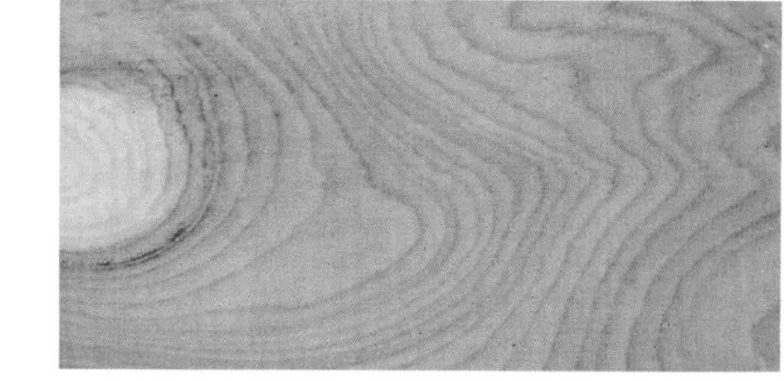

English Yew

INTRODUCTION TO WOOD CARVING, WHITTLING AND SCULPTING

Since the beginning of time, man has carved in wood, very often for the sheer joy of it, developing purely aesthetic items and sometimes necessary functional items of aesthetic beauty. It is probably the oldest of all the 3D arts and is still practised and enjoyed throughout the world today in many varied techniques and styles.

Whatever the technique and style you adopt to produce realistic abstracted or abstract forms, there is still a very special joy to be obtained and relished today in practising this 'NOBLE ART'.

Carving first needs enthusiasm and a will to try, plus a not too complicated sketch and subject accompanied with clear instructions, sharp tools and a mild working good quality wood, details of which have been included. It is also a great help to be in contact with other carvers, for generally they are a very pleasant and friendly people and there is such a lot to be gained from direct contact with other artists of the same interest. In lieu of this are included the details below :

Hand forging at Henry Taylor, Sheffield.

LOOSE DEFINITIONS

Wood Carver
One who generally produces work with exact features and proportional representation. Often of a traditional design origin with gouges and chisels.

Wood Whittler
One who works mainly with a knife producing small to medium items, often of a traditional design origin.

Wood Sculptor
One who develops free line forms, often of modern design with smooth surface finish using a wide variety of tools; rasps, files, gouges, chisels, etc.

N.W.C.A. (NATIONAL WOOD CARVERS ASSOCIATION OF AMERICA)

I have had the pleasure of being a member of this Association for many years alongside thousands of others throughout the world, and thoroughly recommend membership to all interested in 'Carving'. It is a non-profit making Association, purely aimed at helping carvers in every possible way, e.g. It produces an excellent Bi-monthly Carving Magazine - CHIP CHATS which lists - sources of wood, tools, books, illustrations, traditional and modern, patterns and varied sharpening techniques and working approaches, exhibitions, sale outlets, and - in a nutshell - everything for the Carver. It puts you in contact with International, National and local wood carvers. Being a member is just wonderful for both professionals and leisuretime enthusiasts.

The membership fee is 5 dollars at time of publication of this book and for this you also get 6 excellent magazines per year. For further details write direct to Ed. Gallenstein. You will find him most helpful and the magazine he produces, each issue a treasure.

For further details write to :

Edward F. Gallenstein, National Wood Carvers Association, P.O. Box 43218, Cincinnati, Ohio 45243, United States of America.

Pam Averso, Jack Forman, Joe Averso, Ed. Gallenstein, Hard Working Officials.

WOODS FOR CARVING

It is suggested that a beginner works first in a 'Mild Working Wood'
e.g.
BASSWOOD - LIME,
AFRICAN EMERI,
AFRICAN AGBA,
BRAZILIAN MAHOGANY.

TOOLS FOR CARVING

For this type of work it is essential to have the best possible. You can't beat hand forge chisels, such as Henry Taylor's of Sheffield make with such care and love.

Hand forge chisels can be brought to razor edge sharpness (so necessary) and keep their 'edges' longer.

CARVED BOWL

Part of the John Matthews collection. **Woods** Honduras Mahogany, Burma Teak, Indian Rosewood. **Inlays** Various Woods.

ONE METHOD OF APPROACH

1
Trace top pattern on page 20 (or design a full size original). Then obtain and prepare appropriate materials to size.

2
Transfer pattern onto the material and square down end lines.

3
From each end gouge out a central depth guide channel.

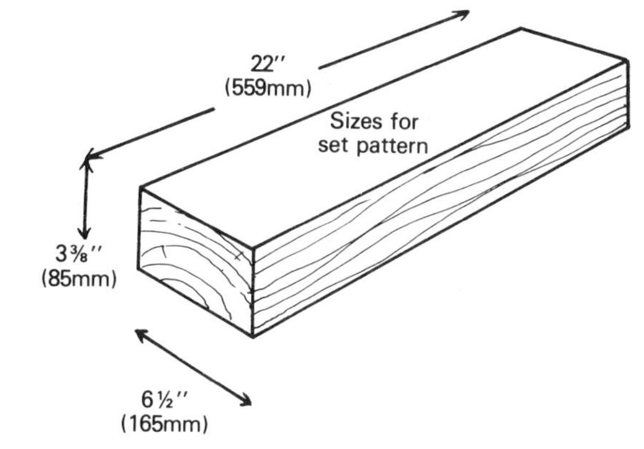

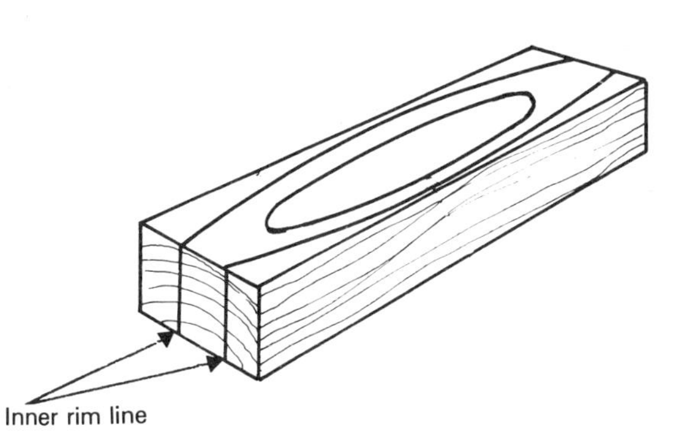

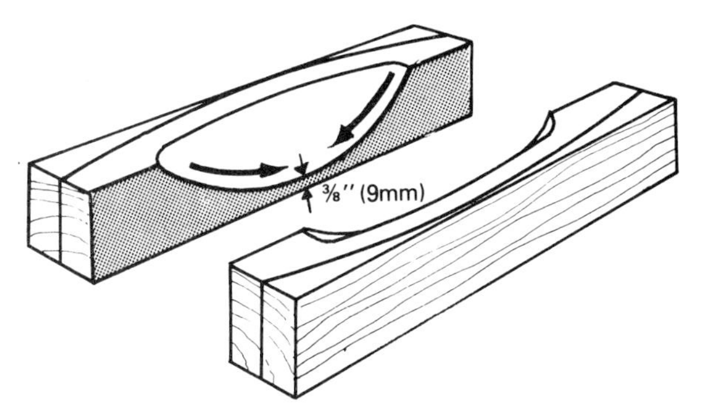

4
Then gouge out the waste back to the inner rim line and down to 'depth'.
Note : Direction of the cuts below. Leave a 'tooled' finish or clean and bring to a smooth finish with abrasives. If you decide to inlay the top - now is the time to do so.

5
Shape back to the outer rim lines. Then underneath mark out, saw and plane off the ends waste. Mark out and remove the sides waste. Clean up with abrasives. Fit and fix a furniture protective pad on the base (leather or felt, etc.). Use a top quality appropriate adhesive, suggest TRETOBOND NON FLAM CONTACT. Apply an appropriate finish.

MARKING OUT DETAILS FOR CARVED BOWL

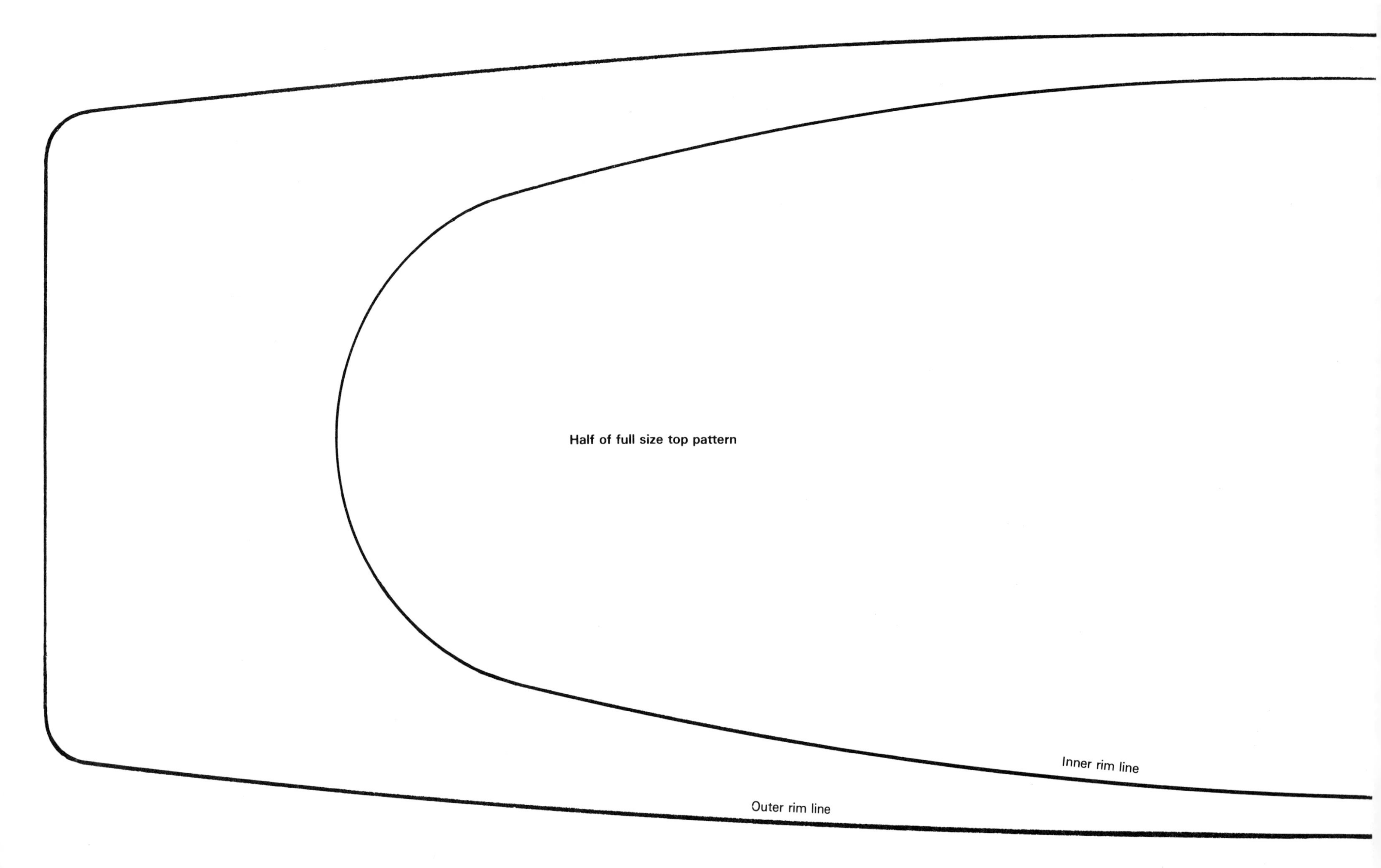

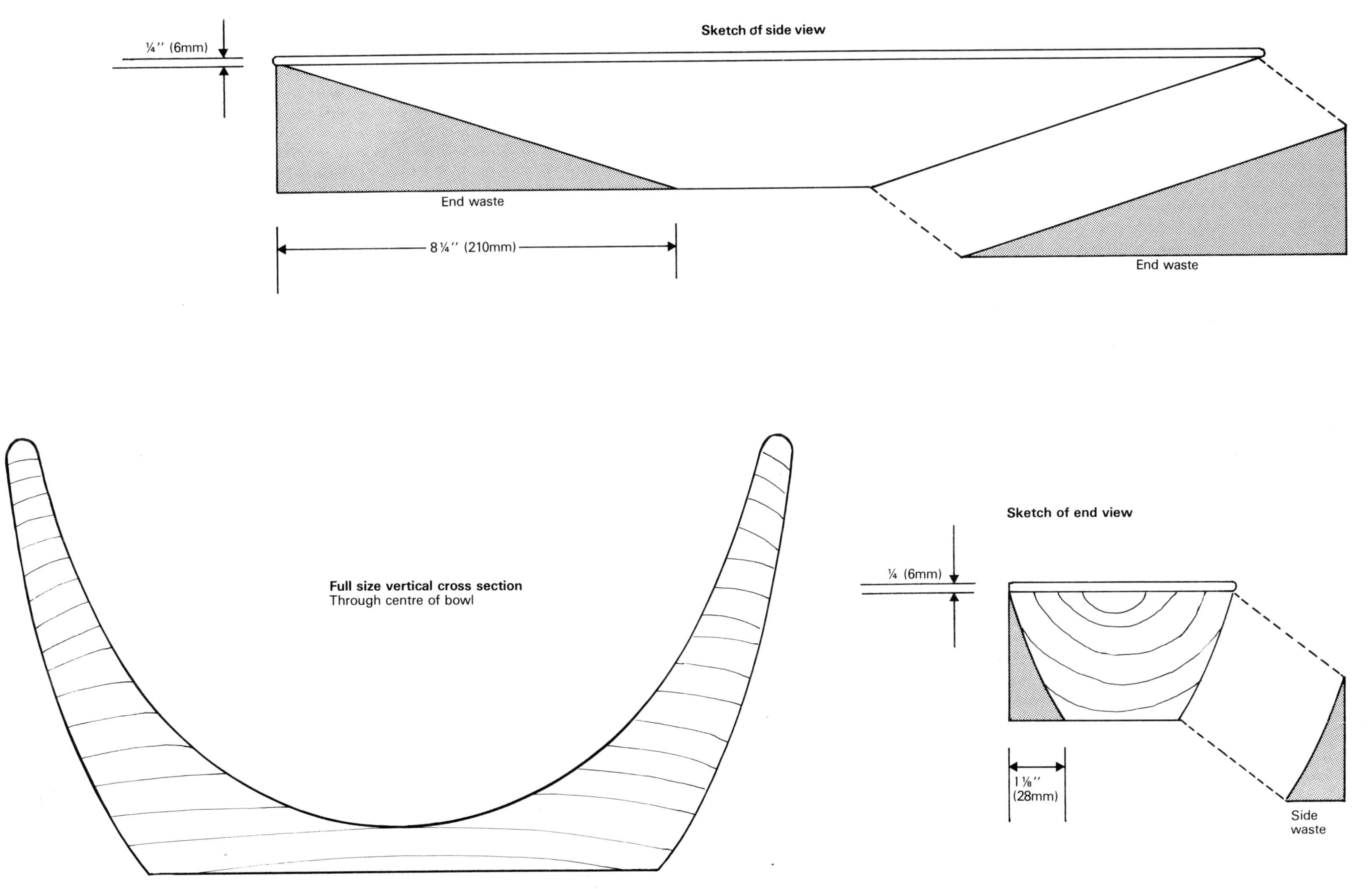
Sketch of side view
¼'' (6mm)
End waste
8¼'' (210mm)
End waste
Full size vertical cross section
Through centre of bowl
Sketch of end view
¼ (6mm)
1⅛''
(28mm)
Side
waste

CARVED HORS-D'OEUVRES TRAY

Owner - Captain Robert White R.A. **Wood** Burma Teak.

This is a shallow varied compartment tray for holding light refreshments, etc., for the special occasion.
The sizes below are just a general guide.

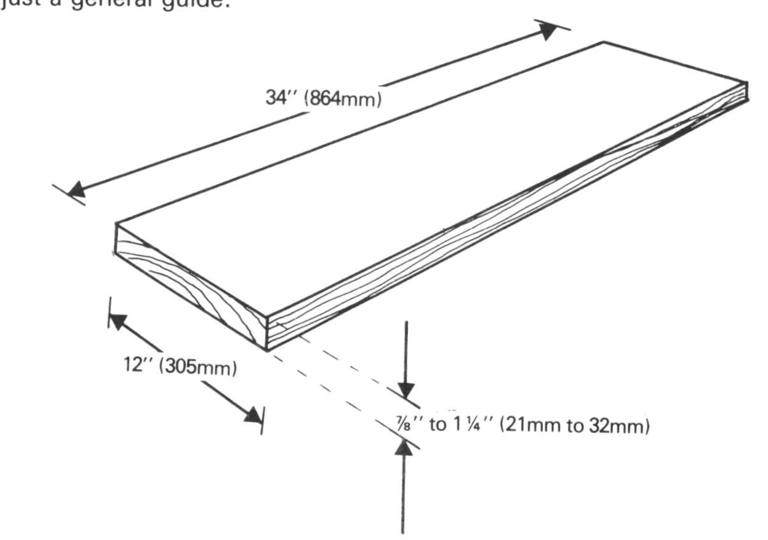

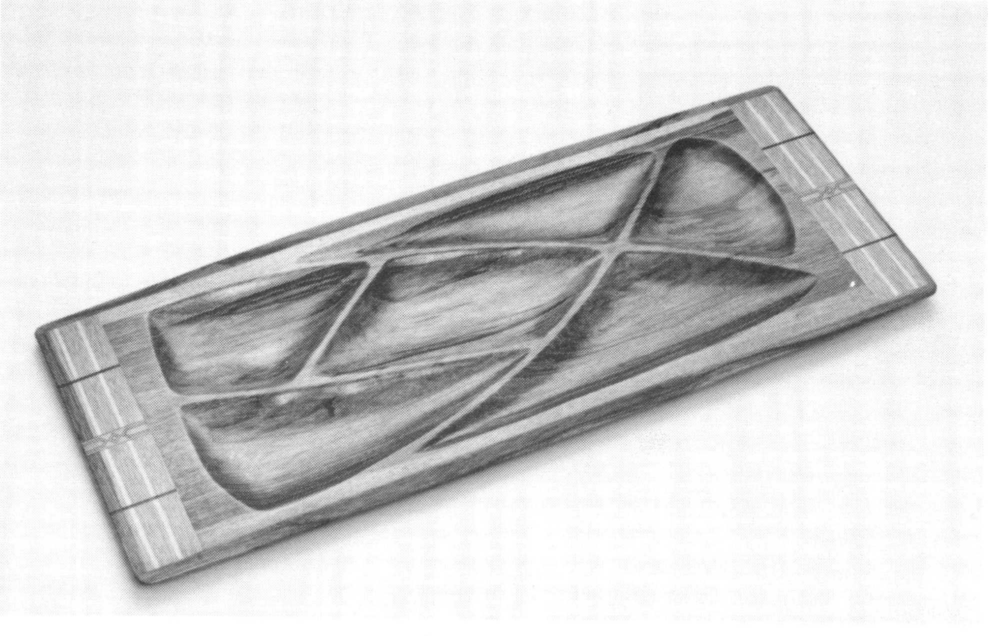

Owner - The Hon. Mrs. Chaworth Musters.
Wood African Limba. **Laminates** English Sycamore. **Inlay** Ebony and Boxwood.

1
You may find it very difficult to obtain a board wide enough and of appropriate material. If so, match up and join together two narrow boards. A top quality appropriate adhesive will do the trick, suggest TIMBABOND No.688.

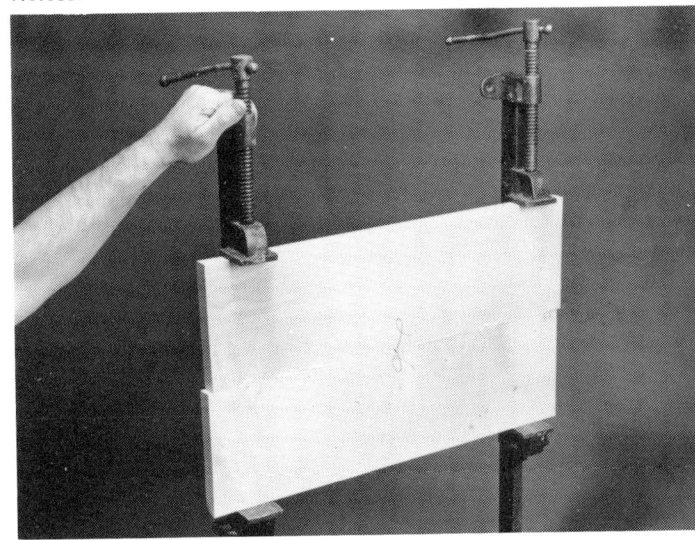

2
On tracing paper, sketch the full size outline of the tray and inside sketch appropriate compartment shapes which integrate in harmony with each other. Then transfer the final layout of the shapes onto the wood.

3
In each compartment gouge out a depth channel. Remove the waste back to the inner rim lines. Leave a 'tooled' finish, or clean smooth with abrasives.

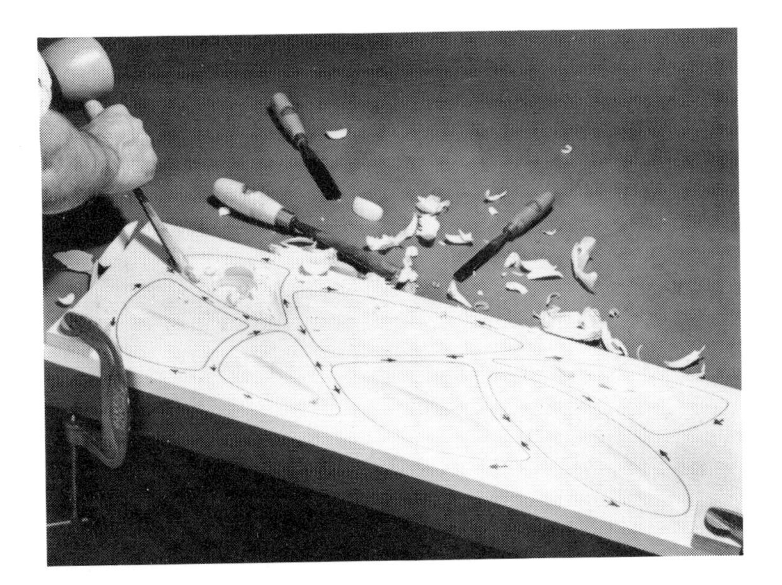

4
Mark out, saw and plane off the ends waste. Mark out and plane off the sides waste. Clean up with abrasives. Fix small furniture protective pads, e.g. leather or felt etc., on the base at the corners and the centre with a top quality appropriate adhesive, suggest TRETOBOND NON FLAM CONTACT. Apply an appropriate finish.

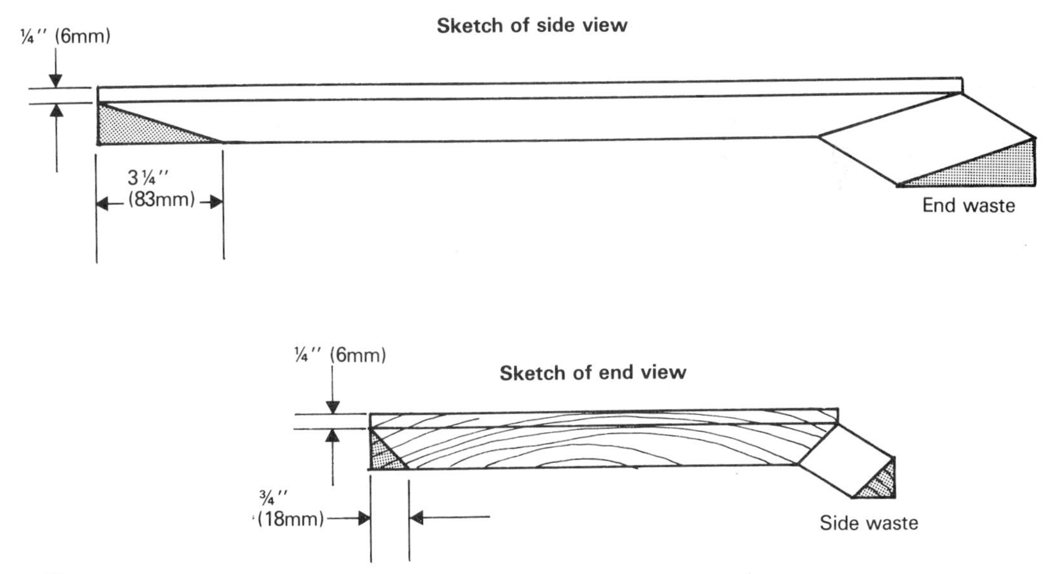

SCOTTIE

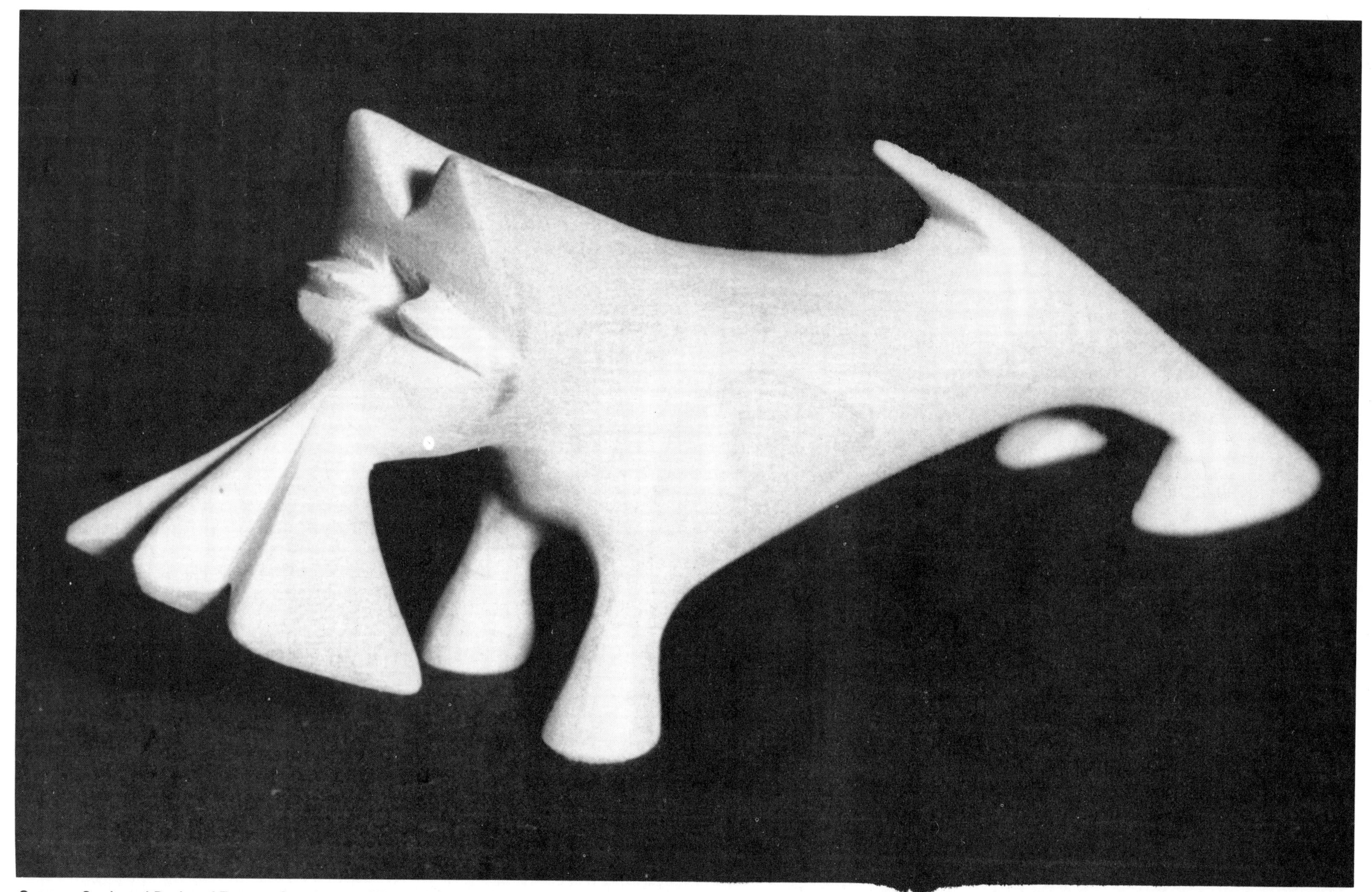

Owners - **Sandy and Denise of Toronto, Canada.** **Wood** African Obeche.

WOOD WHITTLING

The art of Wood Whittling is as 'old as the hills' and is still fervently practised in many parts of the World.

Whittling is mainly done with a knife in a leisurely satisfying manner by peeling slices of wood off, both down and across the grain.

Ideal woods are those of the 'soft easy peeling nature', e.g. Basswood, English Lime, Sugar Pine, African Agba, etc.

Generally the finish is straight from the knife - polished or painted.

Sometimes the items are cleaned up with abrasives for presenting a very smooth finish.

A fine whittled St. Bernard by Tex Hause of New Mexico, U.S.A.

Intricate whittling by Erwin N. Caldwell of Texas, U.S.A.

1
Success in whittling depends very much on having a 'razor sharp' knife. I prefer the permanently fixed blade type which cannot 'jack knife' onto the fingers.
Note : An excellent home made whittling knife can be ground from an old 'cut throat' razor and fixed into a handle shaped to suit your hand.

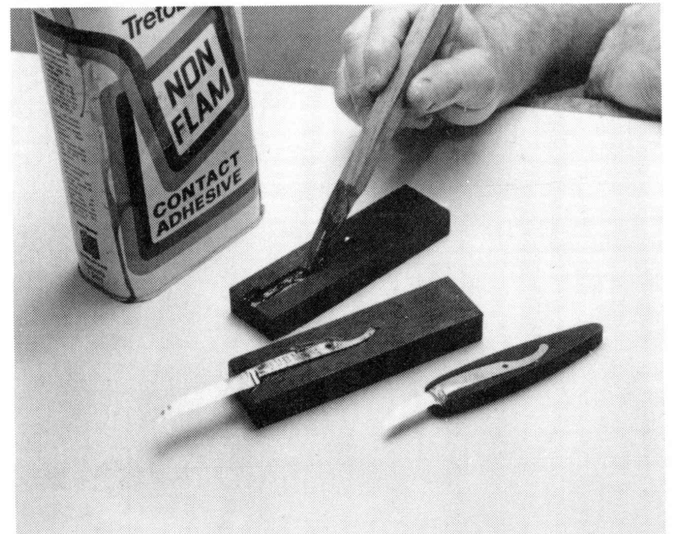

2
Initial shaping can be done on wet and dry paper, Grade No. 120 wrapped and fastened around a strip of wood, e.g. 10" x 1¼" x ½" (254mm x 32mm x 13mm). Move the blade slowly but firmly up and down, keeping the blade as flat as possible to the cutting surface of the wet and dry paper.

3
On a similar strip of wood fasten a piece of fine leather and rub onto its surface a fine grade of Jewellers Rouge and hone to razor sharpness.

ALISTAIR

Full size details of side pattern

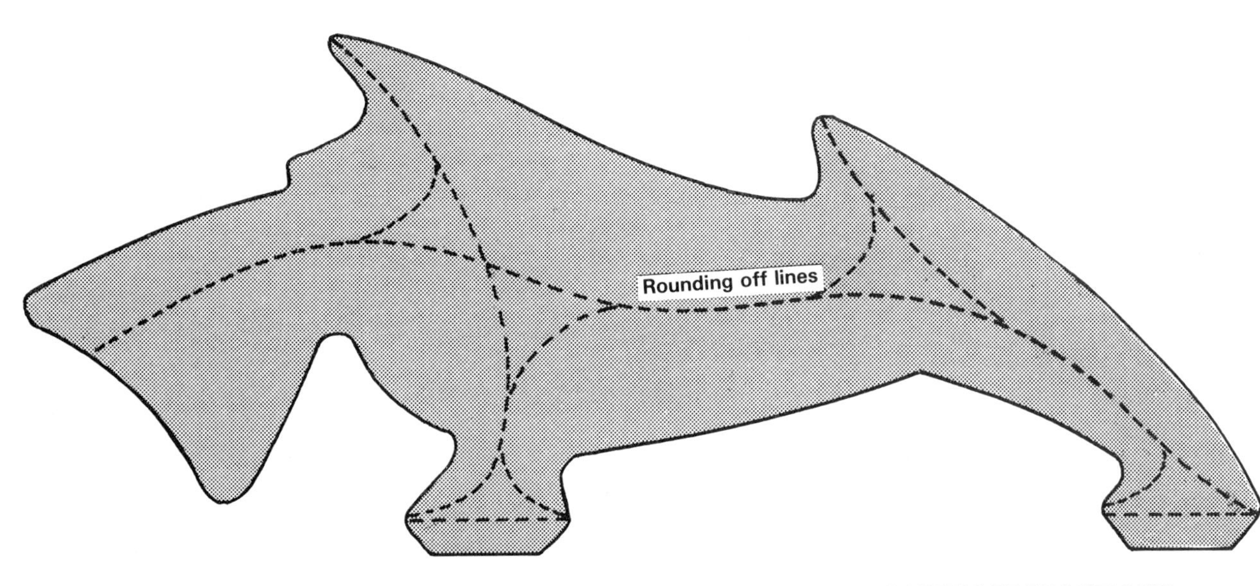

The model - Alistair of Sutton.

SAFETY PRECAUTIONS

1
Whenever possible 'steady' the work on a home made hook support.

2
To prevent injury when peeling inwardly place a thick layer of tape around your thumb end.

3
When breakages occur during whittling these can easily be rectified with a top quality appropriate adhesive. Suggest TIMBABOND No.636. Then cramp in position with elastic bands until the adhesive is thoroughly set.

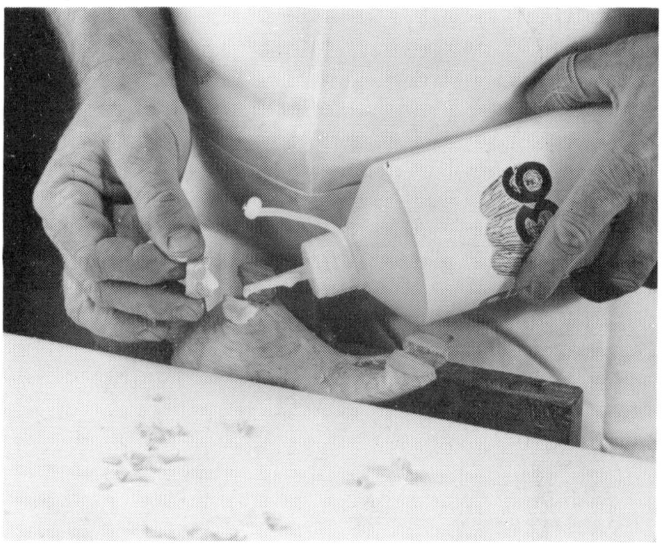

INTRODUCTORY WORKING GUIDE

1
Trace side pattern on opposite page (or design a full size original).
Then obtain and prepare appropriate material to size.
Transfer pattern to prepared material.

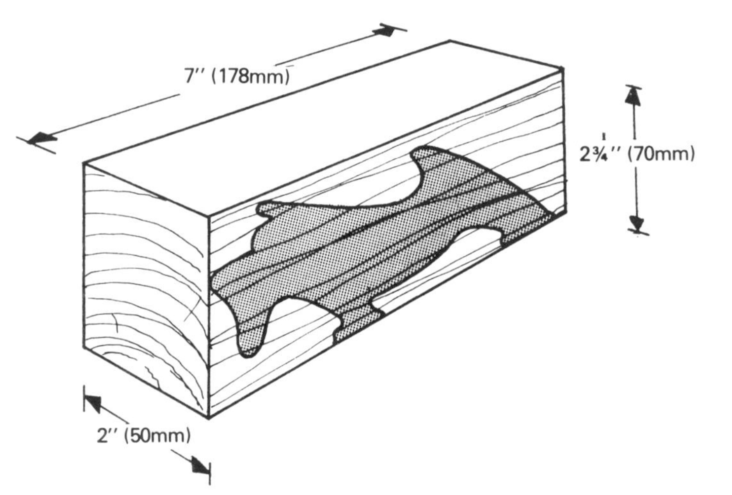

2
Remove the outer waste with a coping or bandsaw

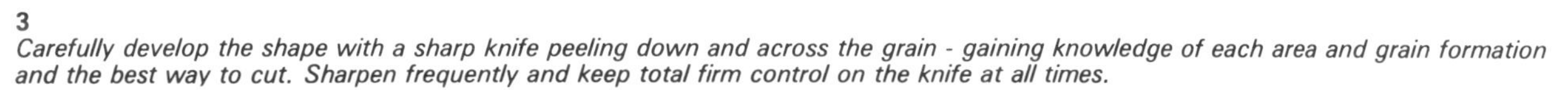

3
Carefully develop the shape with a sharp knife peeling down and across the grain - gaining knowledge of each area and grain formation and the best way to cut. Sharpen frequently and keep total firm control on the knife at all times.

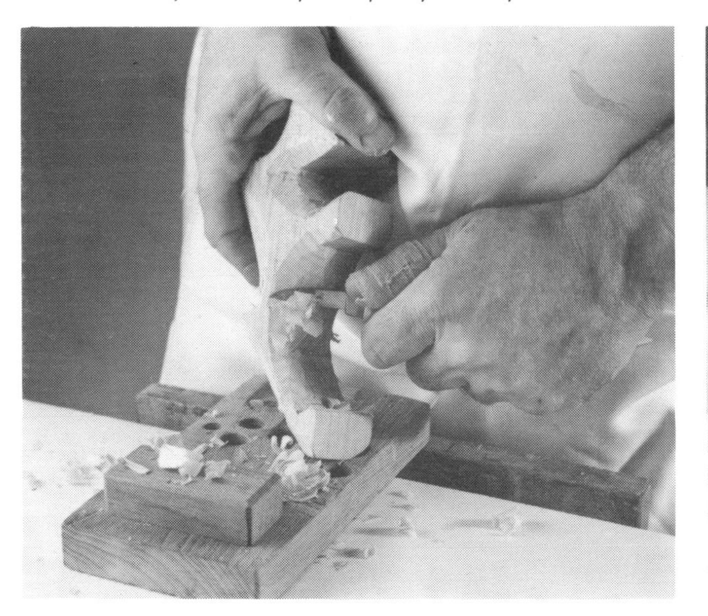

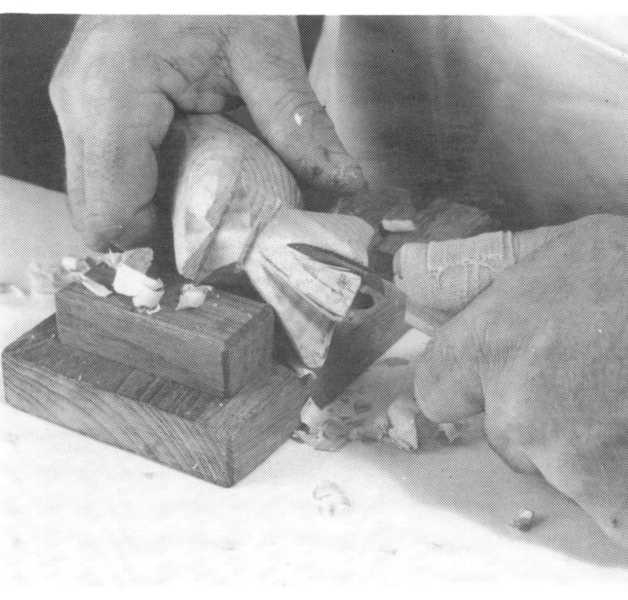

4
An interesting surface developed after knife work with a fine parting tool done by Edward F. Gallenstein of Cincinnati, U.S.A.

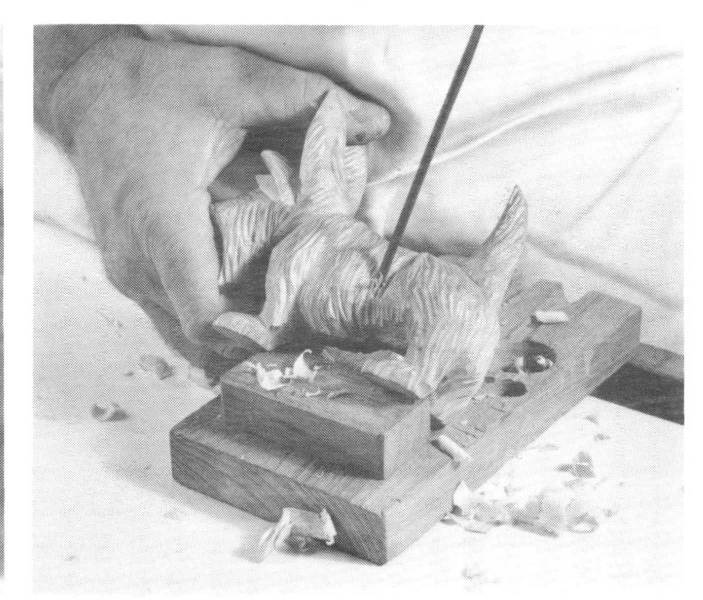

LAMINATED SCULPTING

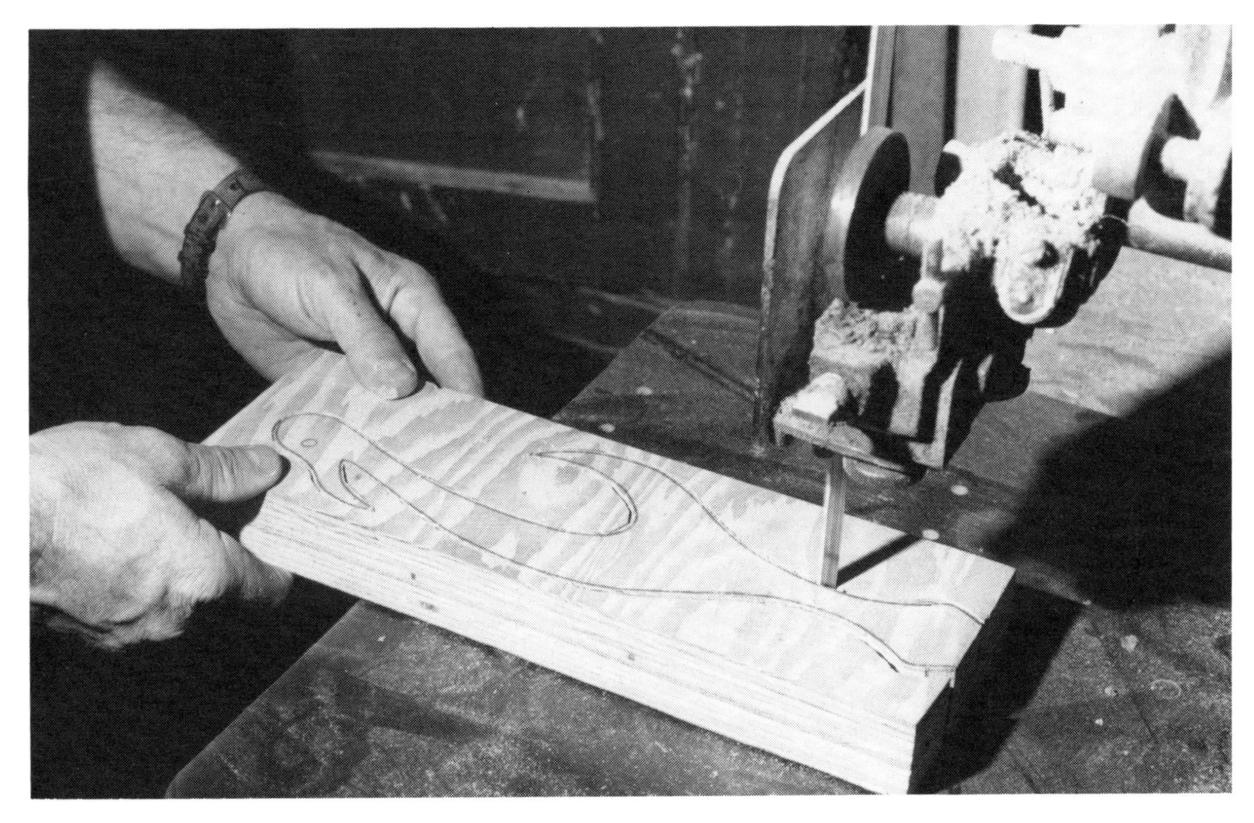

Laminated sculptures are economical to make, attractive, easy to make by simple readily available tools. It is an inexpensive method for producing attractive sculptures from small pieces of plywood waste offcuts available at many D.I.Y. shops and builders merchants etc. The laminated blocks are far stronger in all directions than natural formed wood because of the 'cross bonding' of the plies. This enables the beginner to work a large range of designs with a high degree of success. The pre-formed layers of plies can be easily shaped so that their contours are developed to the best advantage of the particular design. Even delicate features present little problem, because of the overall structural strength in all directions of the laminated items.

The section starts with an introduction to plywood suitable for sculpting, then how to form a laminated block, finishing, and finishes. Then follows a step by step working guide with full size patterns for making a stylised 3D sculpture of a seal.

This is followed by several more examples with full size patterns for your perusal and choice to help stimulate your interest and develop your own designs. Finally, details of abstract work are included.

Note :
When viewing waste offcuts of plywood for sculpting select those with :
HARDWOOD PLIES
THIN PLIES
TWO TONE PLIES
NO PITTED EDGES.

Pitted Edges
Plywood with pitted edges is best kept clear of as where these defects occur it can result in breakages and shaping and filling in difficulties.

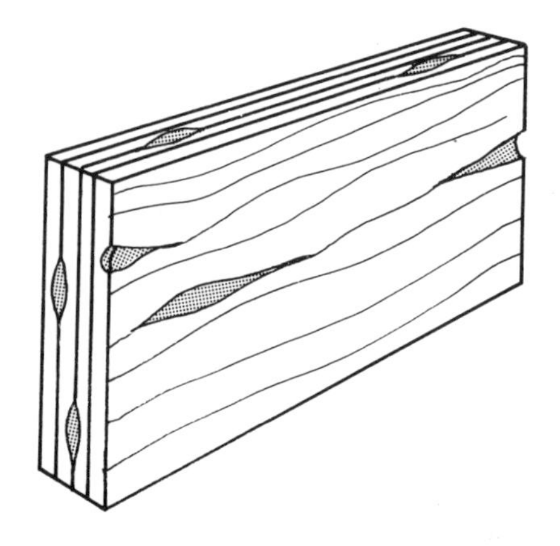

Thin Plies
Plywood with thin plies is generally a better quality than plywood built of thick plies.

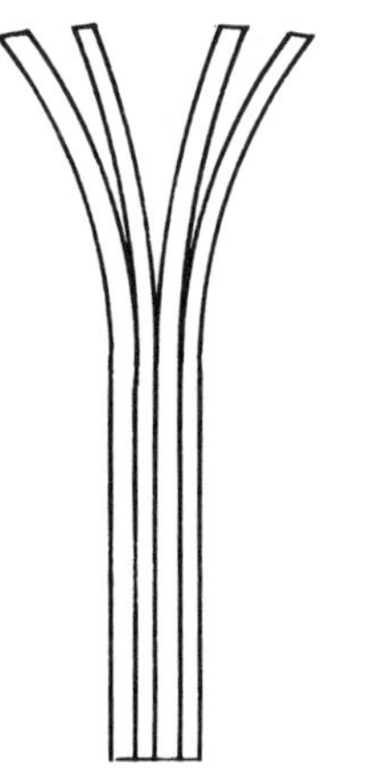

Two Tone Plies
Plywood with different coloured plies often gives an excellent decorative effect.

Plywood with Hardwood Plies
These are often more strong and easier to shape and finish than softwood types.

HOW TO FORM A LAMINATED BLOCK

1
Obtain and saw enough pieces of appropriate plywood to form the required sized laminated block for your sculpture.

2
Remove any edge splinters with an abrasive. Then thoroughly dust off with a brush.

3
Carefully spread top quality appropriate adhesive, suggest for softwood plywood TIMBABOND No.636, and for hardwood plywood TIMBABOND No.688, on each of the plywood surfaces excluding only the two outer faces of the block.

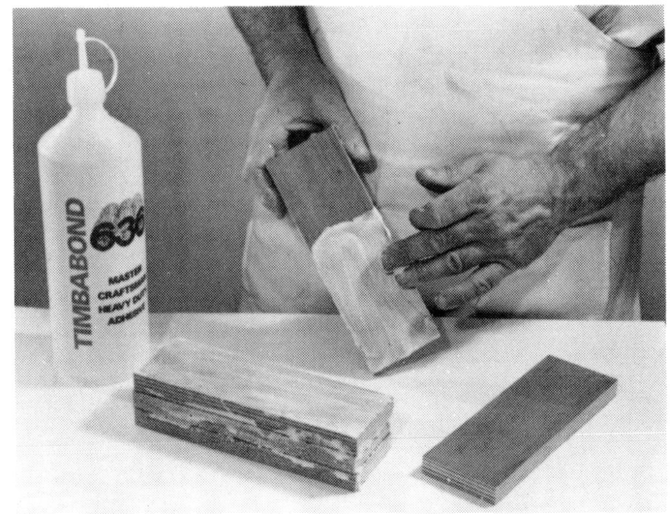

4
Carefully wrap the block in thin plastic sheeting to prevent adhesive running onto the cramping boards which would result in parting difficulties.

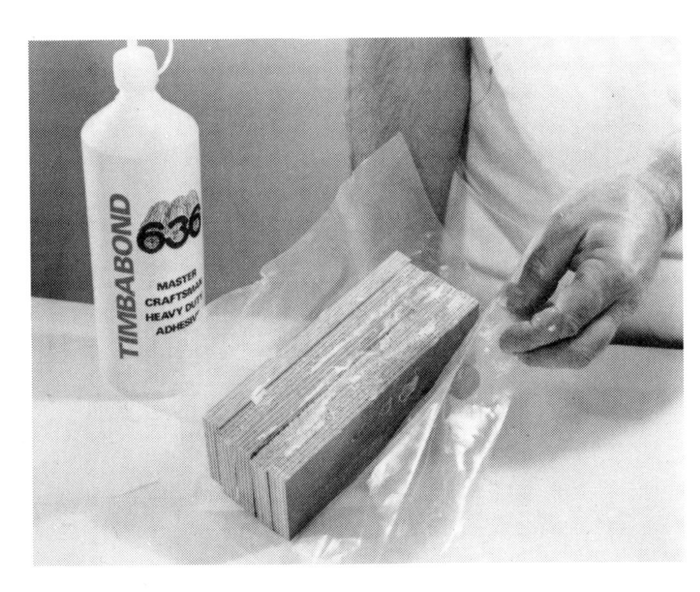

5
Cramp the plywood block between strong boards, applying even pressure all round. Then leave to set thoroughly.

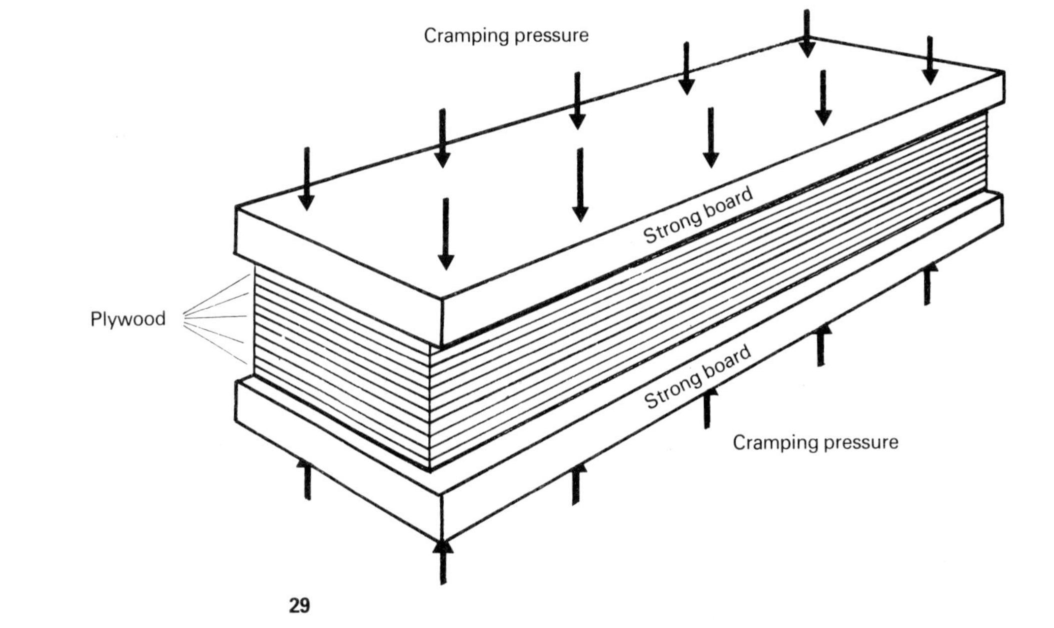

SEAL

This is an introductory working guide for making realistic laminated sculptures. (Example illustrated - laminated seal).

Stage by stage photographs and accompanying instructions will act as a permanent reference and guide to master further items in this highly exciting medium.

INTRODUCTORY WORKING GUIDE

1
Trace patterns on Page No.32 and Page No.33. (Or design full size originals). Then obtain and saw enough pieces of appropriate plywood to form the required size laminated block. (For Seal overall block size is 12" x 3½" x 2½", 305mm x 89mm x 63mm).

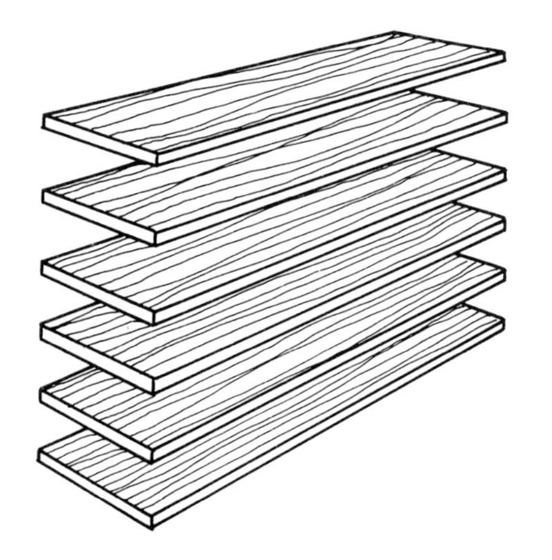

2
On each piece of plywood remove any splinters with an abrasive, then dust thoroughly. Apply a top quality appropriate adhesive, plastic sheeting and strong cramping boards and cramps. Then leave to set thoroughly, after which transfer side pattern.

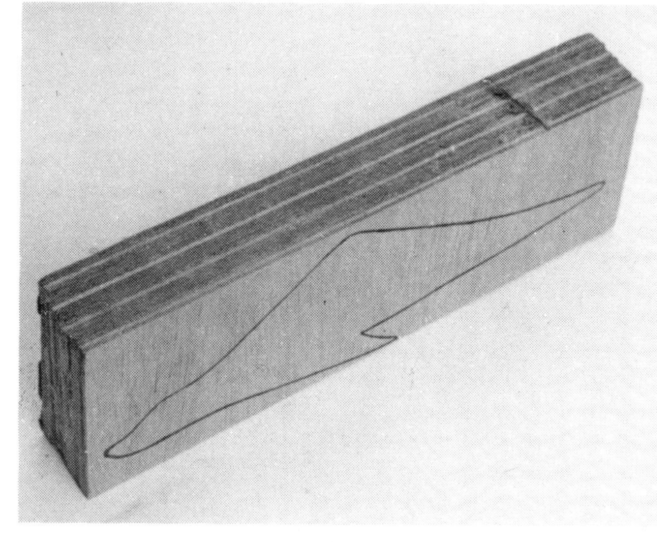

3
Saw off the waste and clean down to the lines with Surform ® Tools. Transfer top edge shape.

4
Remove the waste.

5
Mark out rounding off lines and any features (flappers etc.).

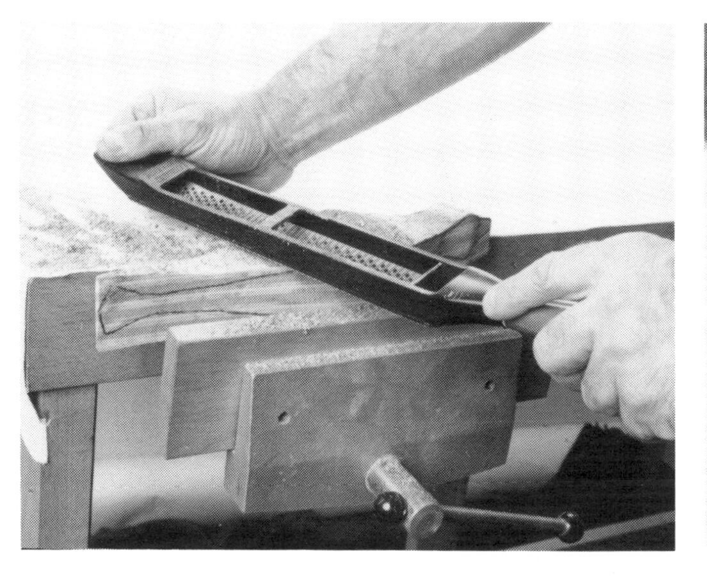

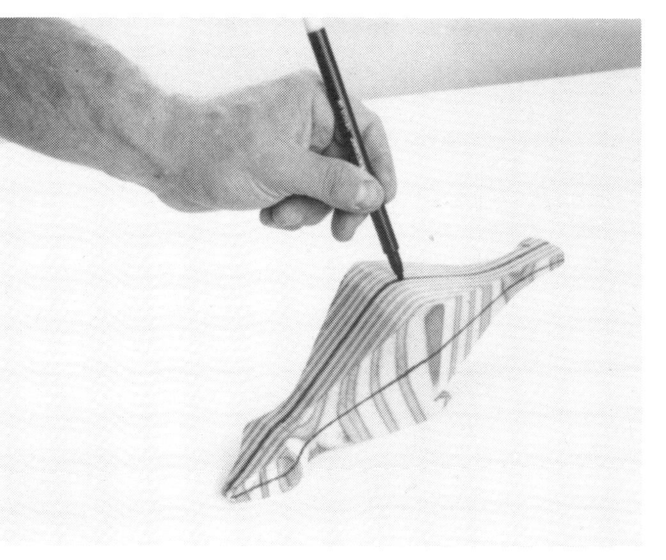

6
Saw between flappers and shape back to the lines carefully developing any features and the plies contours to the best advantage.

7
Make any necessary base of a shape and material which blends appropriately with the sculpture. Test and bore tight fitting holes for metal column in sculpture and base.

8
Test fit together. Clean up with wood files, then abrasives. Apply an appropriate finish.

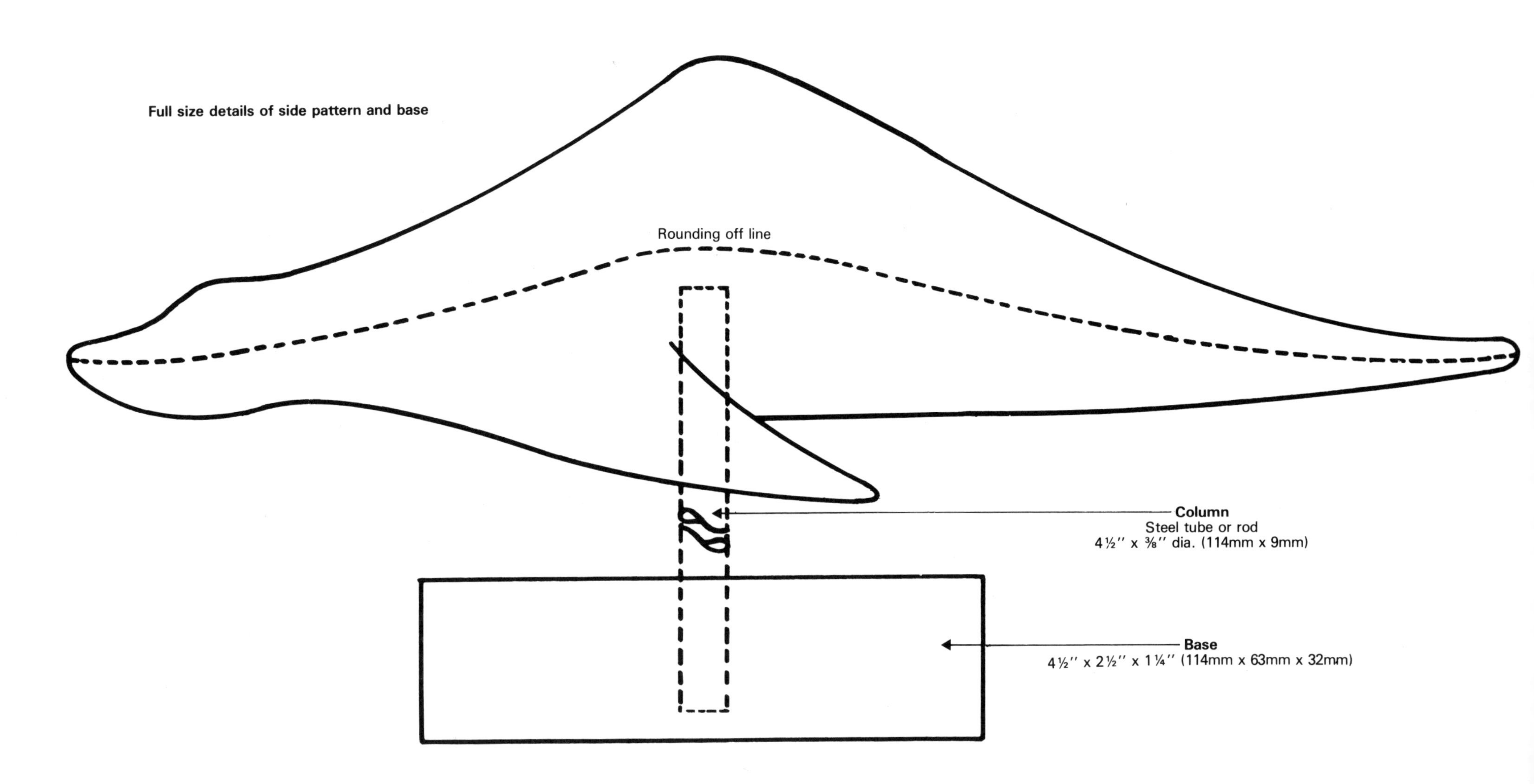

Full size details of side pattern and base

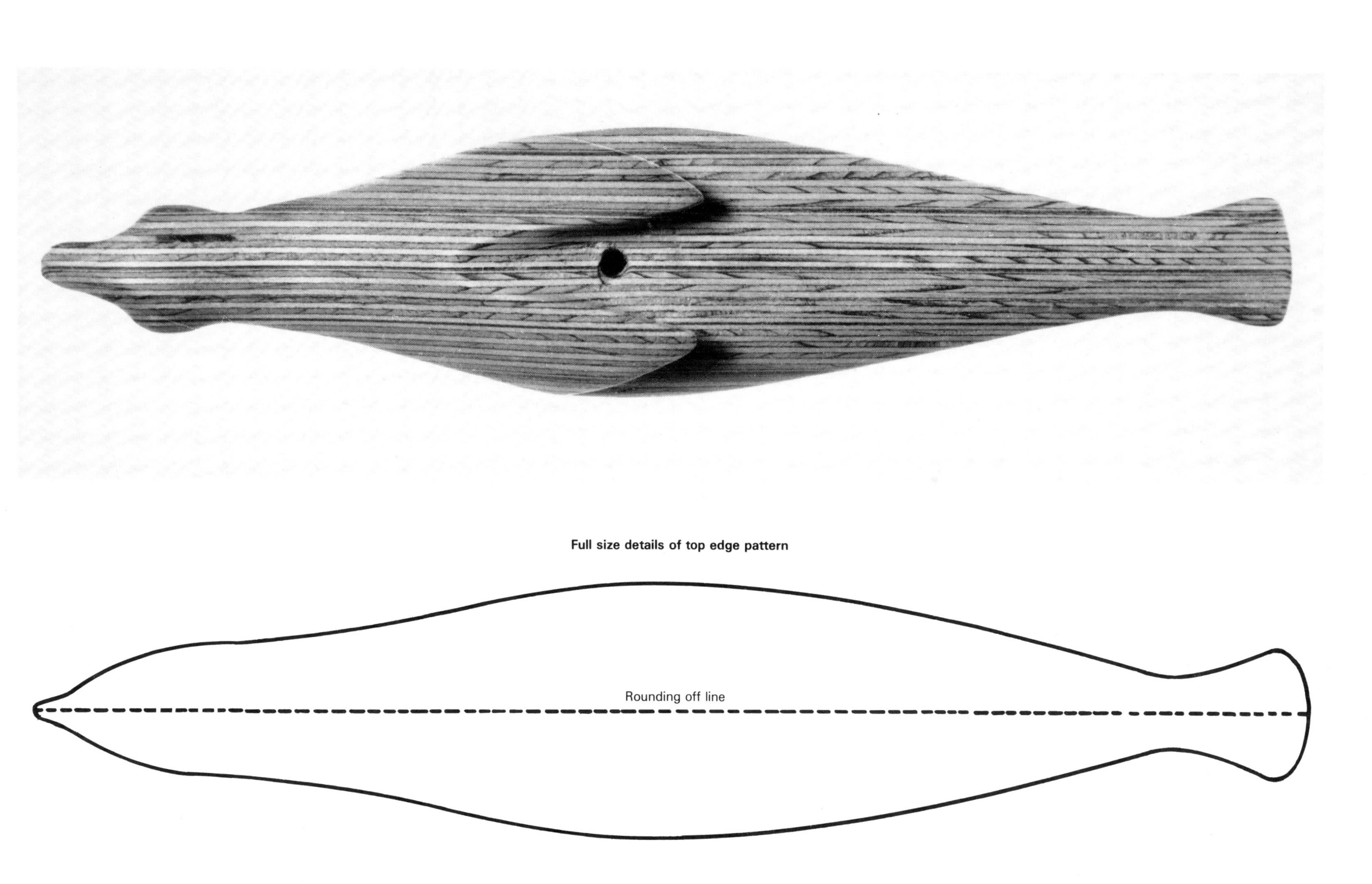
Full size details of top edge pattern
Rounding off line

GOAT

Owner - Her Majesty, Queen Elizabeth II
Presented in the Silver Jubilee Year 1977 at County Hall, West Bridgford, Nottingham, England U.K.

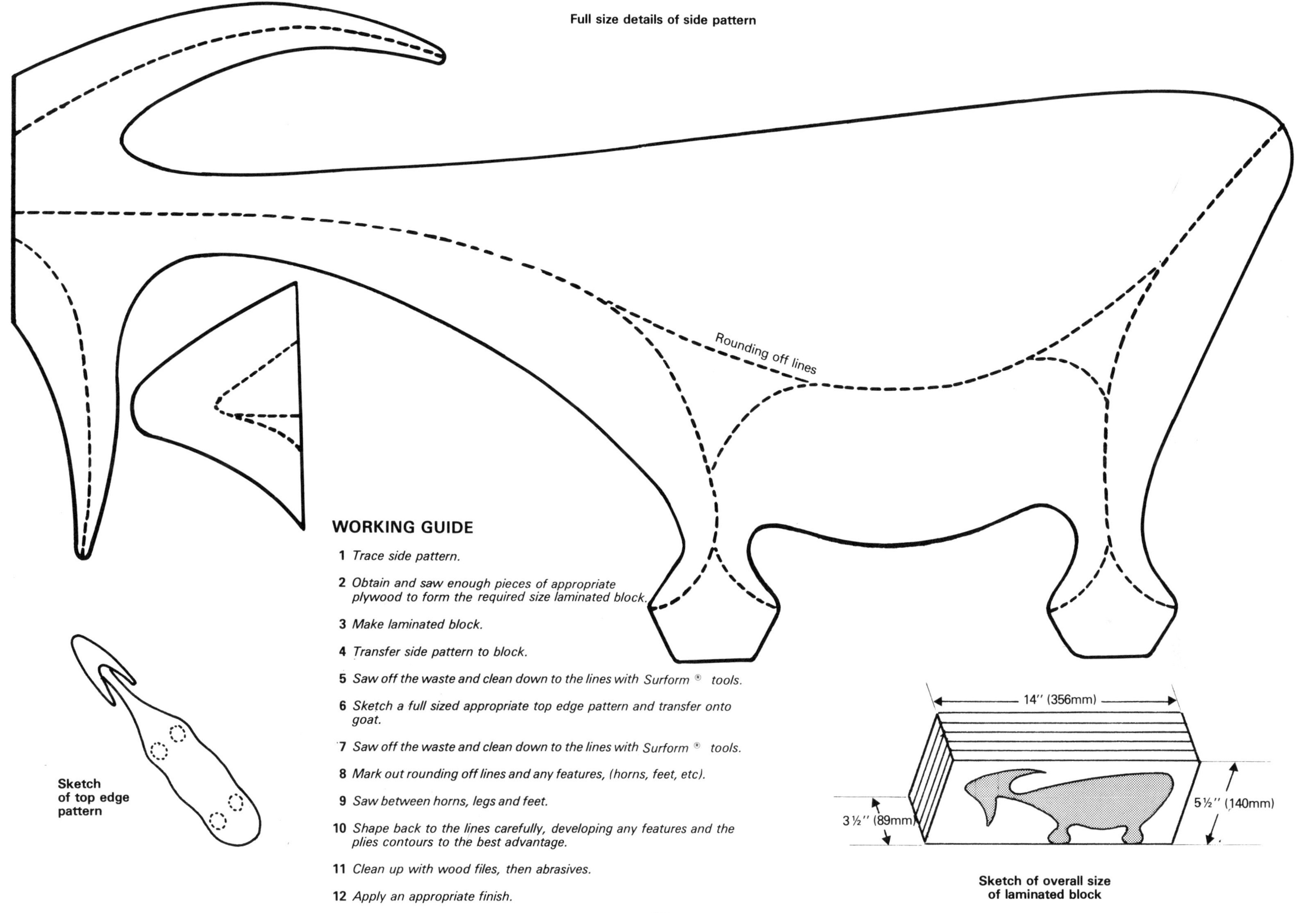

WORKING GUIDE

1 *Trace side pattern.*

2 *Obtain and saw enough pieces of appropriate plywood to form the required size laminated block.*

3 *Make laminated block.*

4 *Transfer side pattern to block.*

5 *Saw off the waste and clean down to the lines with Surform® tools.*

6 *Sketch a full sized appropriate top edge pattern and transfer onto goat.*

7 *Saw off the waste and clean down to the lines with Surform® tools.*

8 *Mark out rounding off lines and any features, (horns, feet, etc).*

9 *Saw between horns, legs and feet.*

10 *Shape back to the lines carefully, developing any features and the plies contours to the best advantage.*

11 *Clean up with wood files, then abrasives.*

12 *Apply an appropriate finish.*

WEASEL

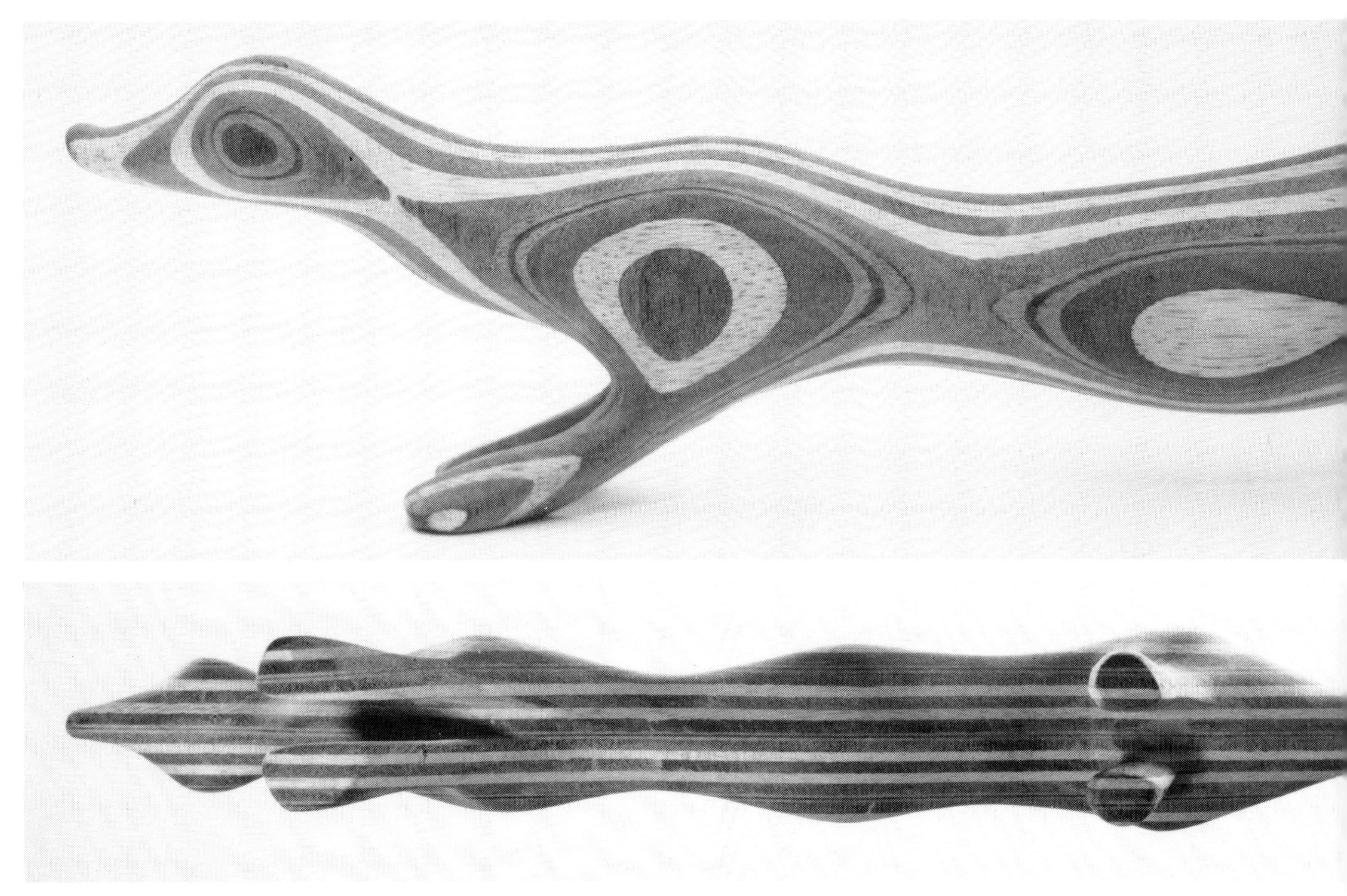

Full size details of side pattern

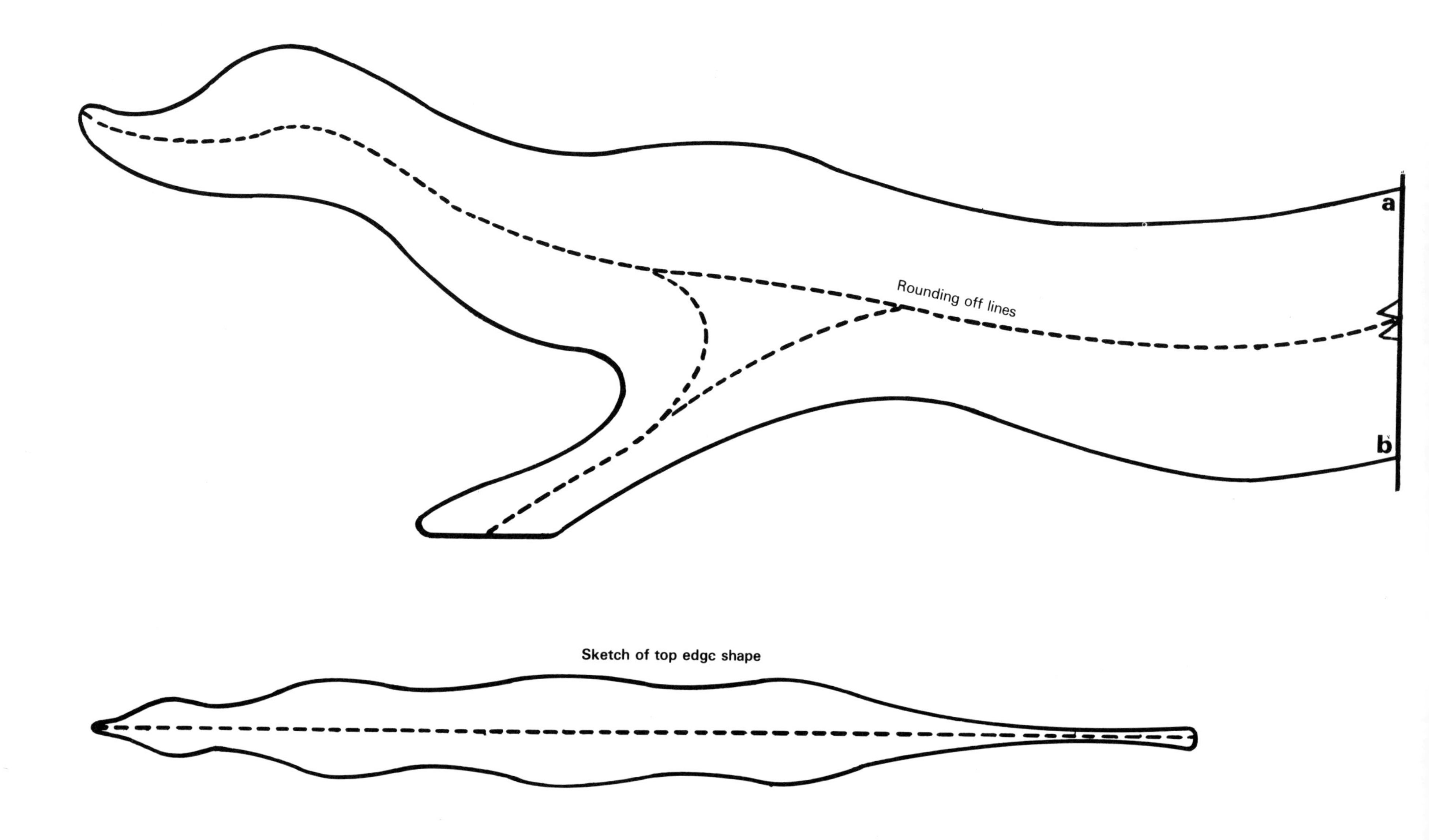

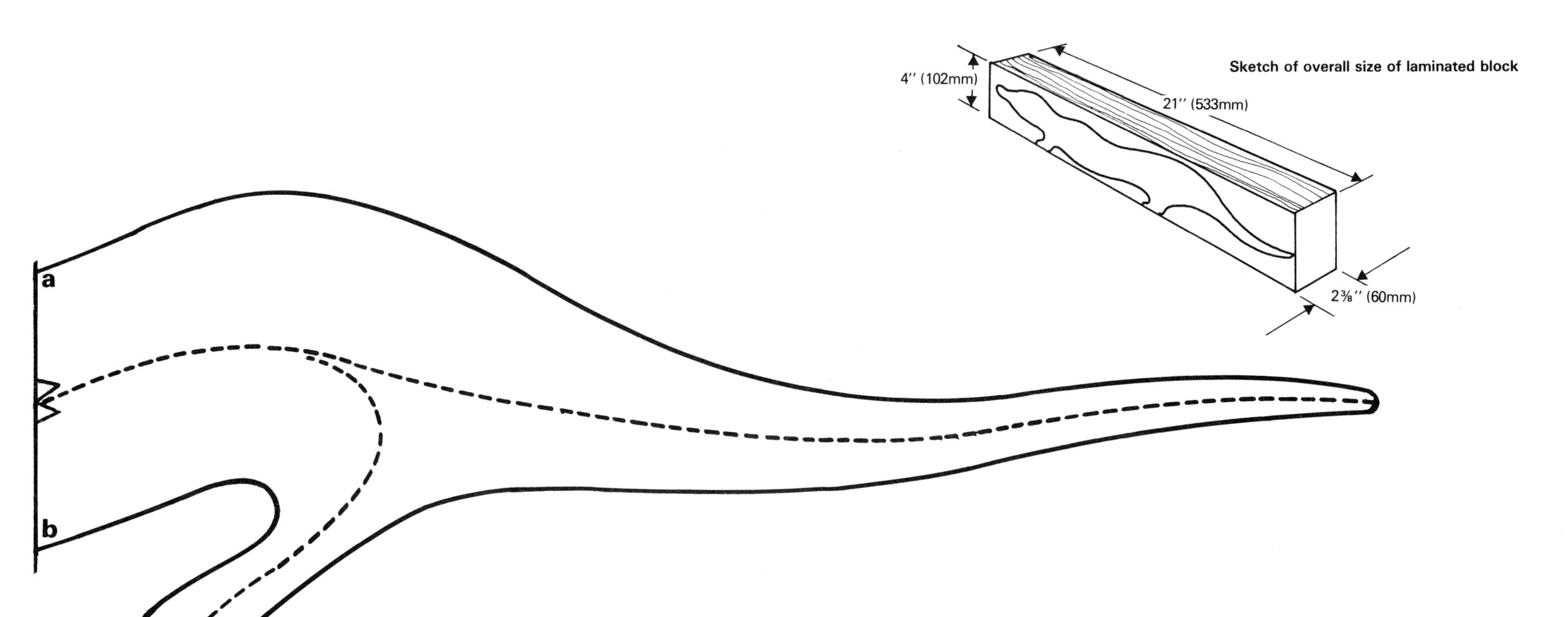

WORKING GUIDE

1 *Trace side pattern.*

2 *Obtain and saw enough pieces of appropriate plywood to form the required sized laminated block.*

3 *Make laminated block.*

4 *Transfer side pattern to block.*

5 *Saw off the waste and clean down to the lines with Surform ® tools.*

6 *Sketch a full sized appropriate top edged pattern and transfer to Weasel.*

7 *Saw off the waste and clean down to the lines with Surform ® tools.*

8 *Mark out rounding off lines and any features (feet, etc).*

9 *Saw between legs and feet.*

10 *Shape back to the lines carefully, developing any features and the plies contours to the best advantage.*

11 *Clean up with wood files, then abrasives.*

12 *Apply an appropriate finish.*

HOUND DOG - OLE BLUE

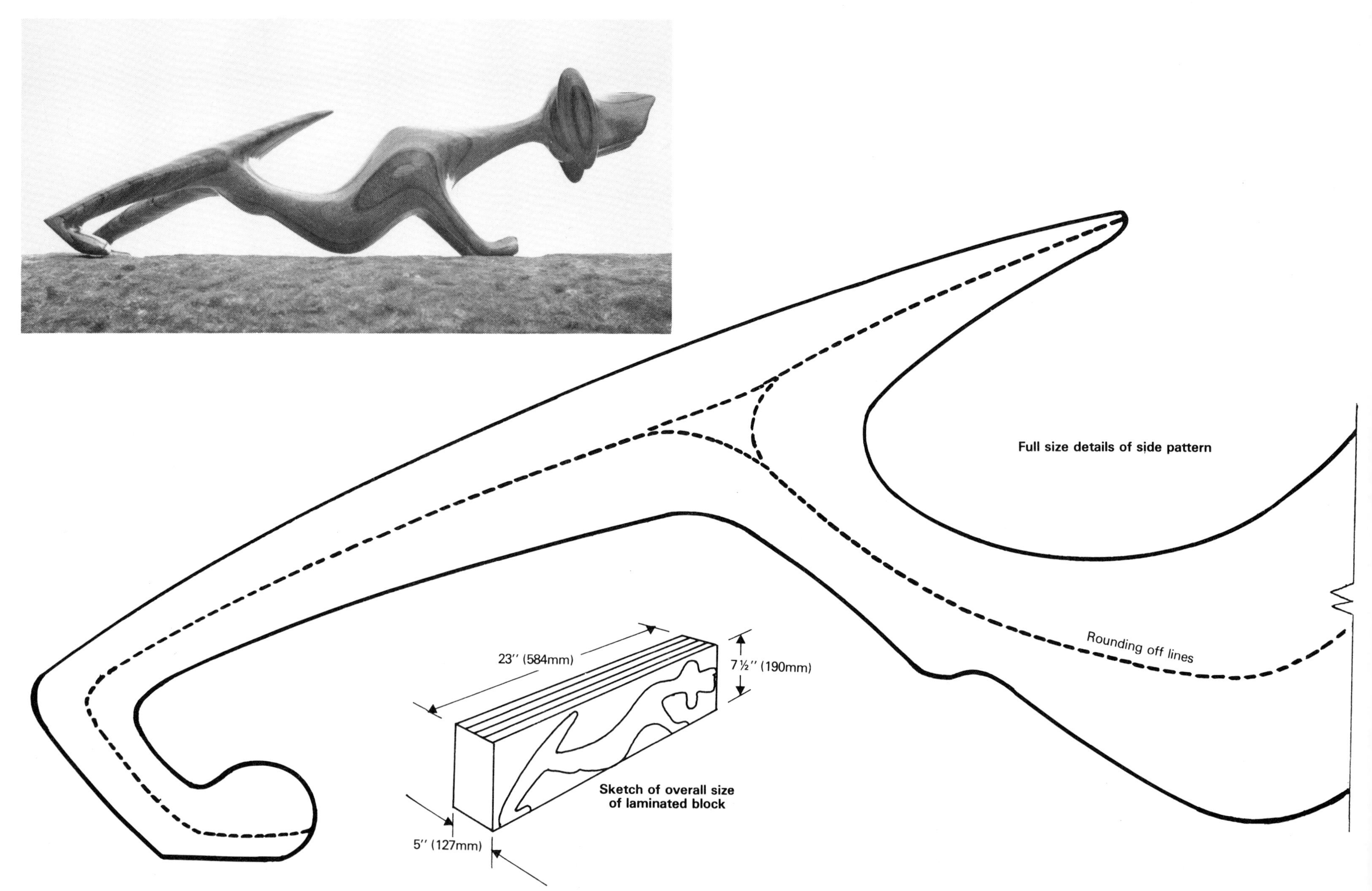

WORKING GUIDE

1 *Trace side pattern.*

2 *Obtain and saw enough pieces of appropriate plywood to form the required sized laminated block.*

3 *Make laminated block.*

4 *Transfer side pattern to block.*

5 *Saw off the waste and clean down to the lines with Surform ® tools.*

6 *Sketch a full sized appropriate top edge pattern and transfer onto Hound Dog.*

7 *Saw off the waste and clean down to the lines with Surform ® tools.*

8 *Mark out rounding off lines and any features (legs, feet, ears, etc).*

9 *Saw between legs and feet.*

10 *Shape back to the lines carefully, developing any features and the plies contours to the best advantage.*

11 *Clean up with wood files and then abrasives.*

12 *Apply an appropriate finish.*

Sketch of top edge shape

ABSTRACT LAMINATED SCULPTING

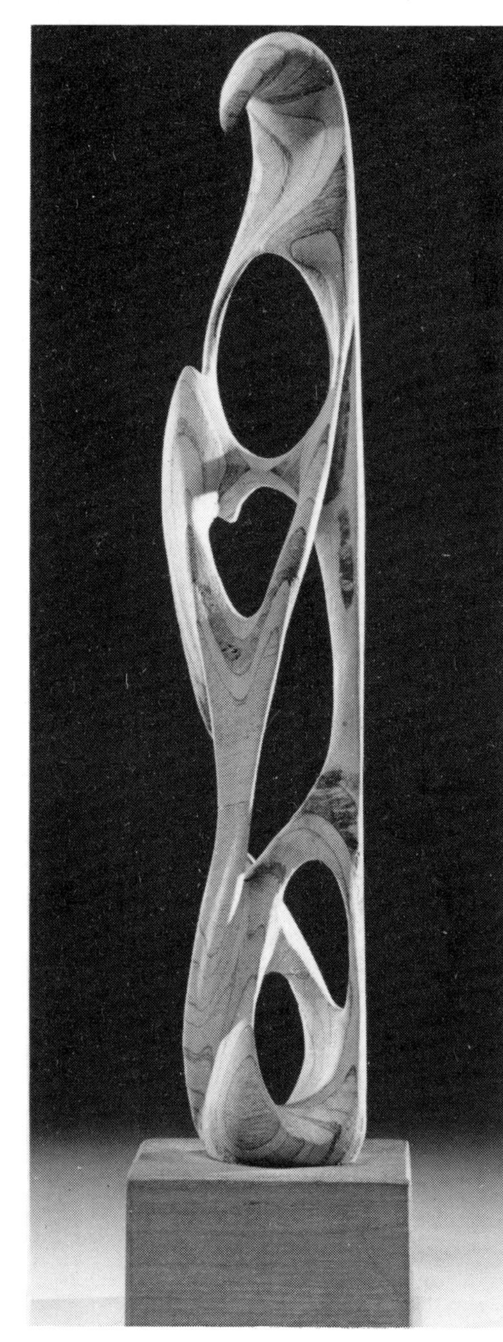

Bird of Prey

Making an abstract sculpture requires careful application of material, tools and throughout all its development.

The method suggested here is one approach - directly with the material.

ONE METHOD OF APPROACH

1 *Make an appropriate sized laminated block using a top quality adhesive. Suggest TIMBABOND No.636 for softwood plywood and TIMBABOND No.688 for hardwood plywood.*

2 *In the block bore various and varied sized holes at interesting positions and angles.*
Note : Bit extensions are very helpful for boring deep holes.

3 *Use carving tools, surform tools cabinet files etc. to make an interesting all round abstract, developing harmonious integrated shapes using the plies contours to the best advantage.*

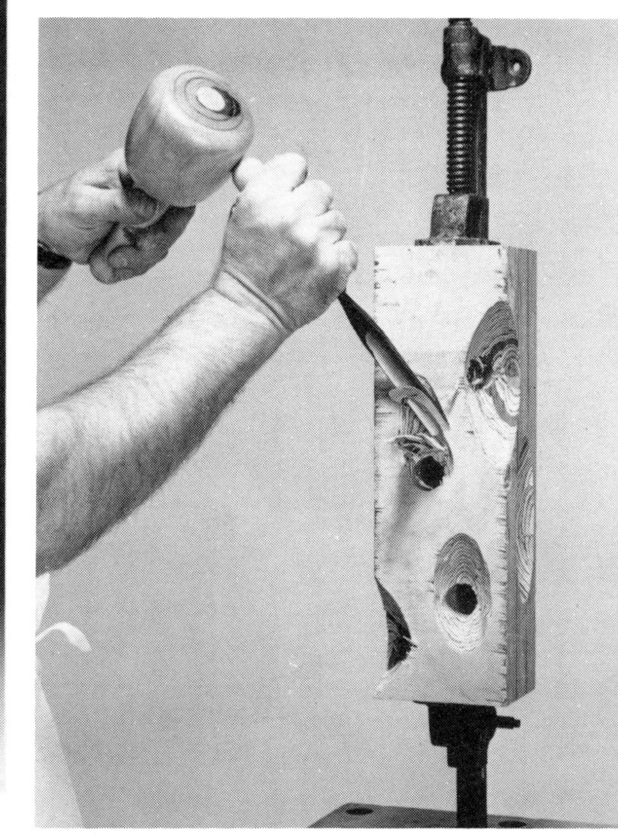

I Got Rhythm
Premium Award Winner 1st 1979 in Laminated Classes at both U.S.A. and Canadian International Exhibitions.

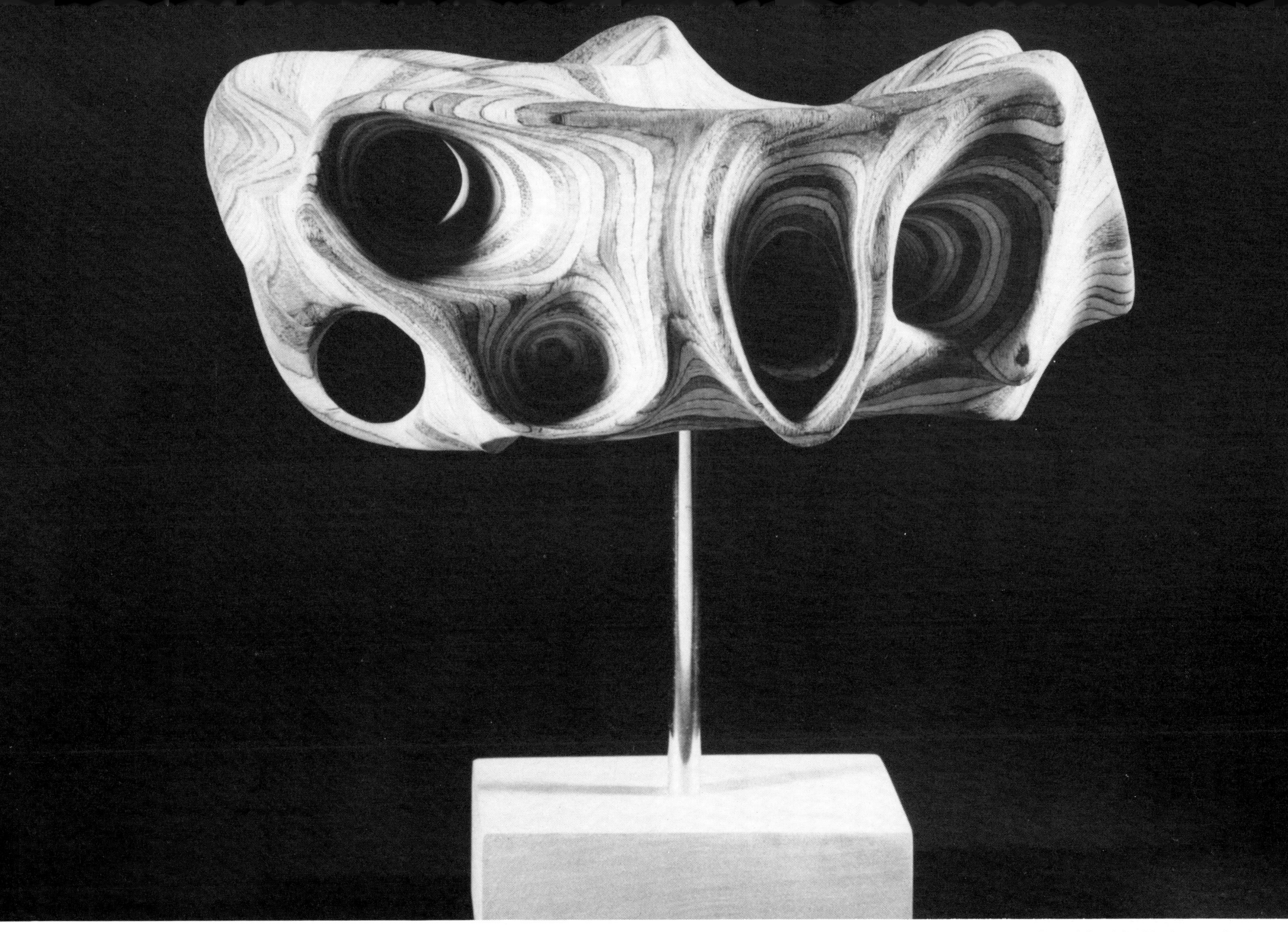

Part of the John Matthews collection.

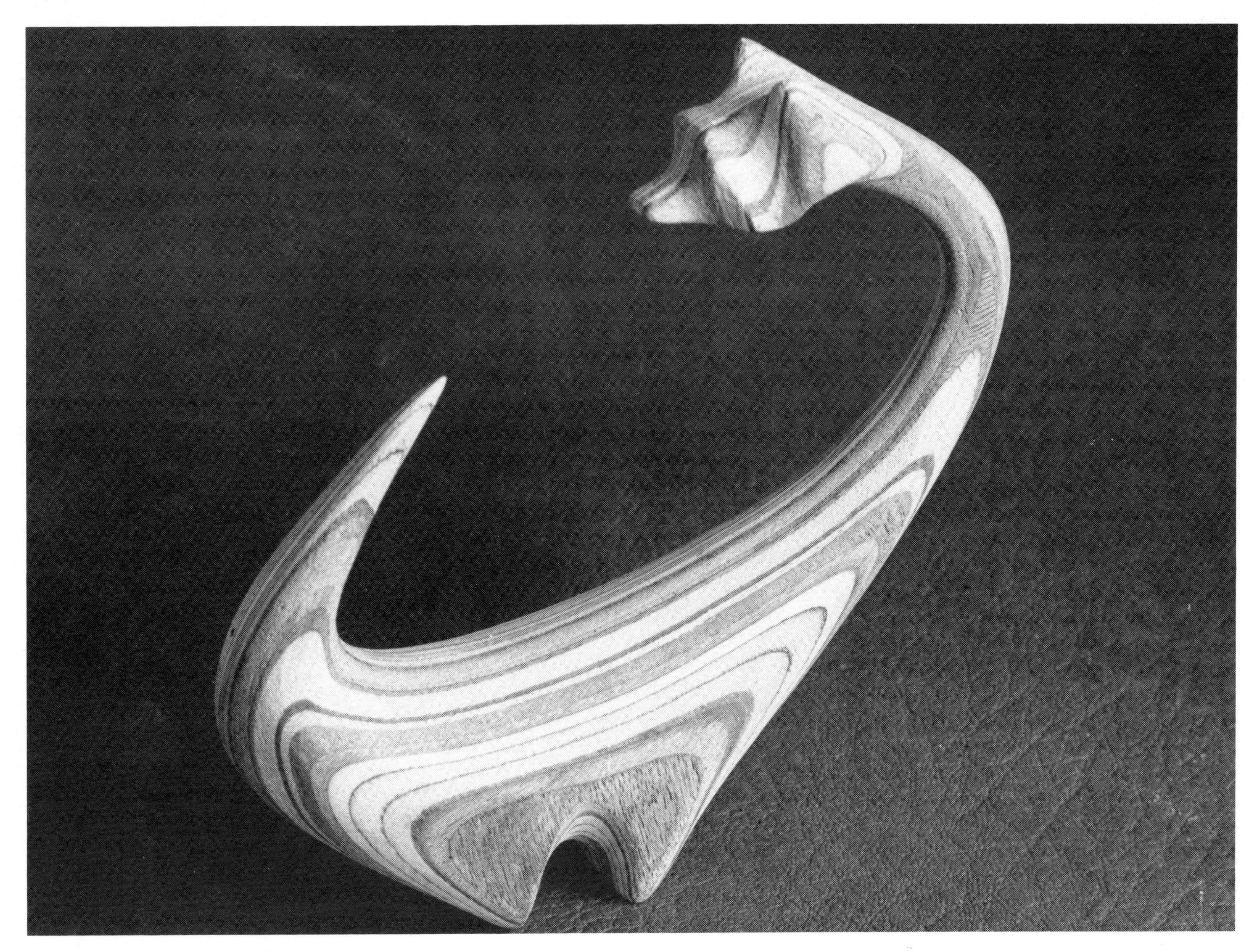

Cat, another fine laminated 3D example.

Giraffe 2D example (with flat backs) for displays on the wall.

A FEW WORDS ON LAMINATED SCULPTING

Laminated sculpting seems to catch the imagination and be very well accepted wherever it is demonstrated and presented as when this Award was given to beauty queen winner, Miss Sheila Walsh of Kirkby-in-Ashfield.
Location at the Blue Boar Inn, Hucknall, Nottinghamshire during the German Festival.

Sculpting at the 'Blue Boar Inn' Nottinghamshire from a live Puma.

◀ On another interesting occasion at the Blue Boar I made a laminated Mountain Lion (Puma) with the live subject present as a model. This proved a risky business as we had quite a job in getting the 'big cat' back into the cage in the adjacent Sherwood Zoo. Not to be recommended unless metal bars are present.

In 1976 I was asked to make and present ▶ on behalf of the local Rotary Club a laminated sculpture to one of the bravest men of modern times - Chay Blythe. I will always consider this a great honour. In keeping with this sea image, the subject I chose was a fearless Tiger Shark. It was very well received by this man who sailed in 1971/72 single handed around the world.

Laminated sculpting was very well received at the ITALIAN NATIONAL EXHIBITION in Rome where I had the pleasure of exhibiting and demonstrating this art form in 1975.
This was in the lovely interior of the Palazzo Dei Congressi. My visit was sponsored by British Airways and it proved very enjoyable and instructive to have the opportunity to work alongside artists of another Country and exchange pleasantries and admire their varied skills, from which there is such a lot to gain in learning and International relationships. The Italian people are great connoisseurs of fine art and craftsmanship and it was wonderful to note their enthusiasm when sculpting in plywood. My host there was the very amiable Lady Natacha de Rossi del Lion Nero for whom I sculpted a laminated abstract entitled 'Coliseum'. (Directly below).

Publicity Shots for British Airways inside The Coliseum, Rome.

Laminated Hound Dog presented to Bob Hope on stage at 'The Canadian National Exhibition', August 1977 in Toronto, Canada.

Rhino

These are two types of highly creative sculpture, generally made by using small pieces of wood and a lot of imagination.

The complex delicate structures rely for positioning and permanent fixing on a top quality contact adhesive - suggest TRETOBOND NON FLAM CONTACT.

These types of sculpture present such a variety of possibilities that it is suggested that much time is spent in thought and taping up 'dry arrangements', before reaching any conclusion and applying a top quality contact adhesive.

EXTENDED RELIEF SCULPTURE

Develop and arrange basic or abstract shapes on a simple background, presenting interesting imaginative and attractive 3D depth formations in harmony with each other. Use shape, colour, texture, balance, line and area and relief to the best advantage. The use and positioning of appropriate background light to this type of sculpture can often add additional dramatic visual appearance.

LINEAR SCULPTURE

Develop sculptural arrangements with good application of imagination in presenting themes. Use colour, texture, balance, line and area to the best advantage. Many attractive fascinating themes can be developed directly with the 'raw material' which may help stimulate abstract thought and produce interesting subjects for viewing and conversation.

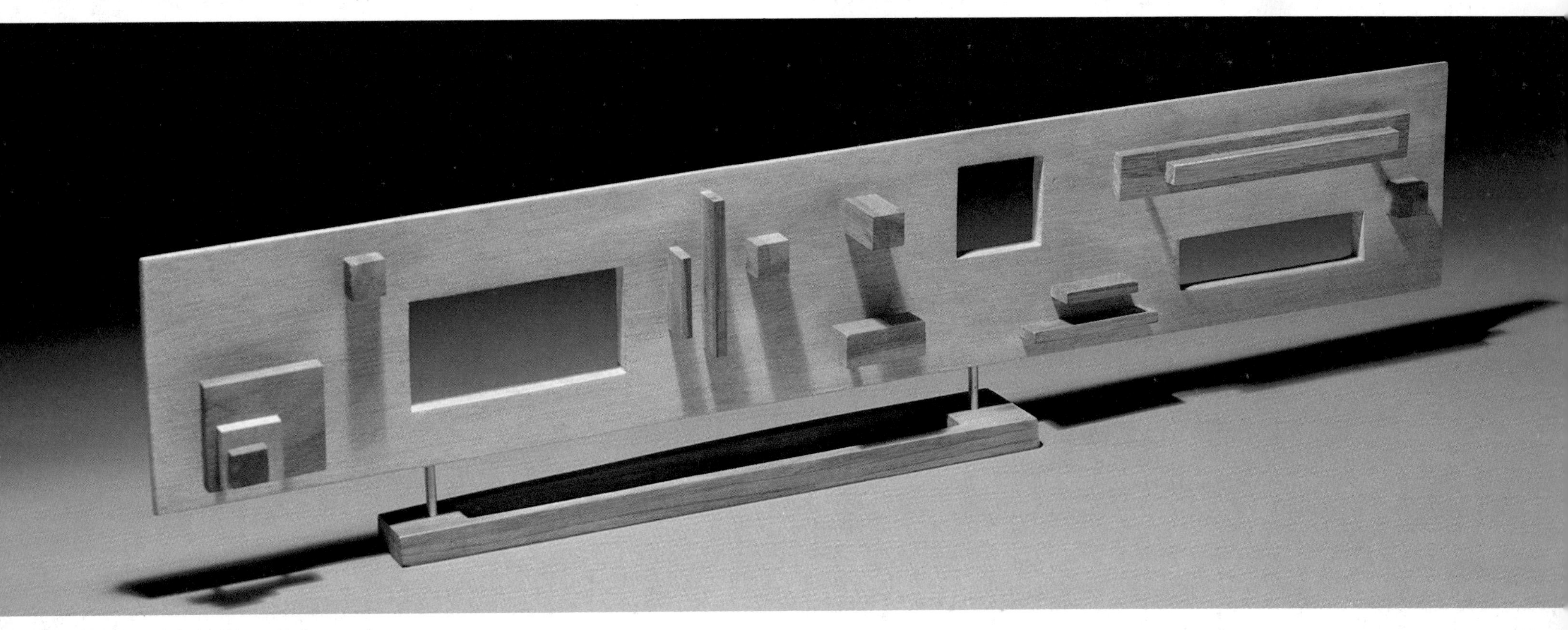

Woods African Limba and Burma Teak.

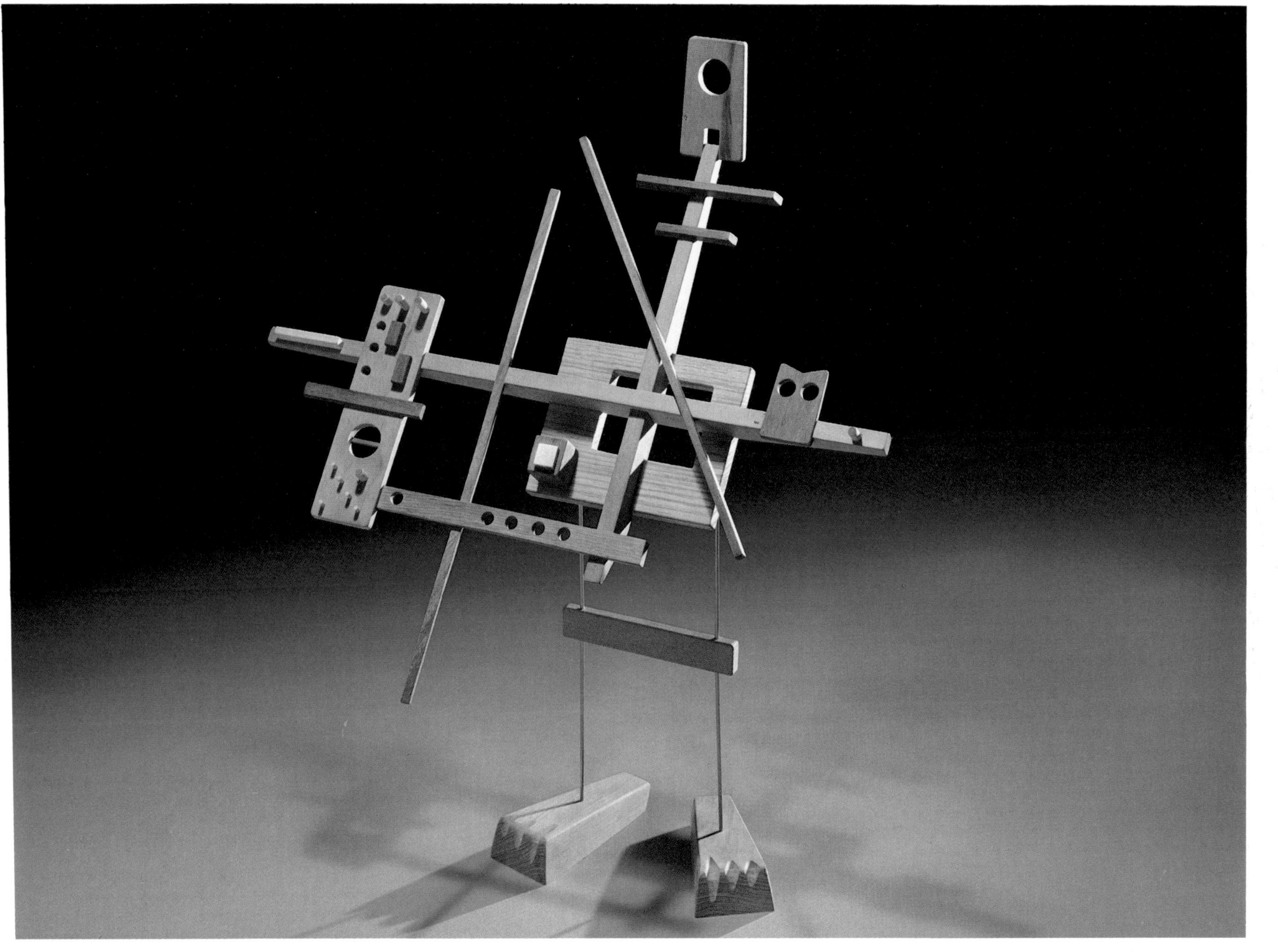

Woods Andaman Padauk, Poplar, Pitch Pine, Indian Rosewood, Burma Teak, English Sycamore.

Part of the John Matthews collection.

WOODEN TOYS

Woods Burma Teak, Red Deal, Beech, African Utile and English Sycamore.

Toys are something very special for the 'Users' and the 'Makers'. The joy of seeing children with toys is wonderful to behold and most especially to the parents, relations or friends when they themselves have made the toys - something not to be missed! Part of the many good experiences in life.

Wooden Toys have always been appreciated. They are strong, safe to use and durable. Items of play, decoration and often of substantial educational value. Long life items passed on from one generation to another and treasured by all.

Today, because of manufacturers' high costs, wooden toys have become somewhat of a luxury item to purchase, but with limited skill, materials and tools, good designs and clear instructions, it is possible to make economical wooden toys which will give good service and be readily appreciated any time of the year.

The toys range in this section includes both entertaining and purposefully educational development toys, each of which is accompanied by an age guide. However, this must remain flexible according to the individual abilities and development of each child.

The section starts with a general forward on basic working instructions. This is followed by a number of full sized varied toy designs accompanied by working guides. The section concludes by illustrating further examples for development.

Most of the toys are made with simple dowel construction, an excellent quick, effective and efficient method.

Note :
These toys are part of a large project intended for The Red Cross Society.

Woods Columbian Pine and Burma Teak.

WORKING NOTES

These toys have generally been made with small power units and safety precautions for their use have been included as a useful reminder.

Do not leave sharp tools and electrical units within the reach of children.

Always check that all power cables, plugs, switches and units are safe to use with no loose, frayed, bare or poorly connected wires etc. Put right any defects immediately!

Protect your eyes with a suitable guard when drilling, grinding, turning etc.

An important safety precaution is to hold the work firmly in a vice or cramped by other means.

Use the slowest speed possible for drilling large holes. This will help to prevent burning out of the temper in bits, thus rendering them useless.

Most softwoods often splinter and generally cannot stand up to the 'hammer' like hardwoods.

Use good quality mild working hardwoods, e.g. Chestnut, Sycamore, Basswood, Walnut, Japanese Elm, Utile, Oak, African Agba, Brazilian Cedar, Honduras Mahogany etc.

Excellent use can be made of good quality plywood, blockboard, laminboard etc. They are extremely strong and can be obtained in large sheets or reasonably priced offcuts.

Planing wood to size can be very time consuming and energy sapping. An alternative is to have it machine planed to size at the source of supply.

When thought appropriate extra length etc. is included in the preparation sizes to allow for comfortable pattern positioning and shaping.

Whenever available use dowelling made of good quality hardwood, e.g. Beech.

Broomsticks make excellent economical large sized dowel, often ranging from ⅞" (21mm dia.) to 1¼" (32mm) diameter.

Initially test bore in a waste piece of wood to find the correct size bit before you bore the 'REAL THING'.

After marking out the centre of the dowel or screw hole with a pencil bore a shallow guide hole with a bradawl to help position the point of the bit easily and accurately.

TIMBABOND No.636 is an excellent adhesive for dowel construction. It's high viscosity helps to prevent runs, and it is not too quickly absorbed by coarse fibres or end grain.

1
For safety round off any prominent dowel ends.

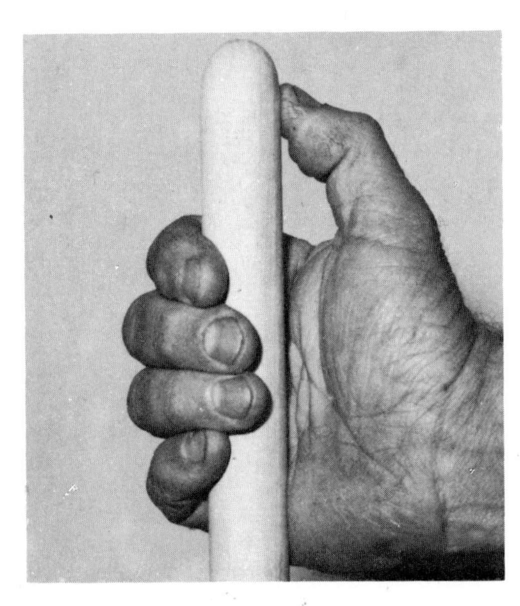

2
Remove the sharp ends of dowel which are to be fitted into holes. This helps easy location and prevents fewer splits occurring.

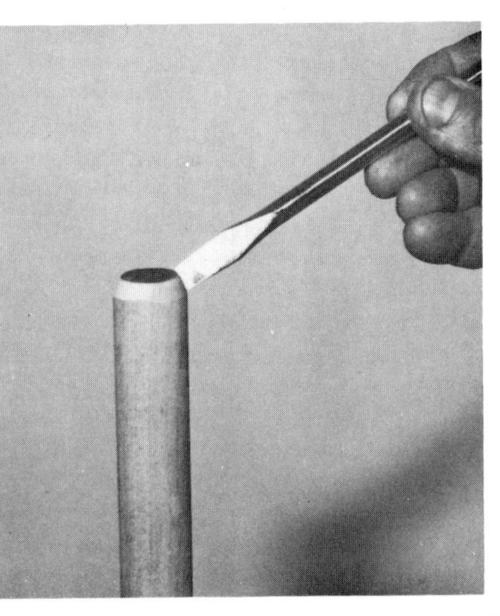

3
When fitting and fixing dowel to prevent damage to their ends place a piece of waste wood over when tapping home with a hammer.

Note:
Remove all sharp edges on the toys with wood files, planes and abrasives. This will make them nice to handle and free from sharp edge splinters.

Dowel sizes often vary slightly and awkwardly, e.g. 1″ (25mm) dia. dowel can be 1″ or 1″+ or 1″– (25mm or 25mm+ or 25mm–). To overcome these odd sizes grind down bits to the required exact dowel sizes and label for present and future use.

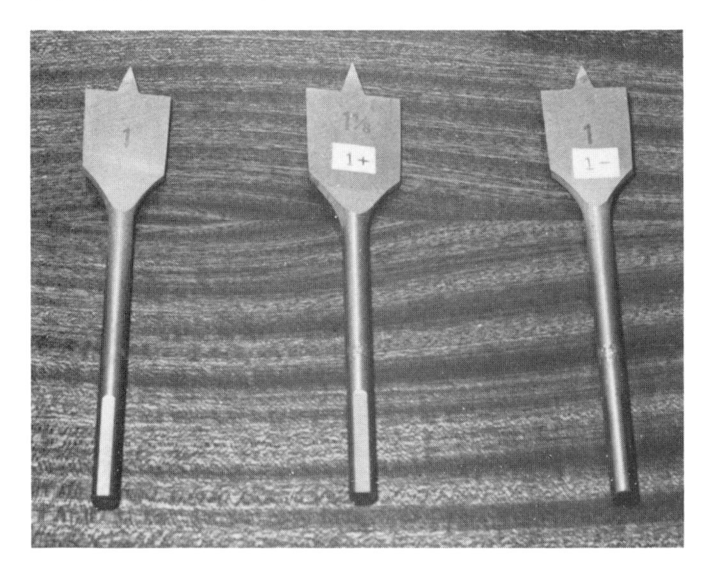

Grind the sides of the bits equally and in keeping with the manufacturers angle.

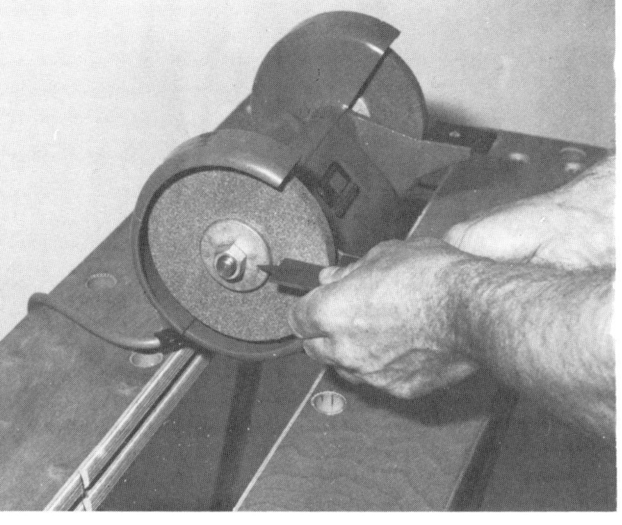

Note this method for boring through dowel. Bore one way until the point of the bit just protrudes: Then turn the dowel over, carefully centre the bit and finish the hole.

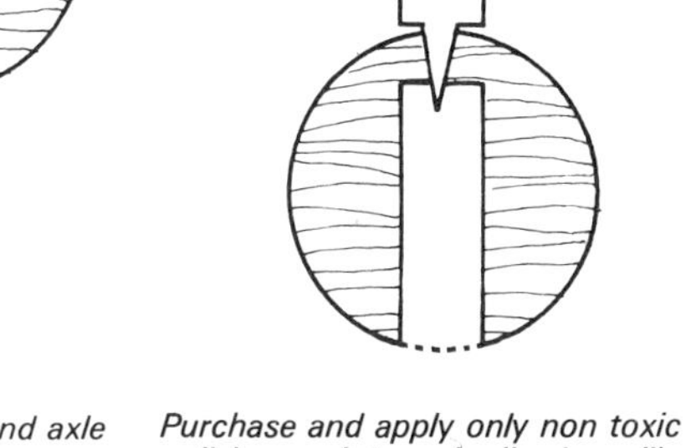

Wheel details

Wooden wheels can be cut by various methods, e.g. Lathes, Drumsaws, Bandsaws, or Tank Cutters etc. Wooden wheels are especially suitable for Indoor Toys.

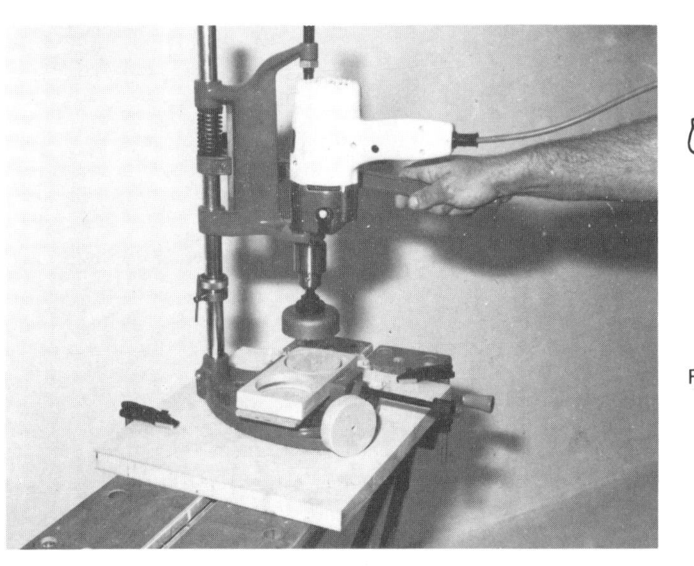

Axle details

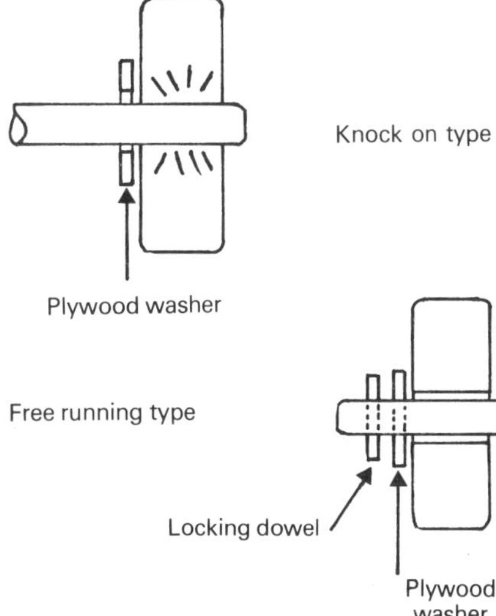

Available at many shops are plastic wheels and axle units. These are especially suitable for outdoor toys and an alternative to wooden units.

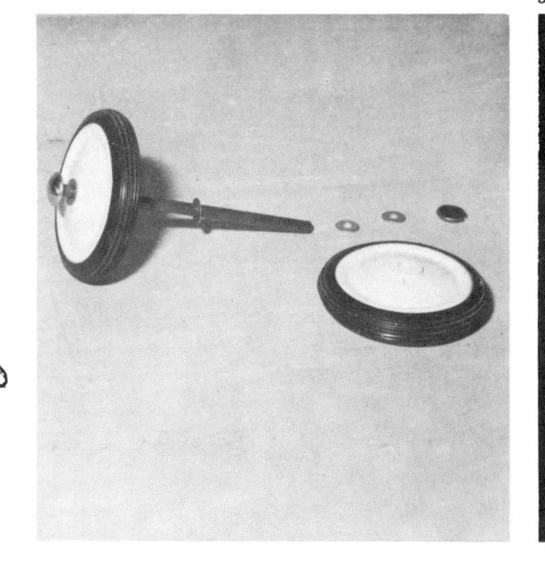

Purchase and apply only non toxic polishes, paints and adhesives, like TRETOBOND LIMITED manufacture as babies and youngsters often chew, suck, bite and scratch the surface of all kinds of toys.

SHUFFLE MOBILE

Wood African Agba.

A large carpet creeper developer, and a pre-walking get-around. After walking has been achieved it can be used just as a ride-about. (Age range 1-4 years).

WORKING GUIDE

1 *Obtain and prepare appropriate materials to size.*

2 *Mark out dowel centres.*

3 *Test, then bore tight fitting dowel holes in body and wheels. (Note : apart from axle holes in chassis and washers. These need to be ⅛" (3mm) larger in diameter than axles).*

4 *Trace and mark out and shape bonnet and boot.*

5 *Shape wheels and washers.*

6 *Clean up with abrasives removing all sharp edges.*

7 *Apply a top quality appropriate adhesive, suggest TIMBABOND No.636 to dowel holes, excluding chassis axle holes and washers.*

8 *Tap construction together.*

9 *Wipe off any surplus adhesive with a clean damp cloth and leave to set thoroughly.*

10 *Clean up with abrasives.*

11 *Apply an appropriate finish.*

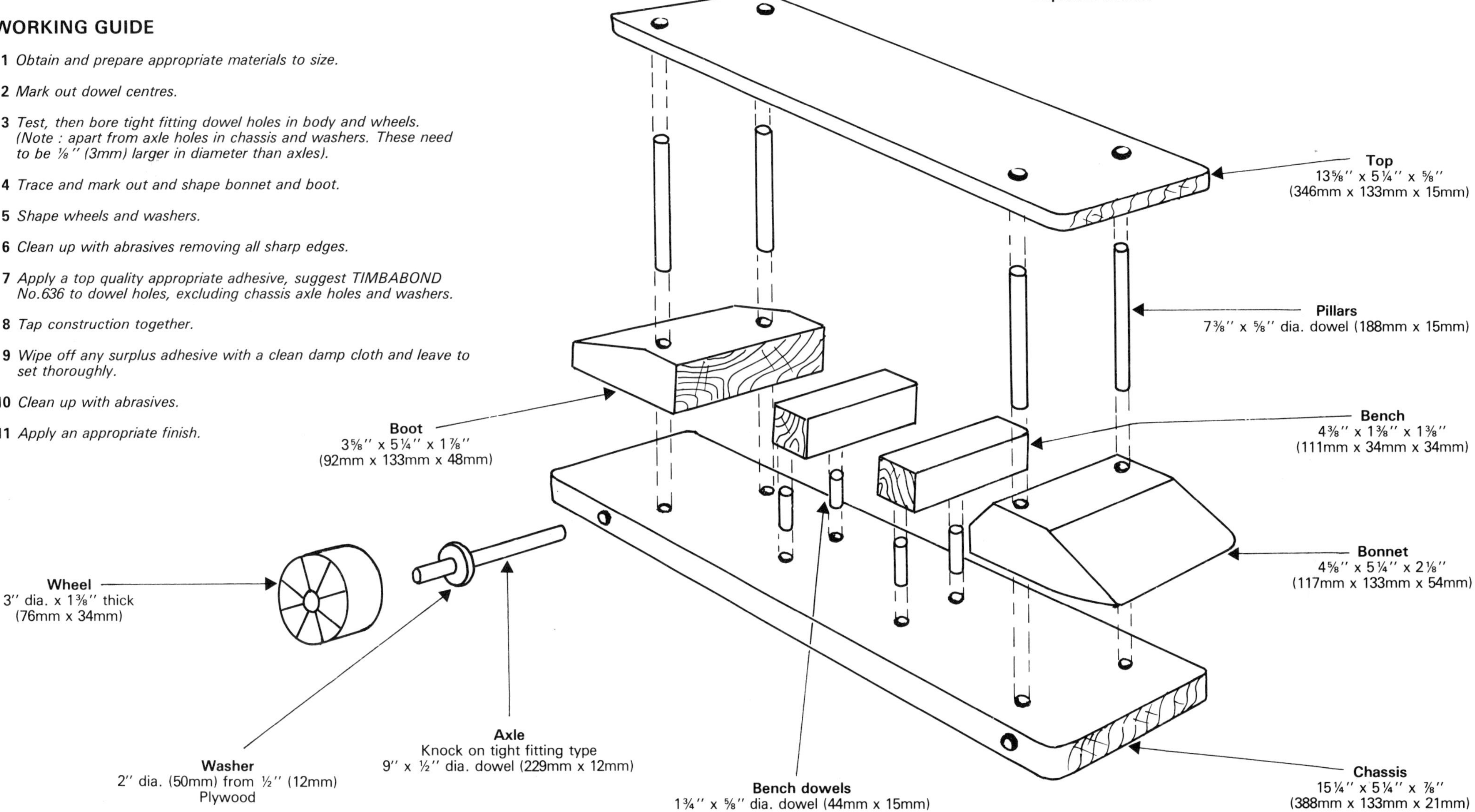

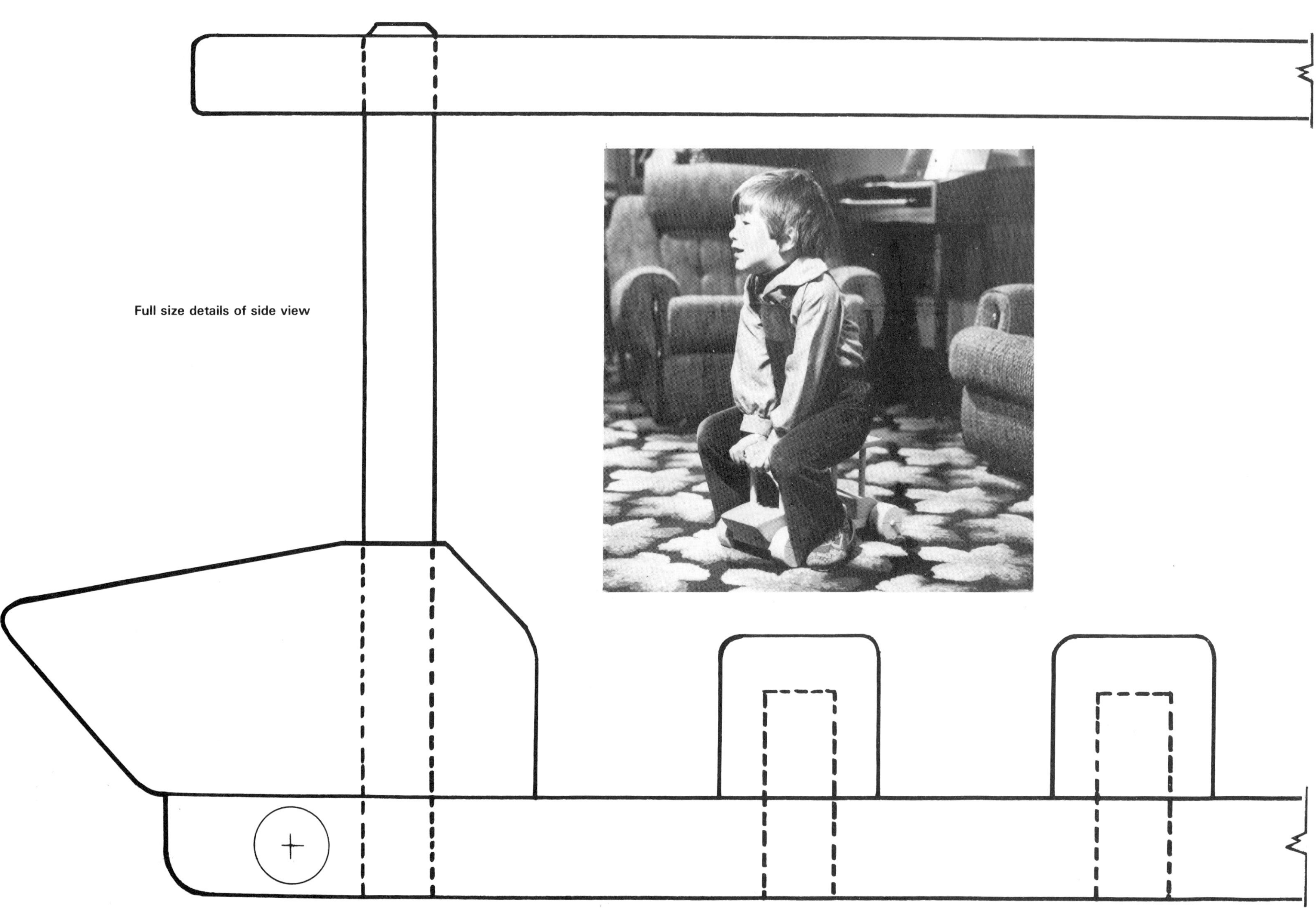
Full size details of side view

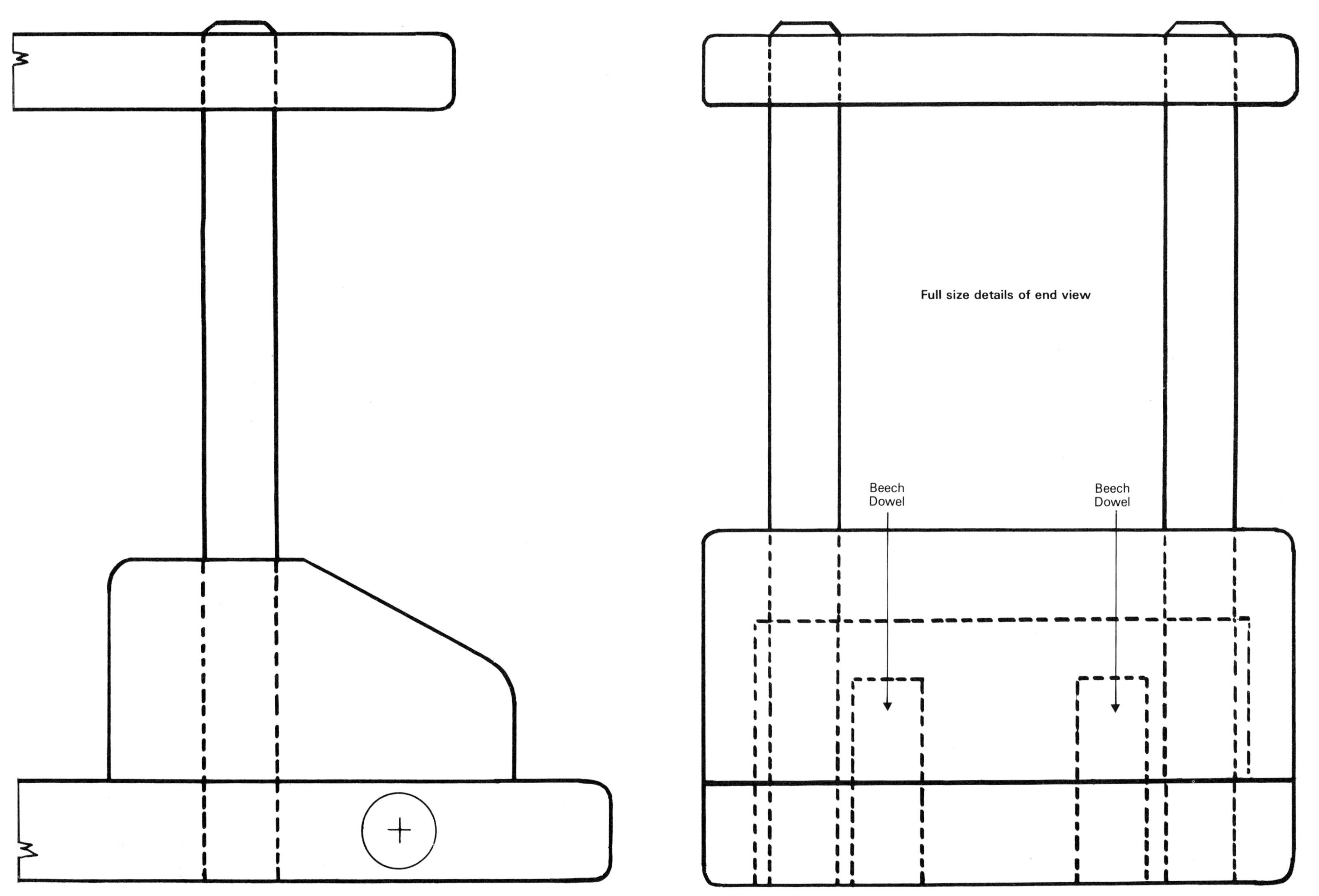
Full size details of end view
Beech
Dowel
Beech
Dowel

STEAM BOAT BILL

Woods Honduras Mahogany and Beech Dowel.

A robust Push-About for use after those first giant steps. An entertaining toy, mainly for outdoor use. For dashing about with and enjoying the freedom of outdoor spaces. (Age range from walking to 5 years plus).

WORKING GUIDE

1 *Obtain and prepare appropriate material to size.*

2 *Trace, then mark out name board, hull and wheels and dowel hole centres.*

3 *Test, then bore tight fitting dowel holes (note : apart from the hull and washer's axle holes - these need to be ⅛" (3mm) larger than the diameter of the axle).*

4 *Shape hull, wheels, washers, name board etc.*

5 *Mark out and shape handle.*

6 *Clean up with abrasives, removing all sharp edges.*

7 *Cut bell beam and central wheel bolt to size.*

8 *Cut, fit and fix paddles and wheels.*

9 *Apply an appropriate adhesive, suggest TIMBABOND No.636 to dowel holes, excluding axle holes in hull and washers.*

10 *Tap, bolt and screw construction together.*

11 *Wipe off any surplus adhesive, with a clean damp cloth and leave to set thoroughly.*

12 *Clean up with abrasives.*

13 *Apply an appropriate finish.*

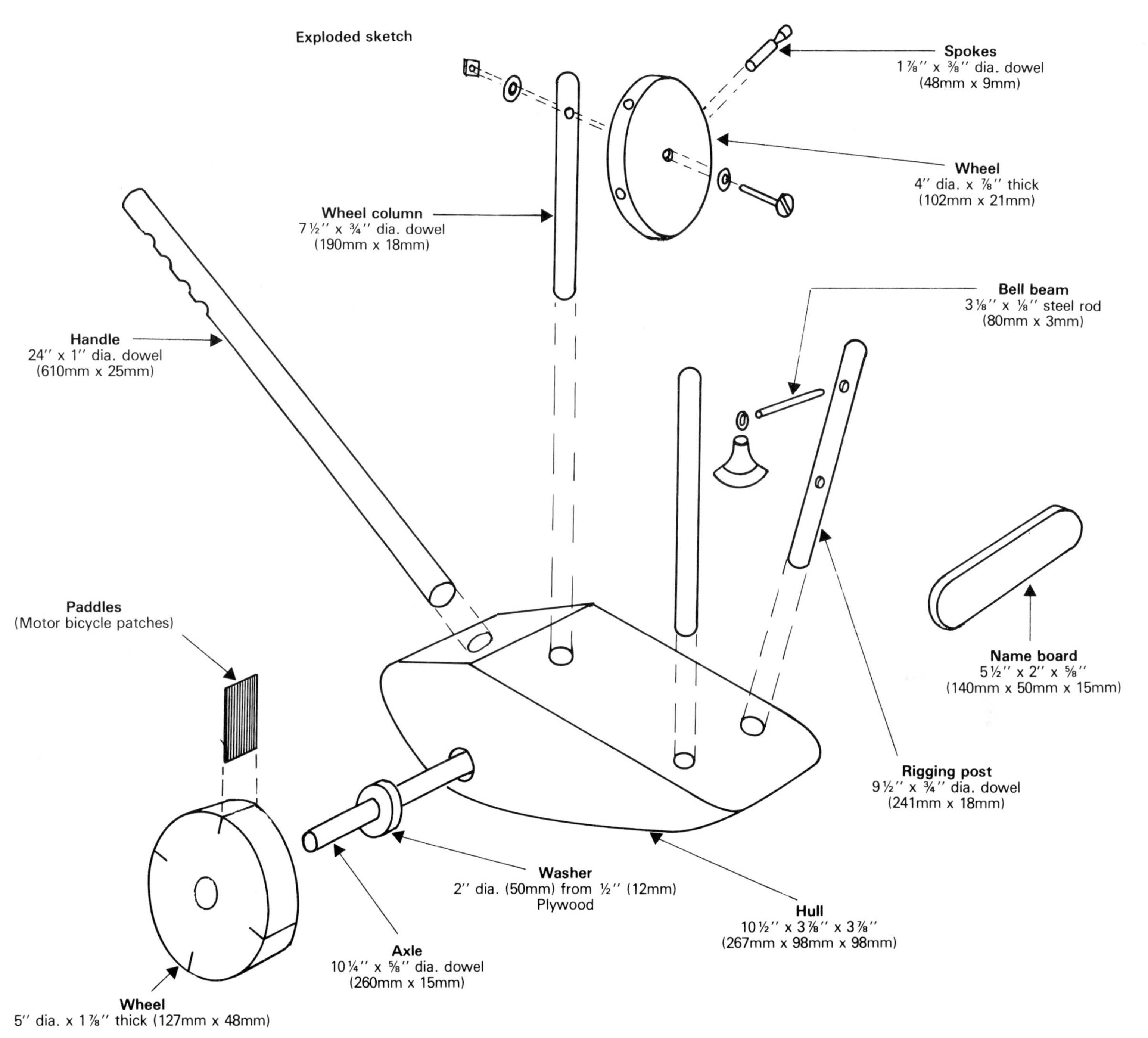

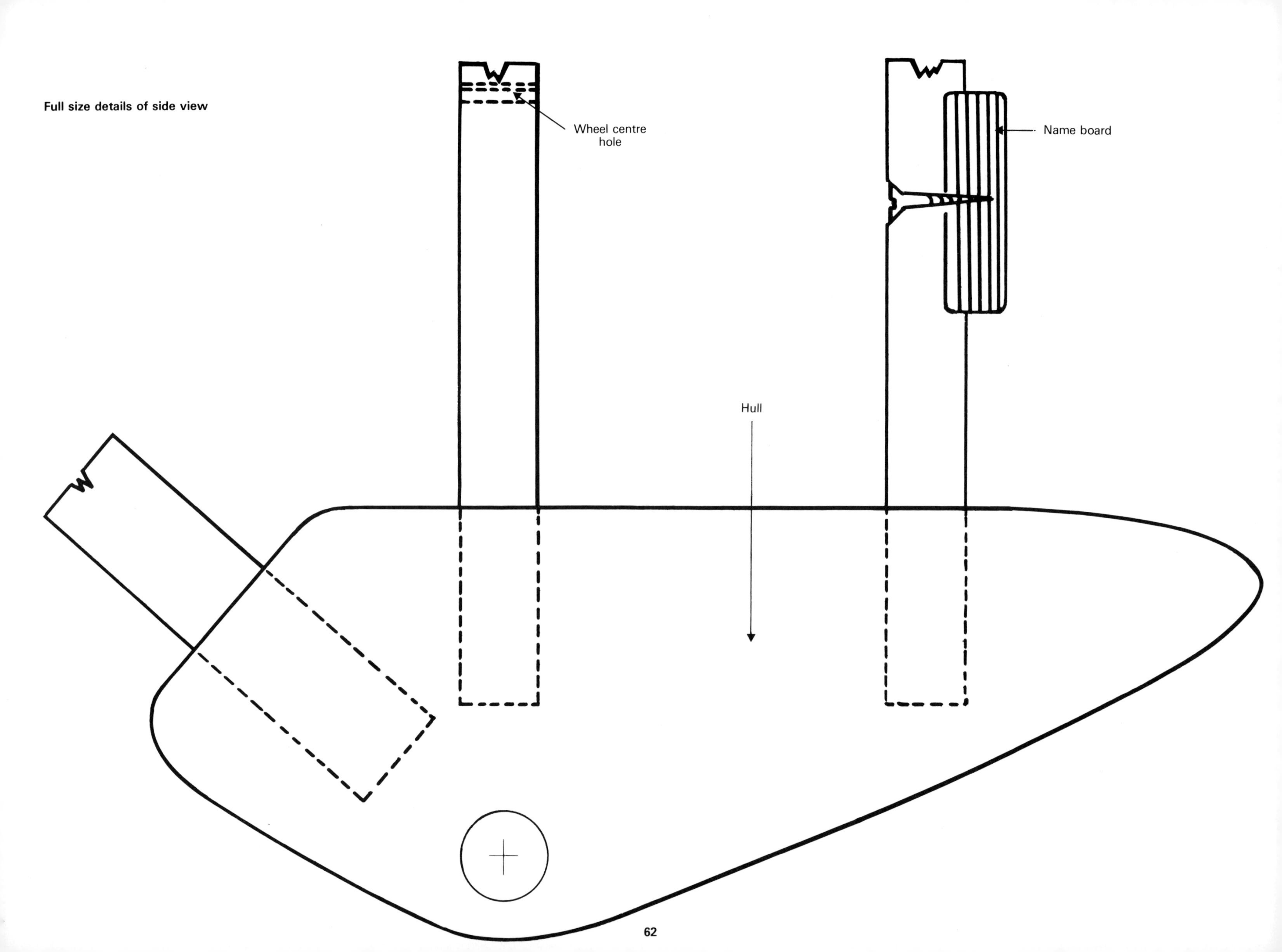
Full size details of side view
Wheel centre hole
Name board
Hull

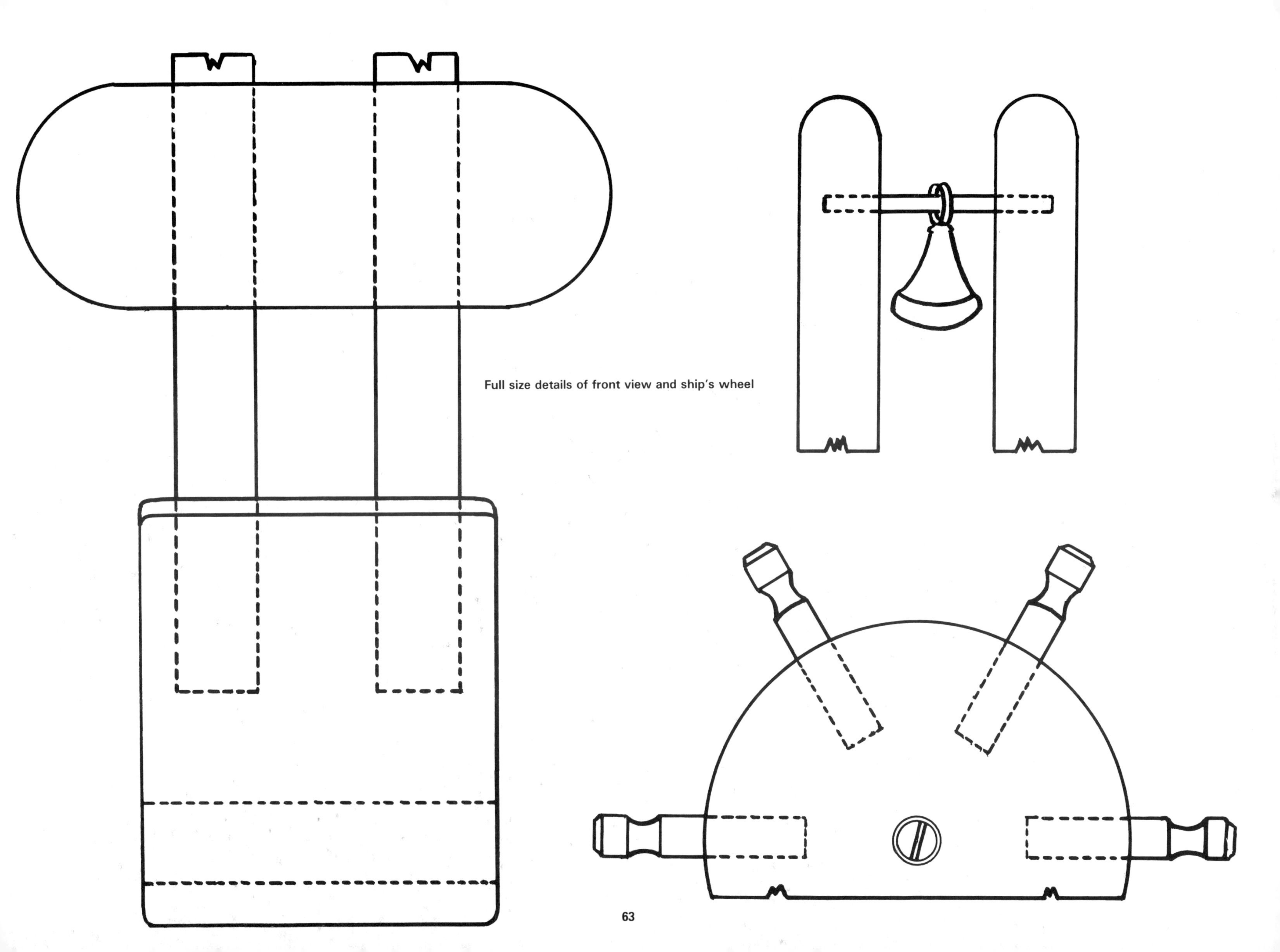

Full size details of front view and ship's wheel

PULL-A-LONG 'SCOTTIE'

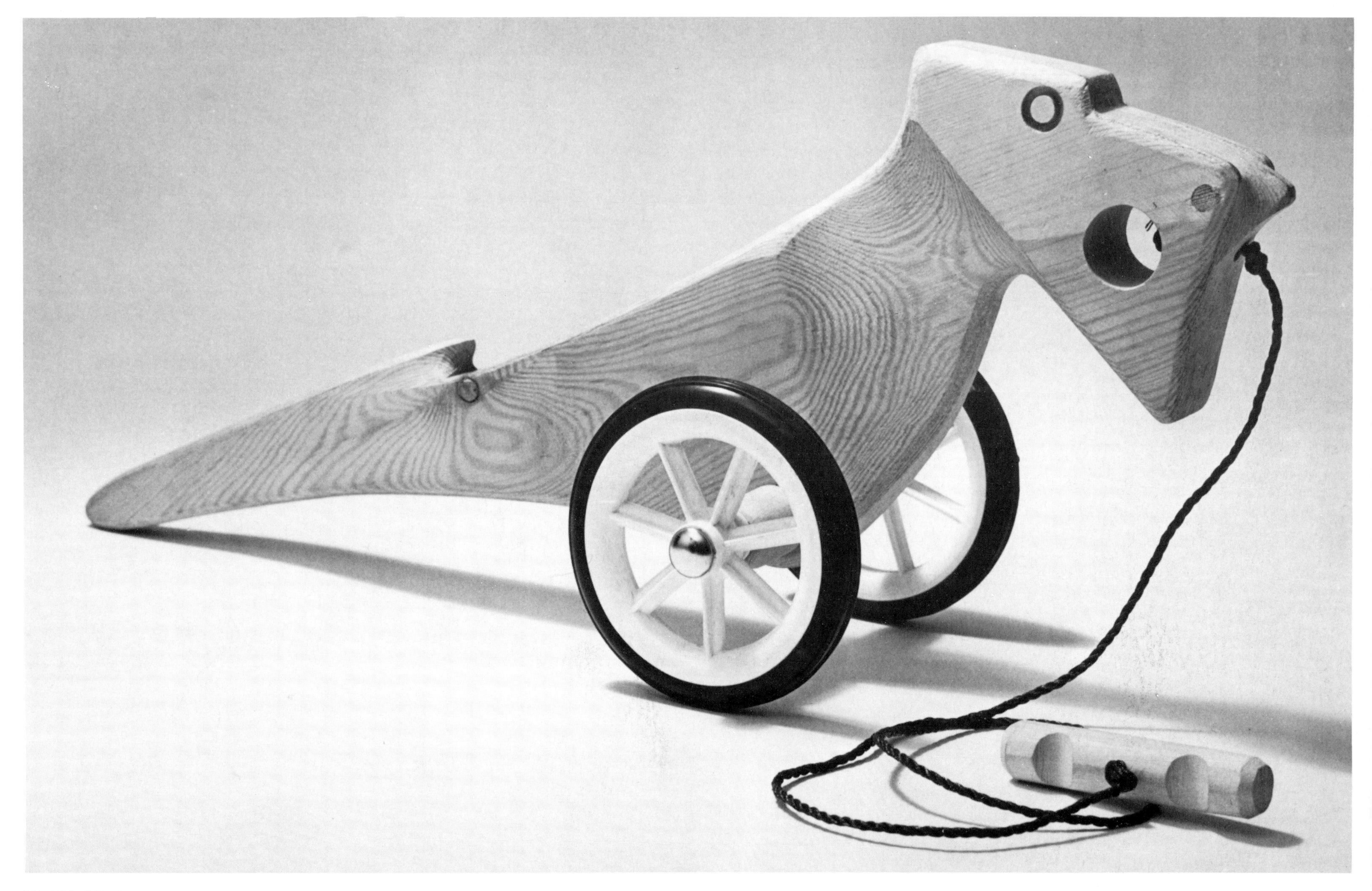

Wood Red Deal.

A robust pull-about toy for the outdoors. Excellent for the energetic youngster to let off steam with and enjoy being in charge of an animated item. (Often easier than the real subject in question). Age range from walking to 5 years plus.

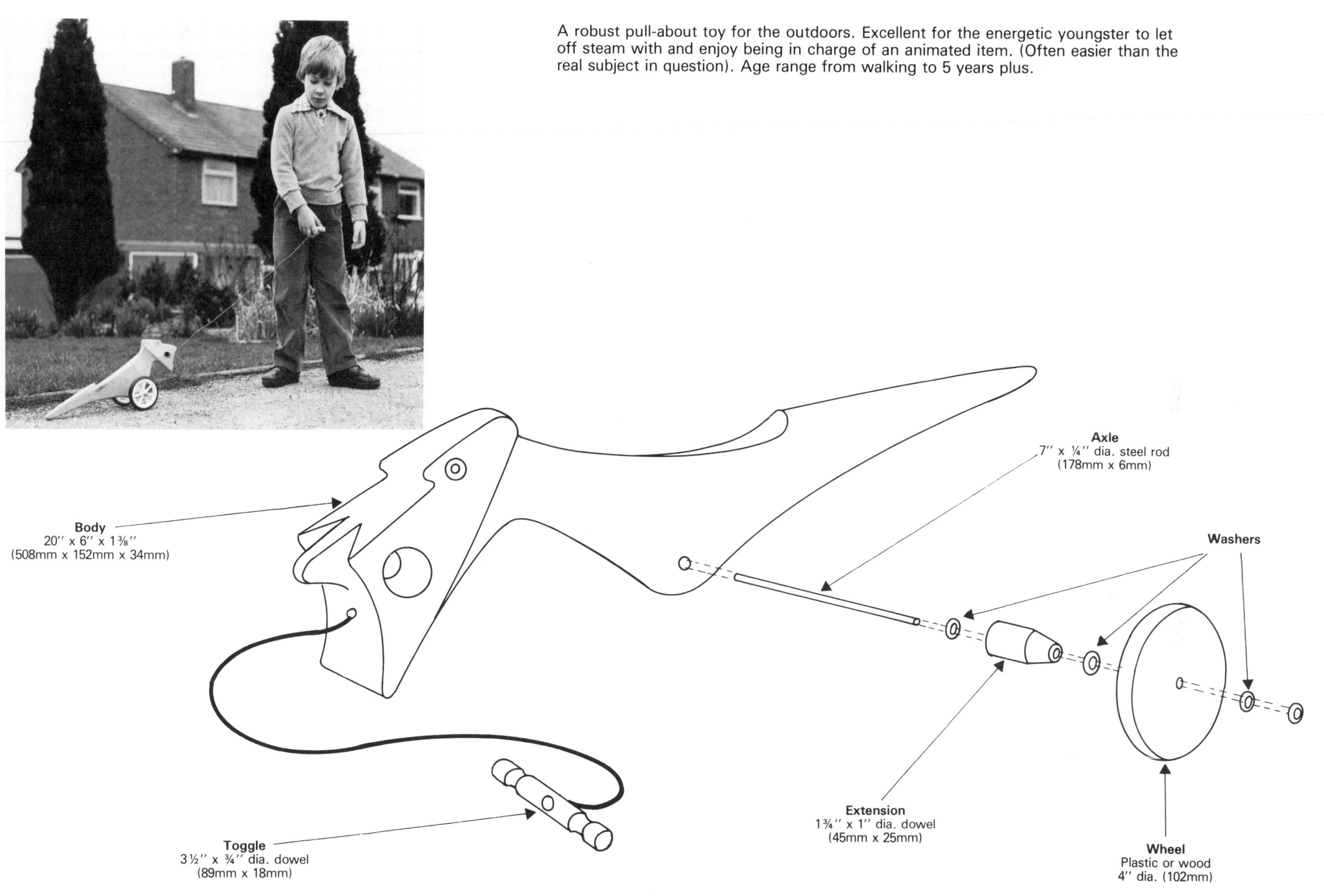

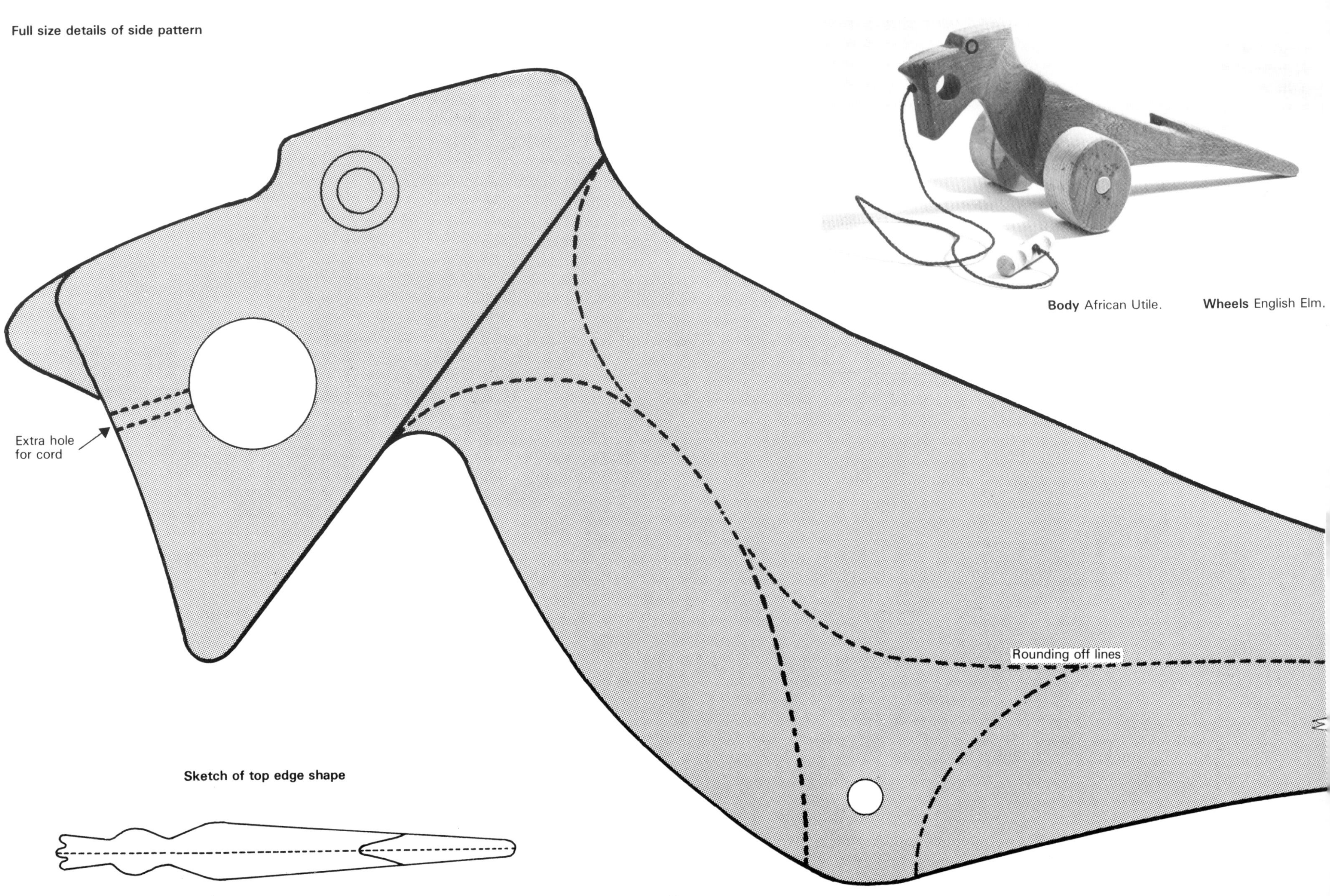

Body African Utile. Wheels English Elm.

Alternative type of wheel
A wooden oval wheel gives that extra dimension of movement.

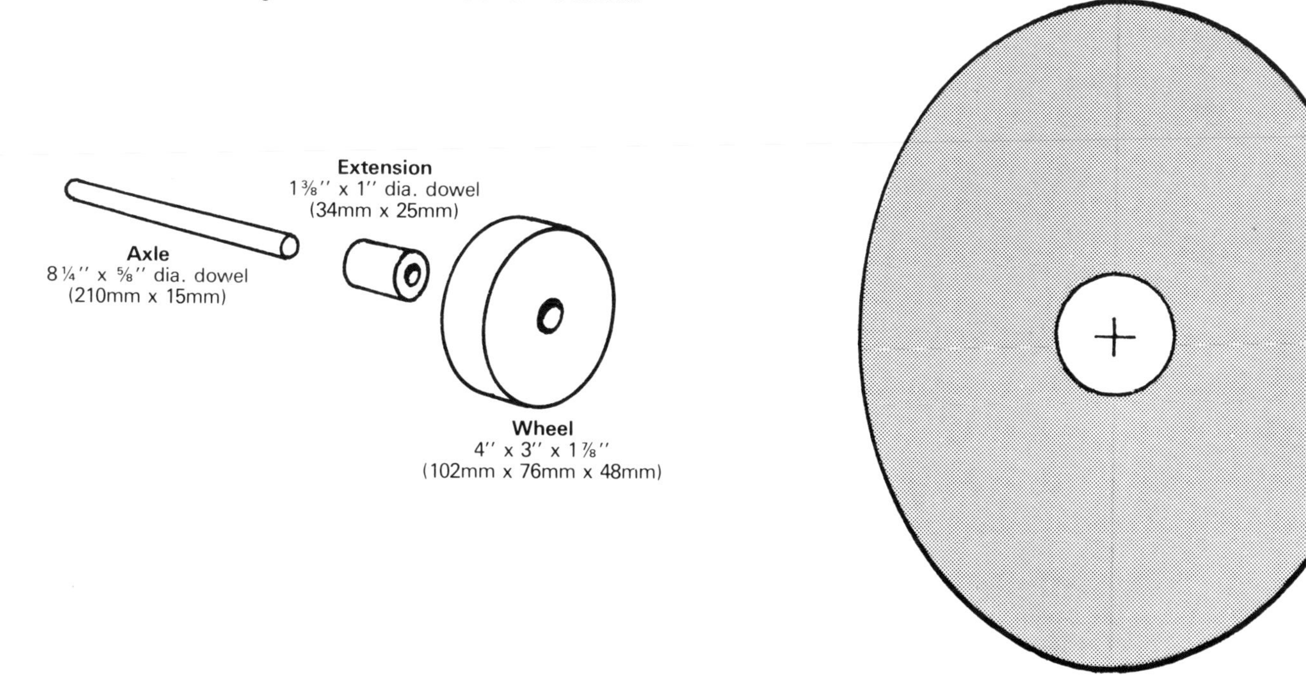

Full size details of wooden wheel

WORKING GUIDE

1 *Obtain and prepare appropriate materials to size.*

2 *Trace and mark out body shape and hole centres.*

3 *Bore mouth and eyes holes.*

4 *Test and bore tight fitting holes for metal axle in body.*
Note : For wooden wheels and matching axle unit mark out, test and bore tight fitting axle holes in wheels, and in the body and extensions bore an axle hole ⅛" (3mm) larger in diameter.

5 *Shape body.*

6 *Clean up with abrasives.*

7 *Fit and fix axle unit.*

8 *Make and fit toggle.*

9 *Clean up with abrasives.*

10 *Apply an appropriate finish.*

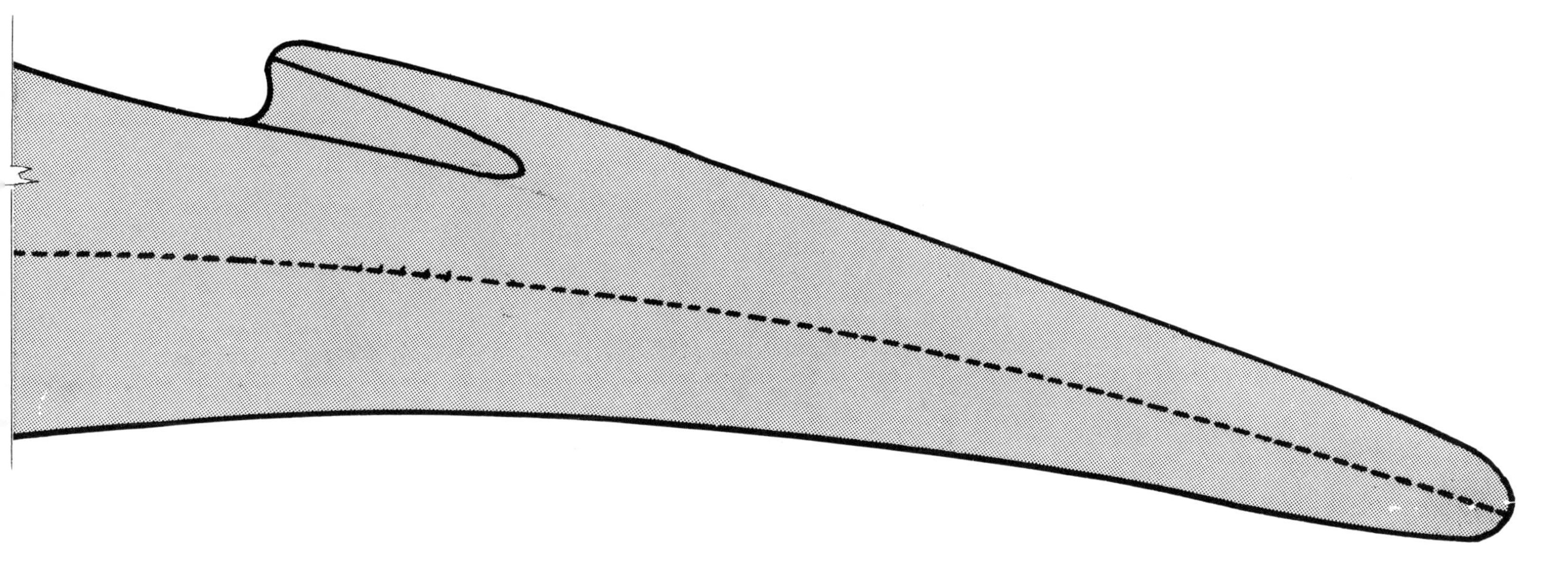

CONSTRUCTIONAL BUILDING TOWER

A simple constructional building toy for the indoors or outdoors on a fine day. A helpful unit for developing active young minds and manipulation skills (age range 18 months to 5 years).

WORKING GUIDE

1 *Obtain and prepare appropriate material to size.*

2 *Trace and mark out base shape.*

3 *Mark out dowel hole centres in base and building blocks.*

4 *Test then bore dowel holes.*
Note : Remember to bore easy fitting dowel holes in base and top part of each building block and tight fitting holes in bottom part of each building block.

6 *Shape base and dowel ends.*

7 *Clean up with abrasives.*

8 *Apply an appropriate top quality adhesive. Suggest TIMBABOND No.636 to tight fitting bottom dowel hole of each building block, then tap in dowels.*

9 *Wipe off any surplus adhesive with a clean damp cloth and leave to set thoroughly.*

10 *Clean up with abrasives.*

11 *Apply an appropriate finish.*

Base Lamin Board. **Building blocks** African Utile.

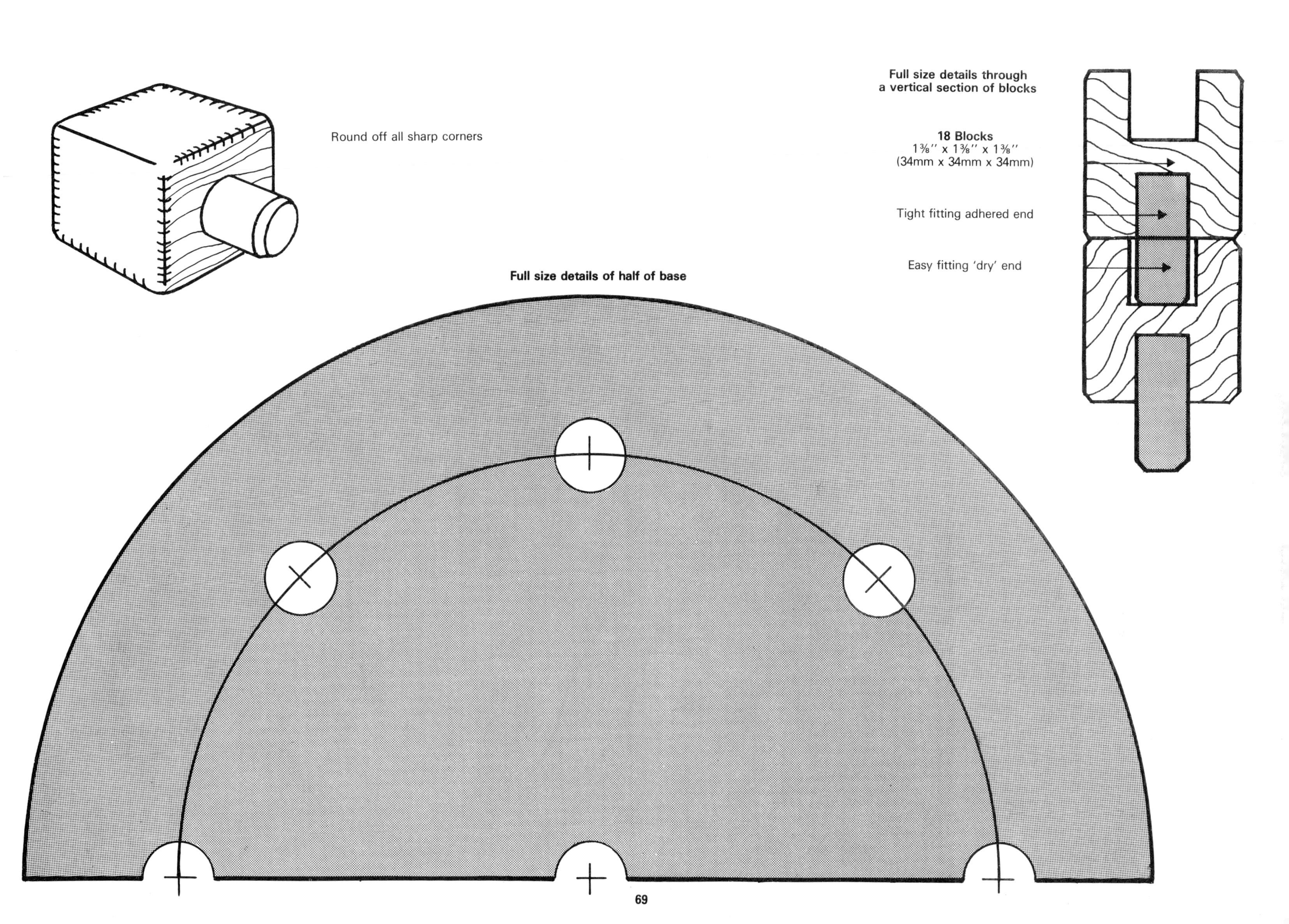
Round off all sharp corners
Full size details through a vertical section of blocks
18 Blocks
1⅜″ x 1⅜″ x 1⅜″
(34mm x 34mm x 34mm)
Tight fitting adhered end
Easy fitting 'dry' end
Full size details of half of base

THE WABASH CANNONBALL

A simple mobile fun toy for constructing and using indoors. A wealth of pleasure can be generated by youngsters as they steam through imaginary 'prairies' and the lounge. (Age guide 1-5 years plus).

WORKING GUIDE

1 *Obtain and prepare appropriate materials to size.*

2 *Trace and mark out engines and carriage shapes, also decorative and dowel hole centres.*

3 *Bore decorative holes and test and bore easy fitting holes for axles in engine and in carriages.*

4 *Test and bore tight fitting axle holes in wheels.*

5 *Shape carriages and engine.*

6 *Clean up with abrasives.*

7 *Fit appropriate sized metal hooks and eyes.*

8 *Apply a top quality appropriate adhesive, suggest TIMBABOND No.636 to funnel holes and wheels.*

9 *Tap construct together.*

10 *Wipe off any surplus adhesive with a clean damp cloth and leave to set thoroughly.*

11 *If desired make and fit a toggle and cord.*

12 *Clean up with abrasive.*

13 *Apply an appropriate finish.*

Three carriages
11½" x 1⅜" x 1⅜" (293mm x 34mm x 34mm)

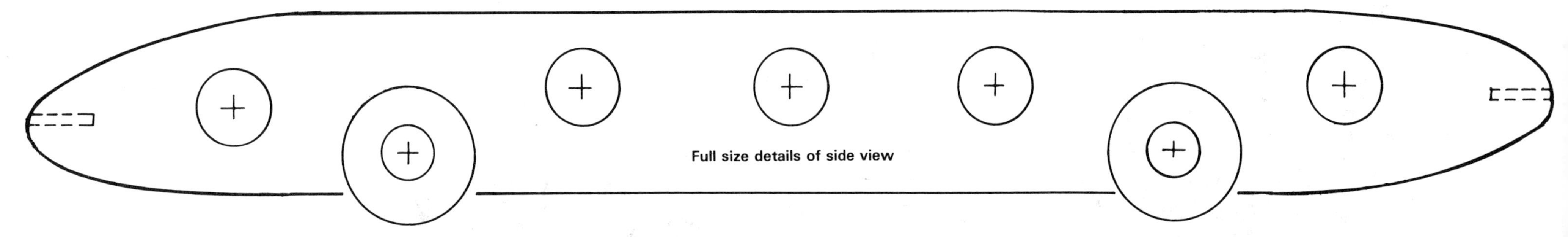

Wood used for train and carriages Honduras Mahogany.

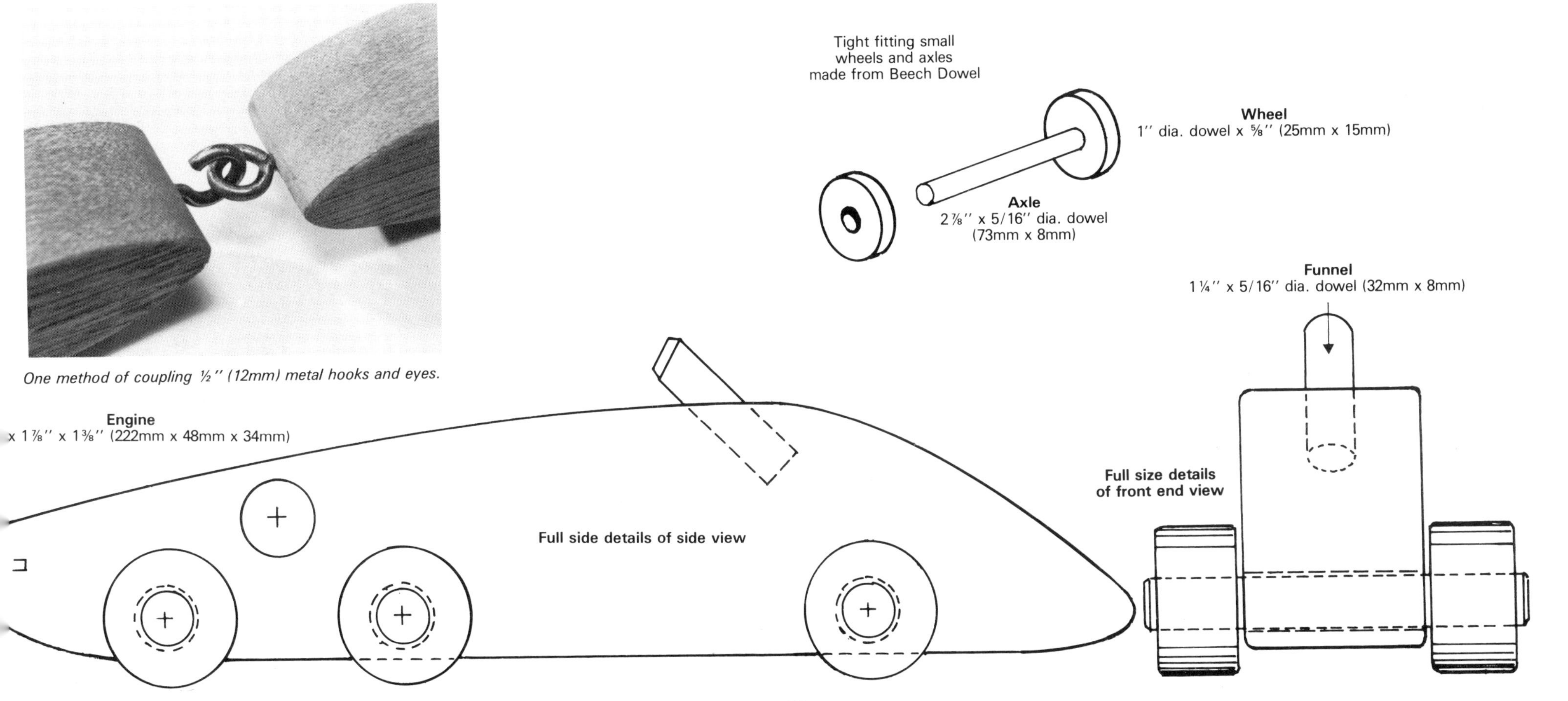

One method of coupling ½″ (12mm) metal hooks and eyes.

LAND RACING YACHT

Hull African Utile.

A strong pull-about highly mobile outdoor toy to help youngsters let off steam and enjoy the exhilaration of being in charge of a racing unit of their own - a great favourite with youngsters. (Age guide - from walking to 5 years plus).

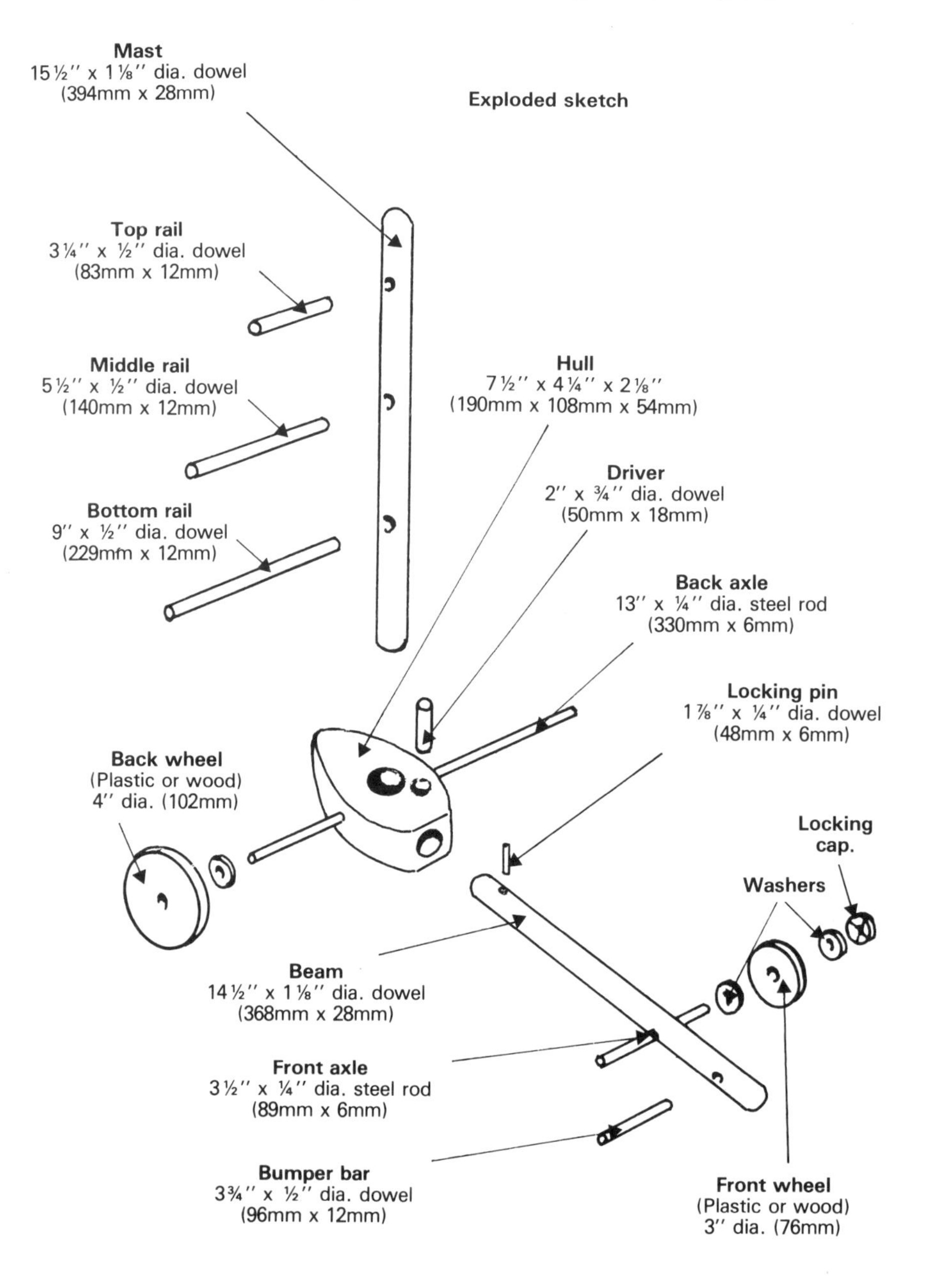

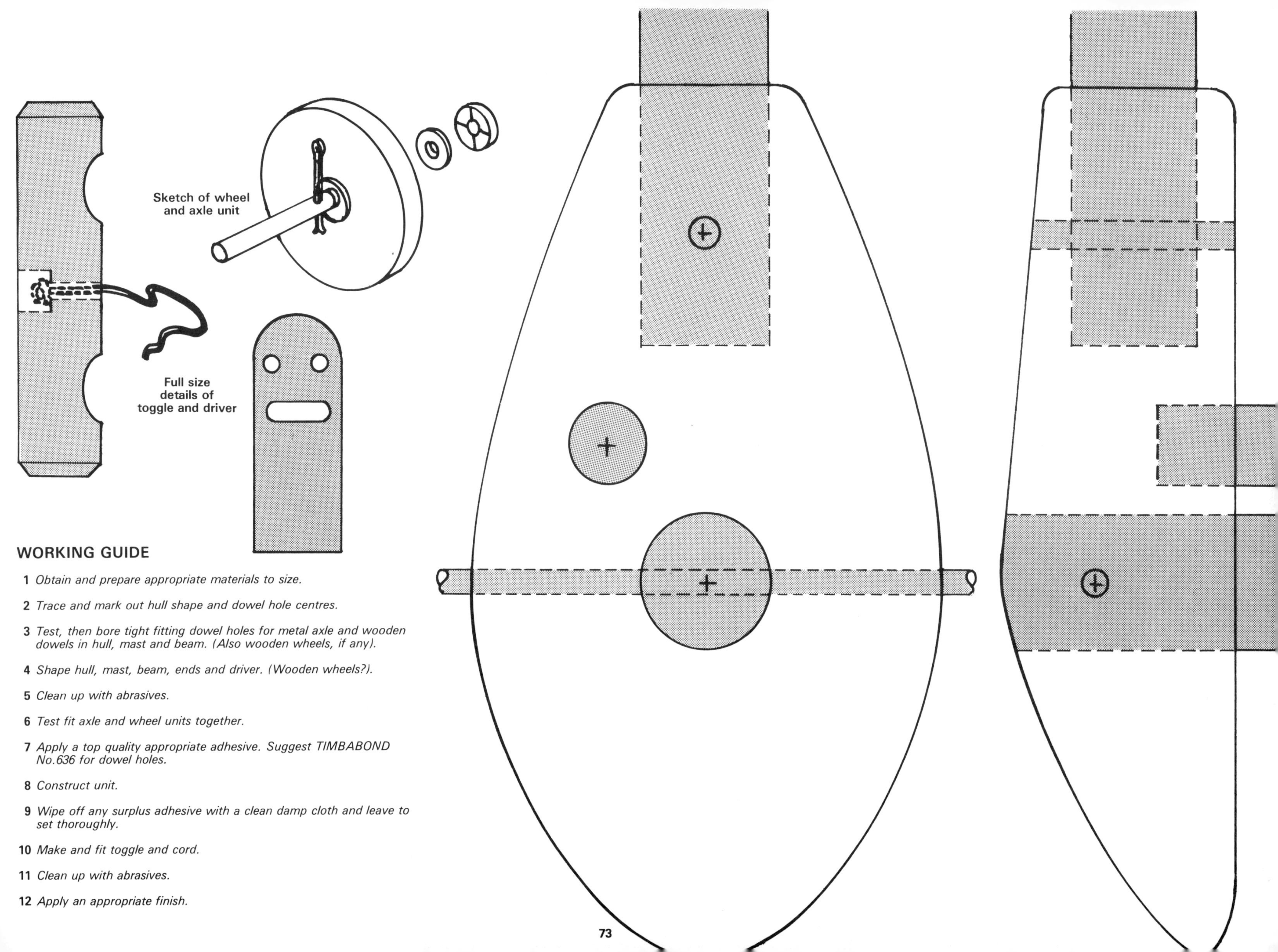

WORKING GUIDE

1. *Obtain and prepare appropriate materials to size.*
2. *Trace and mark out hull shape and dowel hole centres.*
3. *Test, then bore tight fitting dowel holes for metal axle and wooden dowels in hull, mast and beam. (Also wooden wheels, if any).*
4. *Shape hull, mast, beam, ends and driver. (Wooden wheels?).*
5. *Clean up with abrasives.*
6. *Test fit axle and wheel units together.*
7. *Apply a top quality appropriate adhesive. Suggest TIMBABOND No.636 for dowel holes.*
8. *Construct unit.*
9. *Wipe off any surplus adhesive with a clean damp cloth and leave to set thoroughly.*
10. *Make and fit toggle and cord.*
11. *Clean up with abrasives.*
12. *Apply an appropriate finish.*

SWISS CHALET - DOLLS HOUSE

Most of the structure is made from ½" (12mm) Teak faced Plywood.

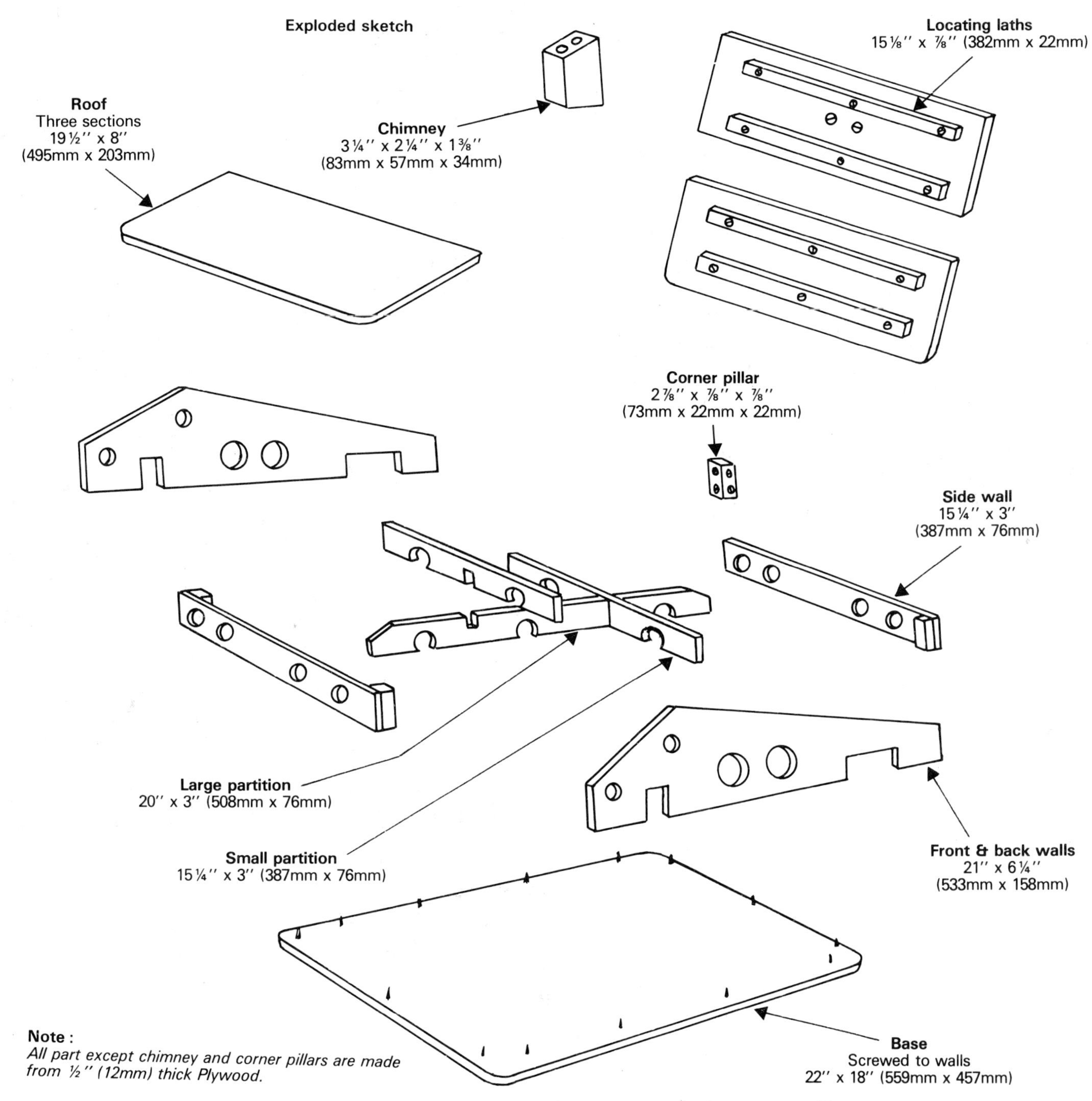

Note :
All part except chimney and corner pillars are made from ½" (12mm) thick Plywood.

A versatile, modern dolls house with a moveable roof for easy access.

A simple unit to make and use indoors and kit out with small home-made items of furniture etc.

An excellent assembly for individual or group use. (Age guide 18 months to 5 years plus).

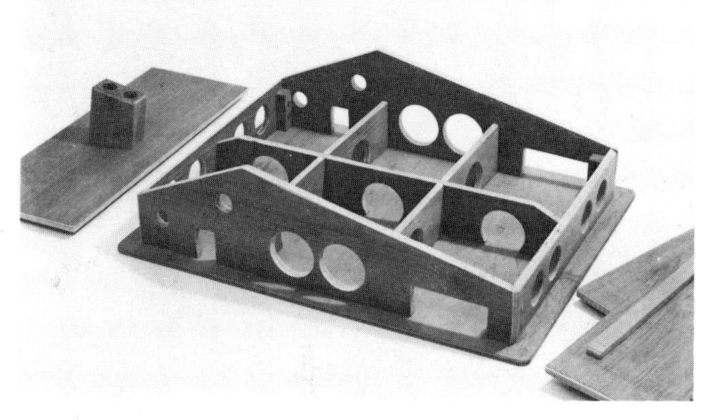

WORKING GUIDE

1. *Obtain and prepare appropriate materials to size.*
2. *Mark out walls, partitions, doorways and windows and chimney hole centres.*
3. *Mark out centres of screw holes in base and corner fillers.*
4. *Bore, saw and shape walls, doorways, windows and chimney.*
5. *Bore and countersink screwholes.*
6. *Saw partition cogged joints.*
7. *Test fit together and number each part and adjust where necessary.*
8. *Unscrew and clean up with abrasives.*
9. *Apply a top quality appropriate adhesive.*
10. *Construct.*
11. *Wipe off any surplus adhesive and clean with damp cloth and leave to set thoroughly.*
12. *Clean with abrasives.*
13. *Apply an appropriate finish.*

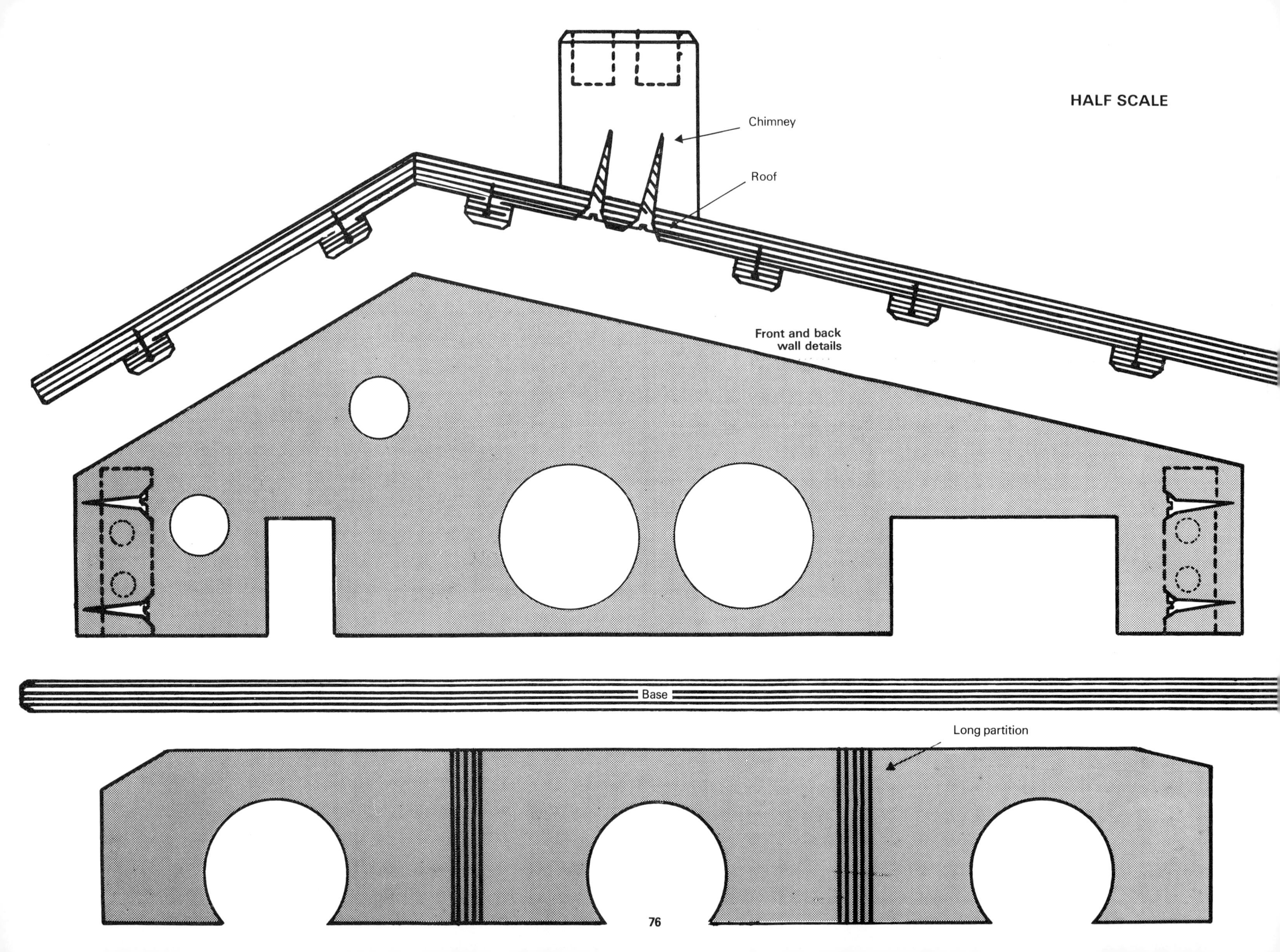
HALF SCALE
Chimney
Roof
Front and back wall details
Base
Long partition

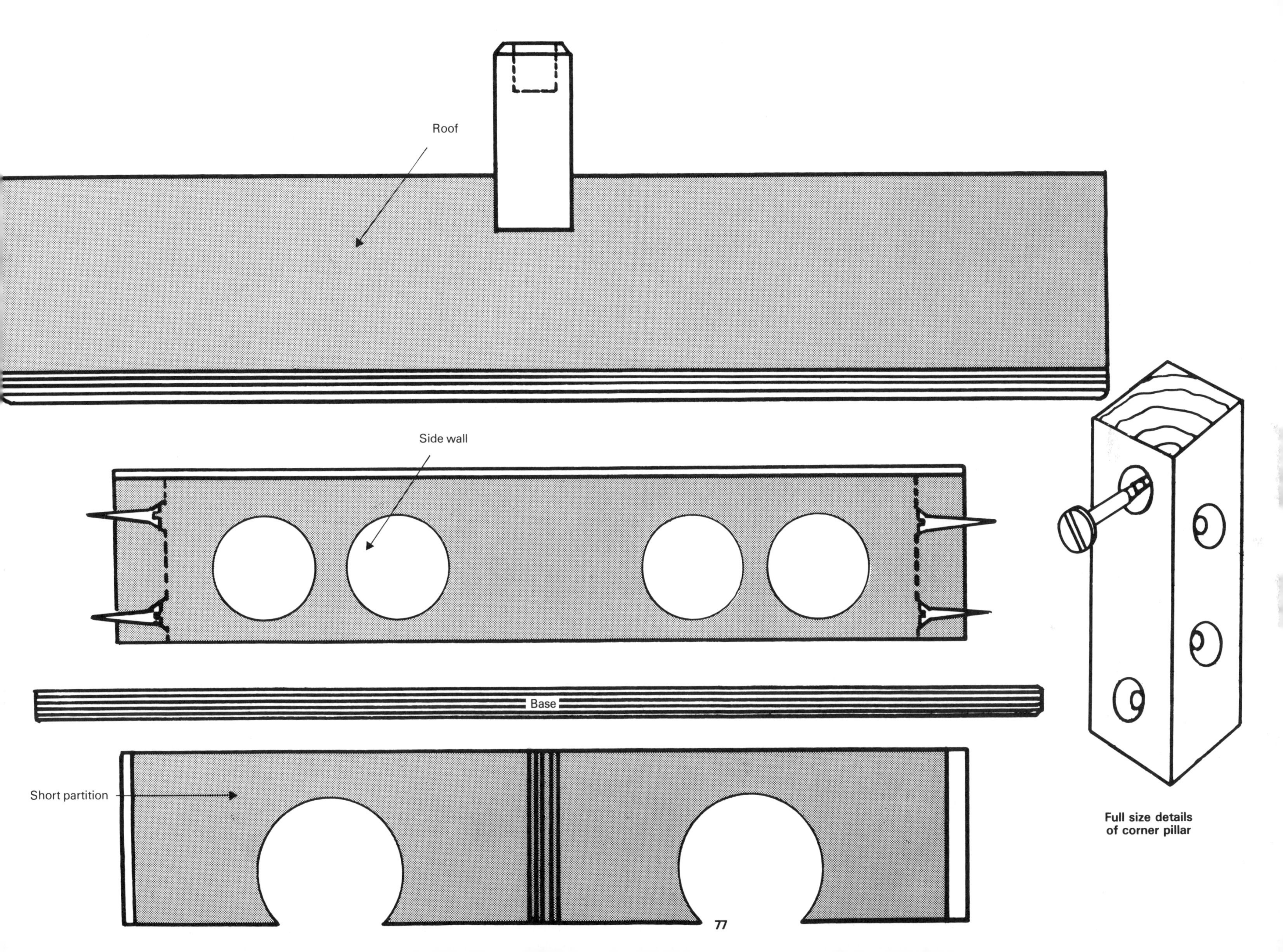

Full size details of corner pillar

CAR PARK AND RAMP

This toy fitment can be used actively indoors with the very popular die cast metal car models. It can act as a high rise car park and variable height exit ramp on which the cars can speed down. After play it can be used as an excellent display and stacking unit. Highly suitable for individual or group use.
(Age range 1-5 years plus).

Base Burma Teak. **Staging** Teak faced Plywood ½'' (12mm) thick.

MOTORWAY MOTEL

Another excellent fitment for use with the very popular small toys. So many different types of simple fitments like these can be made for exciting activity play and are especially useful when the weather is bad and youngsters are confined to the indoors. Excellent for individual or group use.
(Age guide 1-5 years plus).

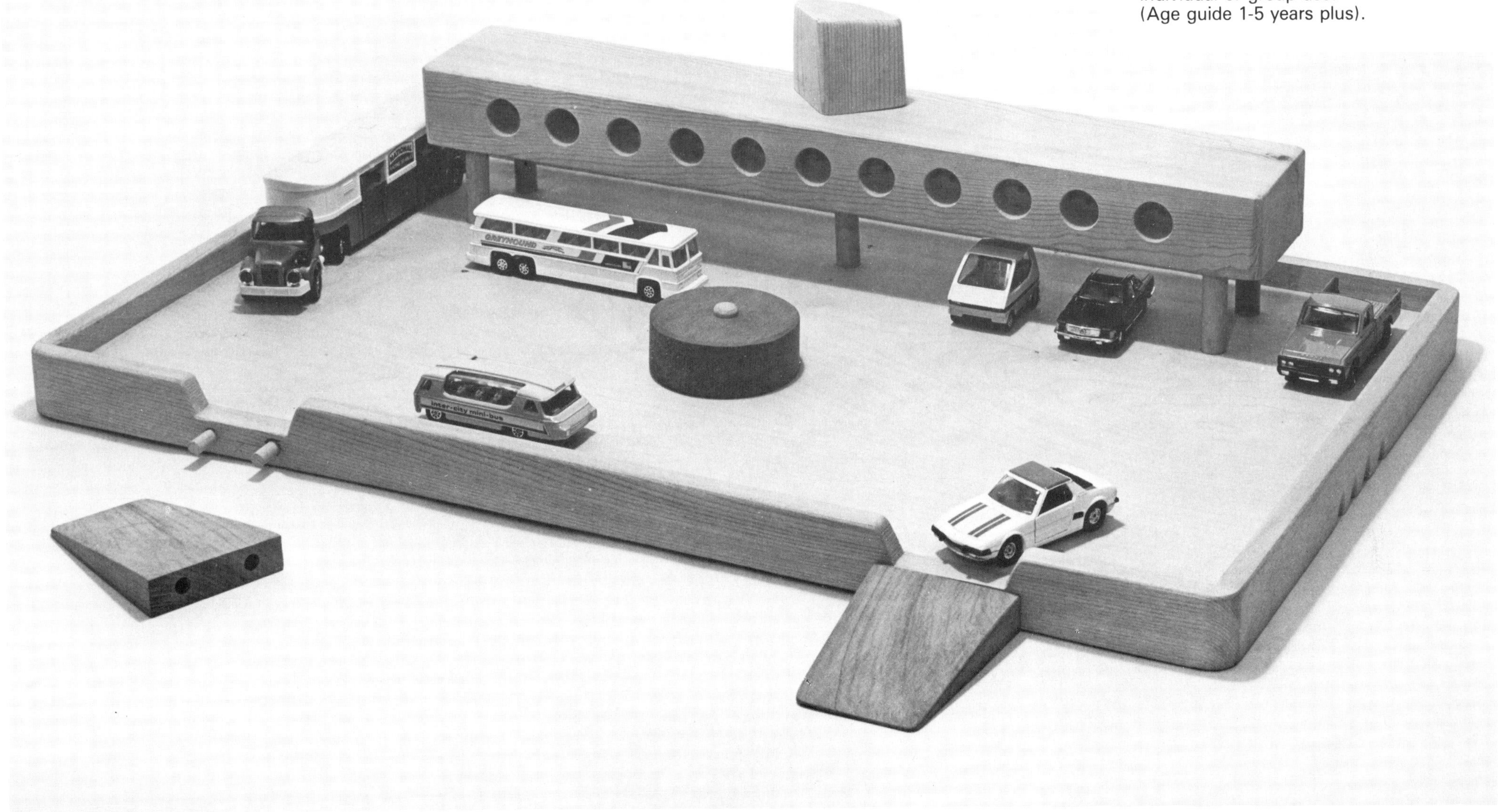

Base Blockboard. **Motel** African Utile.

LIGHT DUTY TRANSPORTER

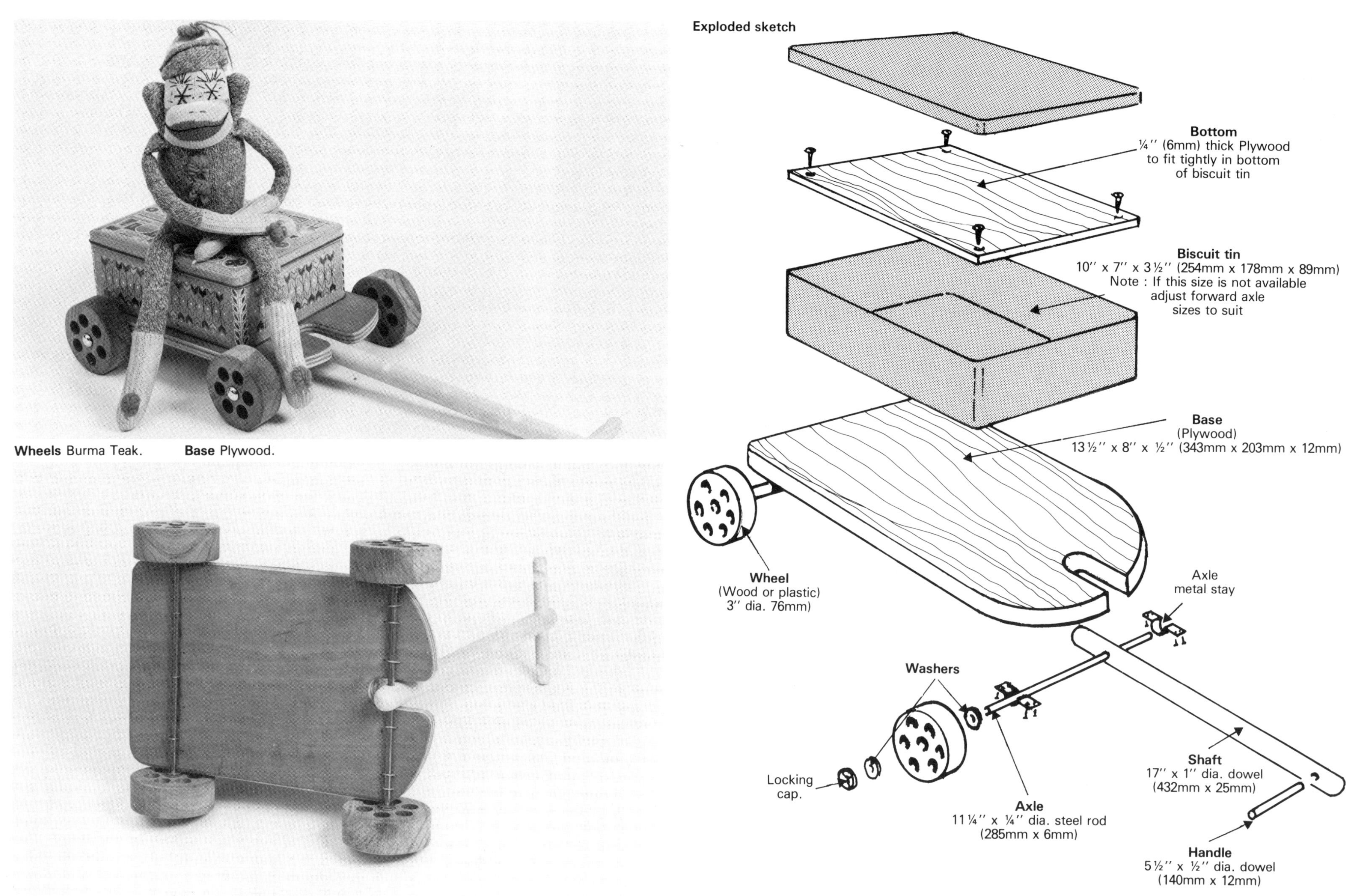

Wheels Burma Teak. **Base** Plywood.

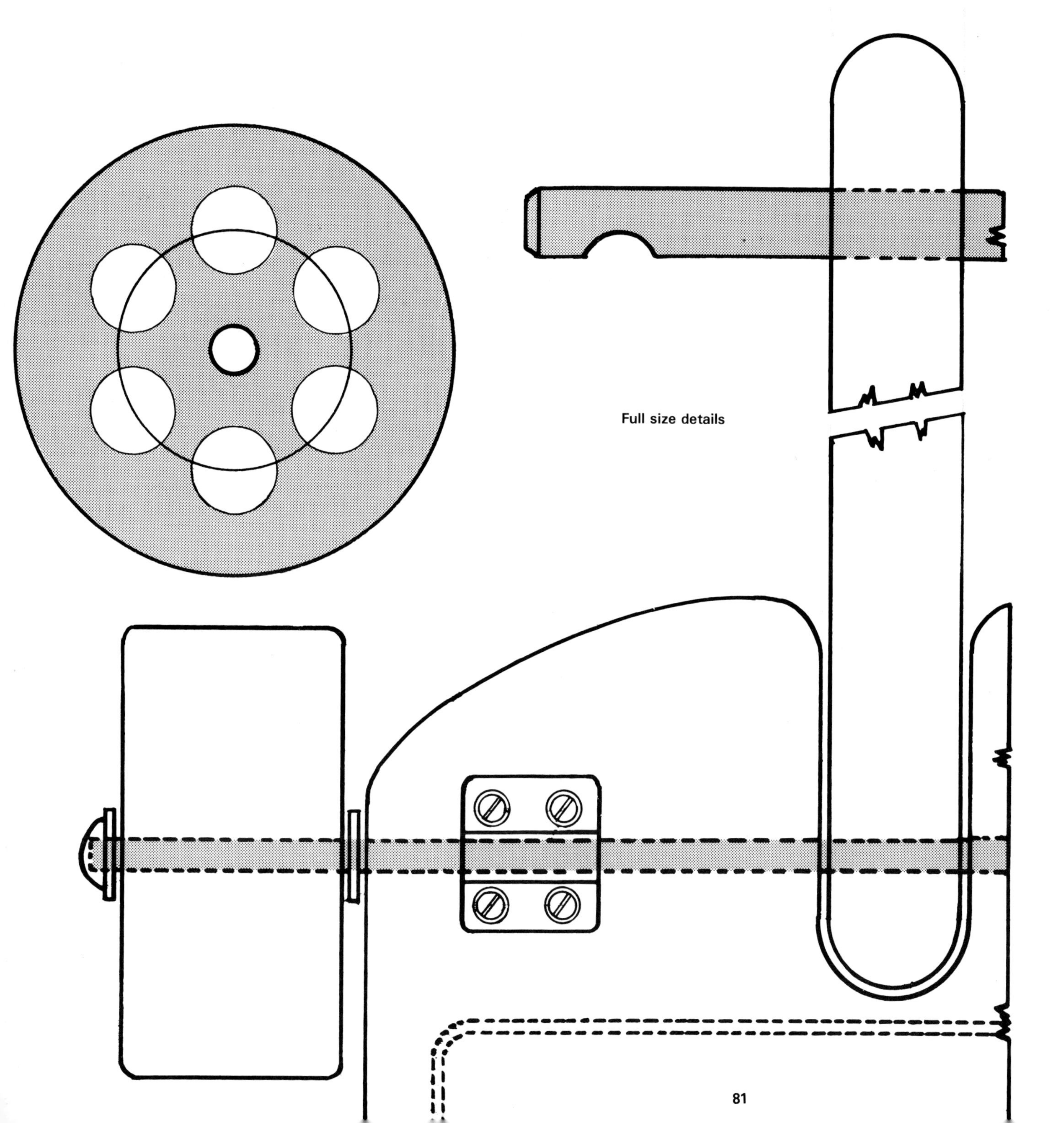

A Light Duty Transporter mainly for indoor use. The simple framework is surmounted with a decorative biscuit tin to act as a lightweight container and conveyor of 'Favourite Things'.
(Age guide 1-5 years plus).

WORKING GUIDE

1 *Obtain and prepare appropriate material to size.*

2 *Trace, mark out and shape base.*

3 *Mark out and bore decorative holes in wheels and test then bore easy running holes for metal axles in wheels and shaft.*

4 *Shape wheels.*

5 *Mark out test and bore a tight fitting hole for handle in shaft.*

6 *Shape shaft.*

7 *Clean up with abrasives.*

8 *Fit bottom in tin and screw through to base.*

9 *Apply a top quality adhesive, suggest TIMBABOND No.636 to handle hole.*

10 *Wipe off any surplus adhesive with a clean damp cloth.*

11 *Construct unit.*

12 *Clean up with abrasives.*

13 *Apply an appropriate finish.*

TRAIN AND WAGON

Woods English Sycamore and African Iroko.

Another of the many excellent toys which can be developed using subsidiary materials alongside wooden frameworks, e.g. note the use of strong decorative kitchen tin and wine coasters in making this excellent large attractive train and waggon set.

INLAID WOODEN JEWELLERY - PENDANTS

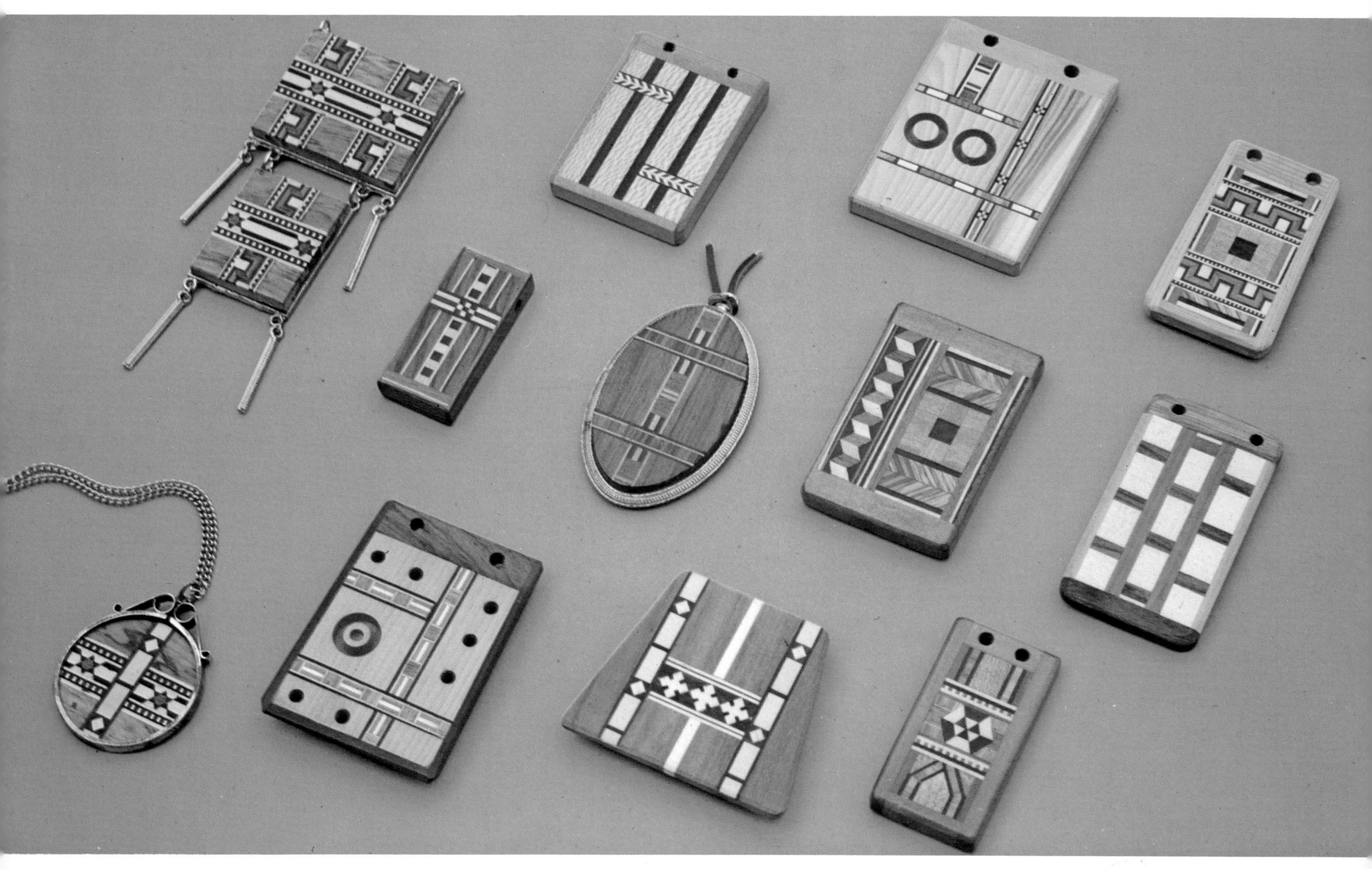

Part of the John Matthews collection.

INLAID BRACELETS, RINGS AND NECKLACE

Wood Popular. **Inlays** Various woods. **Part of the John Matthews collection.**

GENERAL WORKING NOTES

According to your design and skill carefully consider these different methods of edging jewellery.

Examples

Plain edge

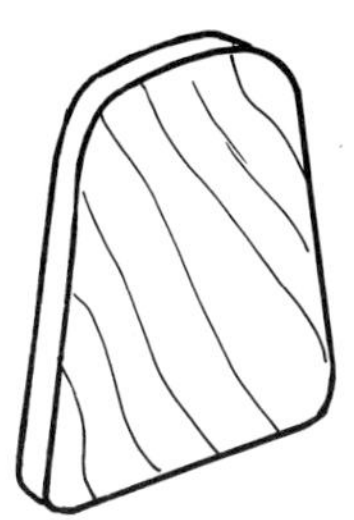

Top edged

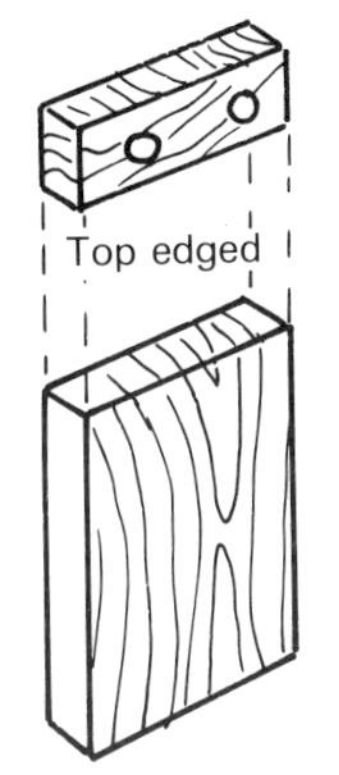

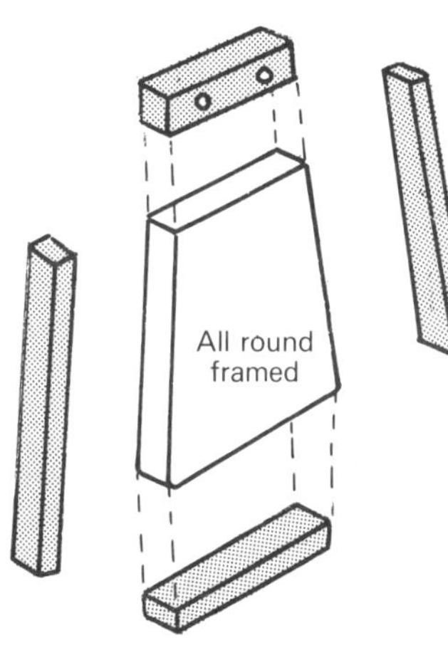

Various methods of thonging

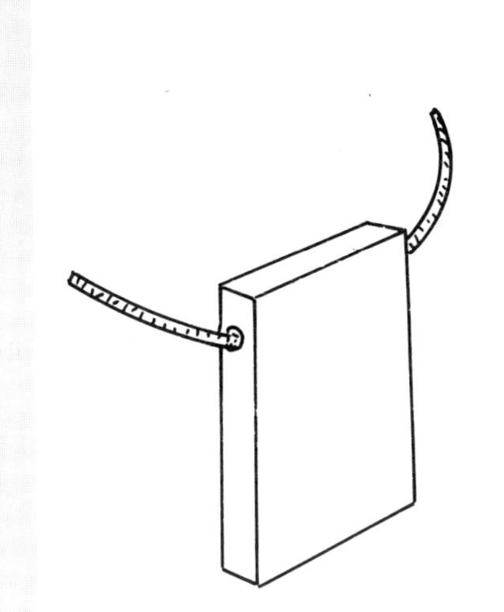

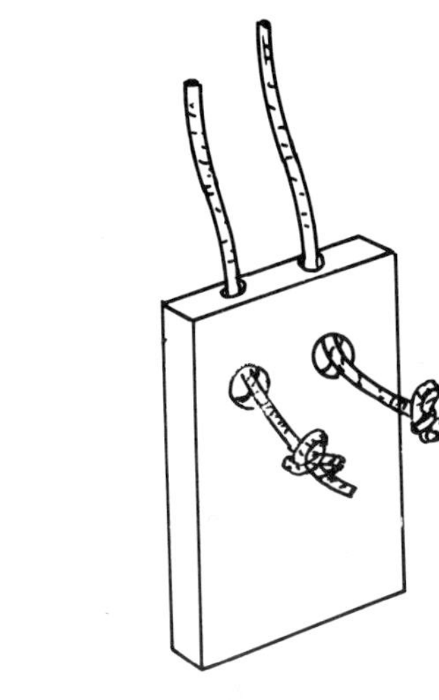

Keep an eye open for small pieces of decorative wood. When designing incorporate decorative features to the best effect.
Note the example below using varying colour of Heartwood and Sapwood to good effect.

Make sure you use a top quality appropriate adhesive, suggest TRETOBOND NON FLAM CONTACT ADHESIVE for fastening wood to metal. Findings etc. For small work hair clips can be utilised as excellent cramps.

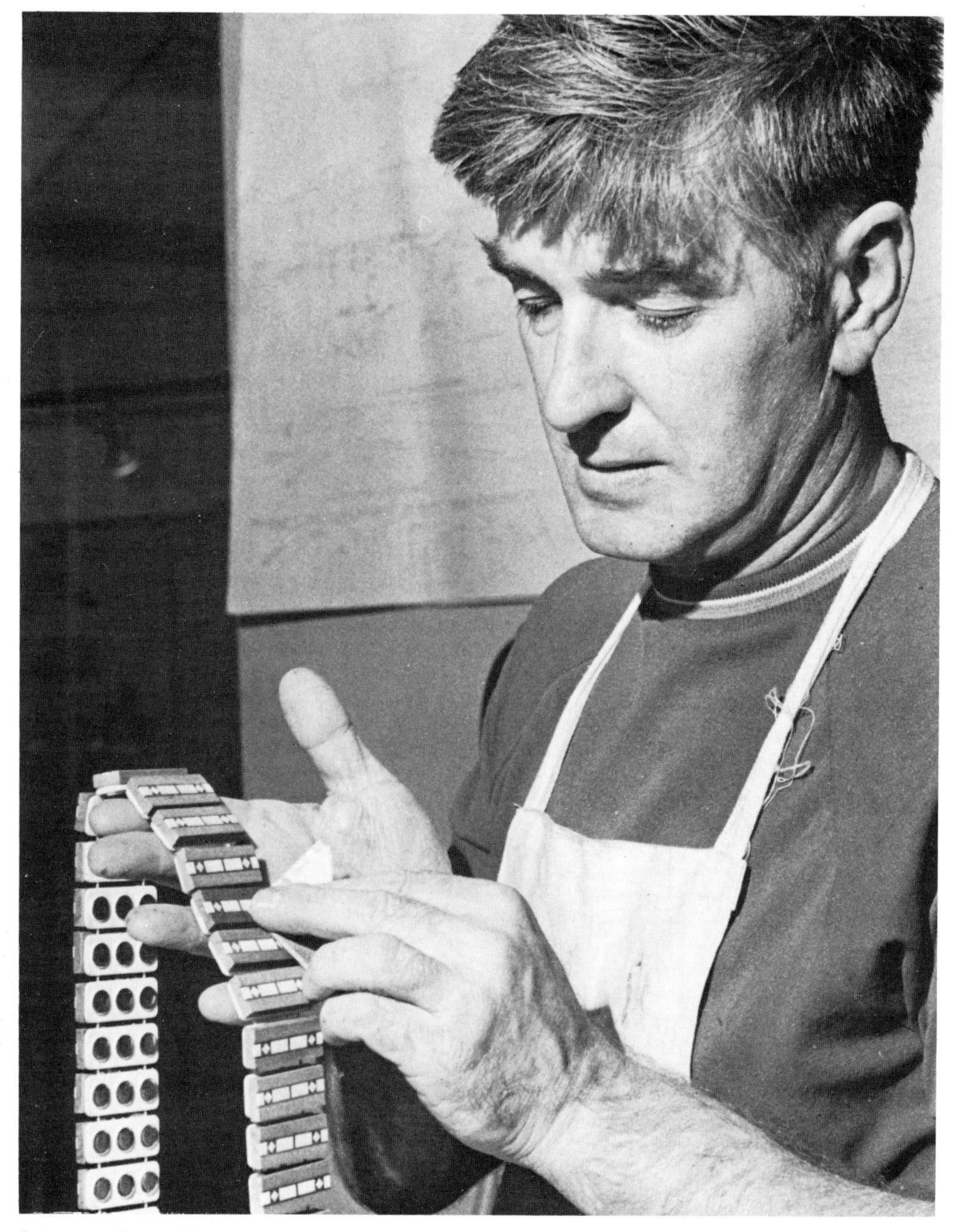

Demonstrating making Inlaid Belt at the U.S.A. International Exhibition, Davenport, Iowa. August 1976.

This type of work can be stimulating and financially rewarding in this age of ever developing awareness and appreciation of the value of hand made items and the prevailing fashion of wearing pendants, rings etc. for personal adornment on many varied occasions.

Such a lot can be achieved with very small pieces of decorative wood, inlay, jewellers findings and leather tongues etc.

My favourite woods for this type of work are - English Yew, Rio de Janeiro Rosewood, Padauk, Walnut, Teak, Ebony, African Limba, Sumach and Lacewood.

The tools required are of a limited range and it is easy to make a scratch stock for inlaying.

Inlaying, like all worthwhile processes needs practice and in time if the beginner will follow the basic instructions included in this section the skill will soon be acquired.

For Christmas and birthdays, this type of work is enthusiastically received.

Neatness, appropriate quality adhesives, woods and jewellers findings presented with loving care often mean a great deal to the receiver.

ADDRESSES FOR OBTAINING INLAYS

U.K.
Fitchett and Woollacott Ltd.,
Willow Road, Lenton Lane,
Nottingham NG7 2PR.

U.S.A.
Constantine,
2050 Eastchester Road,
Bronx, N.Y. 10461.

ADDRESSES FOR OBTAINING JEWELLERS FINDINGS (METAL FITMENTS)

U.K.
DRYAD, P.O. Box 38,
888 Northgates,
Leicester LE1 9BU.

U.S.A.
Roch Haven Art Metal Co.,
Box 8,
Whitefield N.H. 03598.

EXAMPLES OF BANDINGS AND STRINGINGS AND JEWELLERS FINDINGS

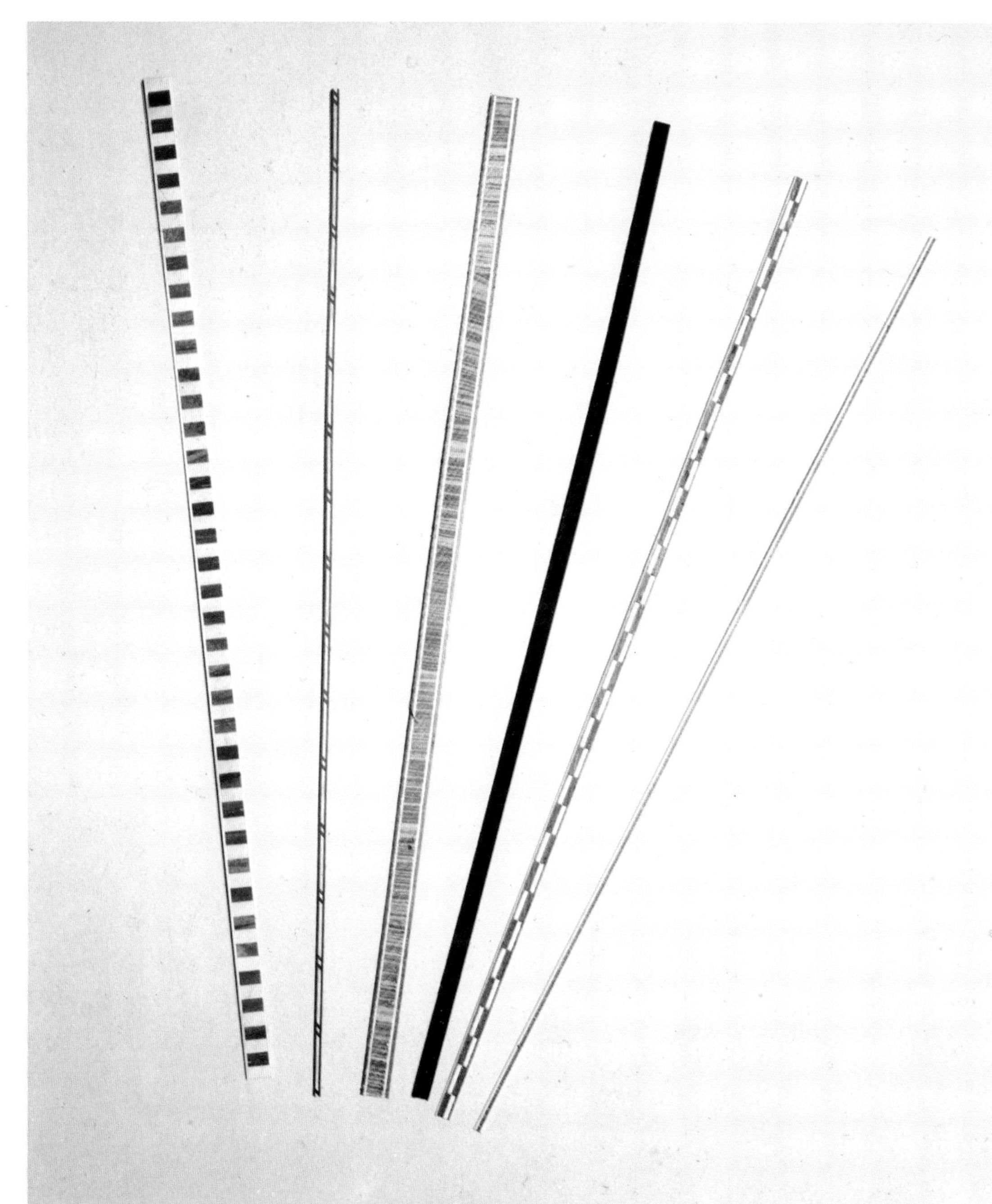

INTRODUCTION TO INLAYING

1
Inlaying medium to long lengths of wood with the grain is best done by a scratch stock tool. Apply this with a scrubbing action and heavy side pressure.

Sketch of a home made scratch stock

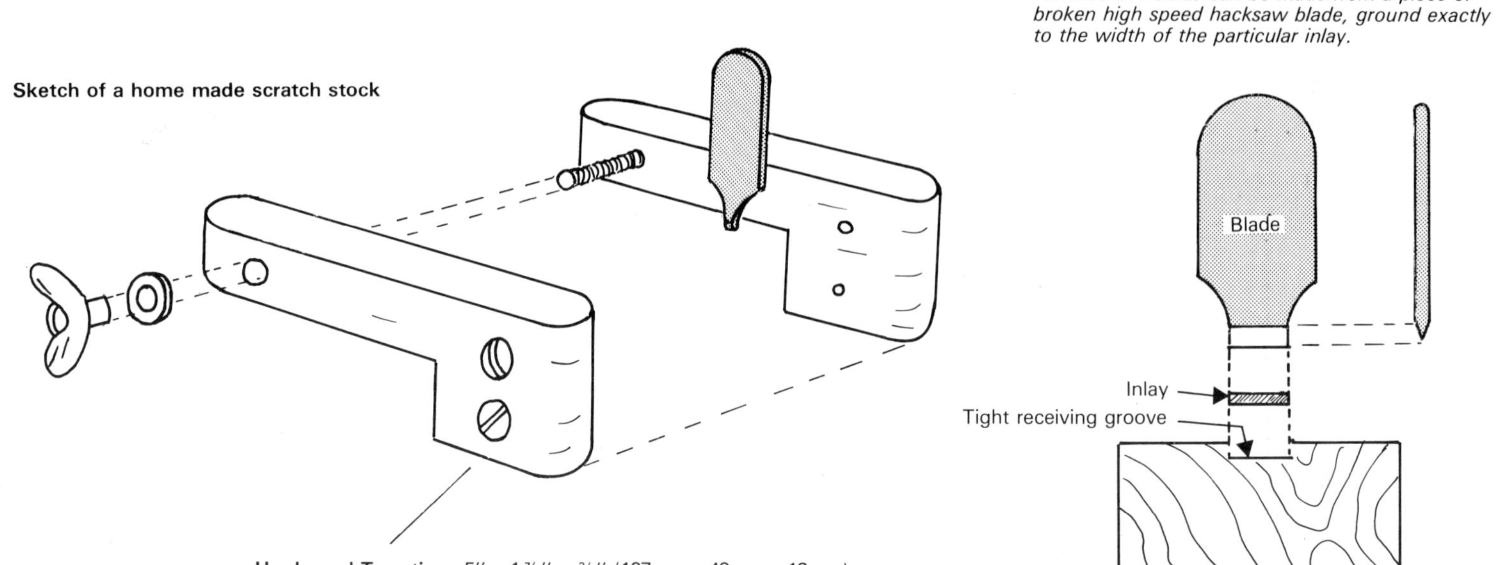

Hardwood T-sections 5″ x 1⅞″ x ¾″ (127mm x 48mm x 18mm)

Blade details
An excellent blade can be made from a piece of broken high speed hacksaw blade, ground exactly to the width of the particular inlay.

2
After cutting the groove down the grain apply a top quality appropriate adhesive, suggest TIMBABOND No.688. Then press in the inlay. Tape over the inlay and wrap in plastic sheeting. Apply strong cramping boards and cramps and leave until the adhesive is set thoroughly. Remove the tape and clean up with an abrasive.

3
Inlaying across the grain is generally best done with a sharp knife by cutting two lines the width of the inlay apart and removing the waste in between down to depth with an appropriate chisel. Then apply a top quality appropriate adhesive, suggest TIMBABOND No.688 in the groove. Press in the inlay and tape over. Wrap in plastic sheeting and apply strong cramping boards and cramps and leave to set thoroughly.

LAMINATED RINGS

Beverley

From an appropriate piece of close grained plywood ⅜" (9mm thick) mark out a suitable design for your particular finding. Cut out this shape with a coping saw.

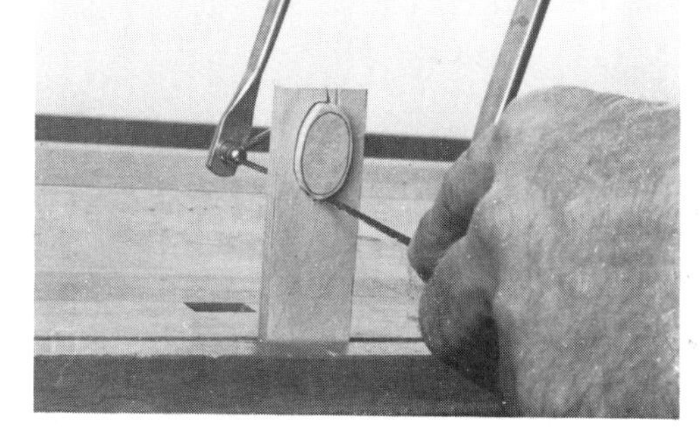

Round off the outer surface developing the contour lines of the ply to the best advantage. Clean up with abrasive. Fit, then fix with a top quality adhesive. Suggest TRETOBOND NON FLAM CONTACT ADHESIVE. Apply an appropriate finish.

Note :
Screw a waste block on backside of ring for gripping in vice allowing easy shaping of the surface.

PENDANTS

Wood English Yew.

Part of the John Matthews collection.

Here are some examples without inlay where just the natural grain has been utilised in harmony with the outer edge shape.

Often, interesting attractive appropriate sized 'natural pictures' occur in wood like English Yew, African Limba, Mazar Birch etc.

Note below this natural grain formation depicting a bird's head.

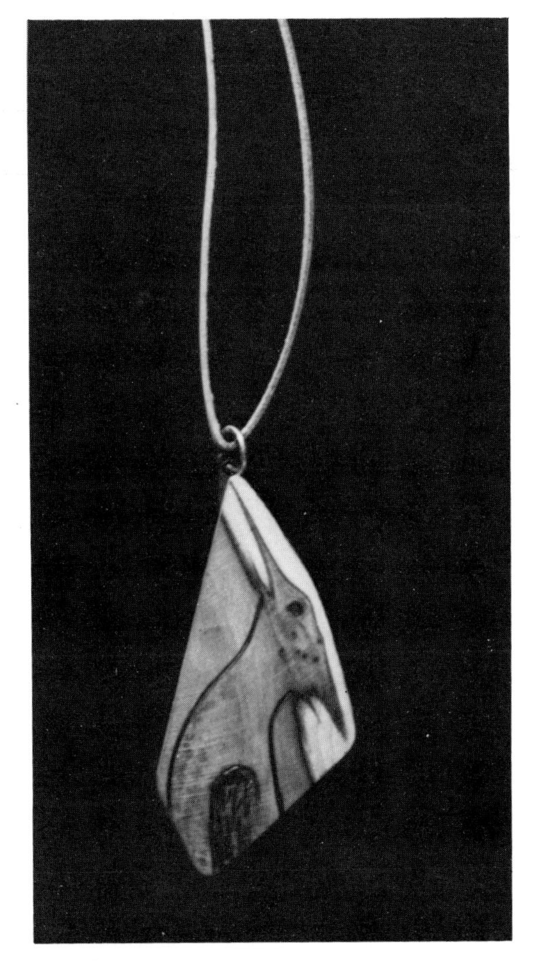

English Yew

Elizabeth

Full size examples

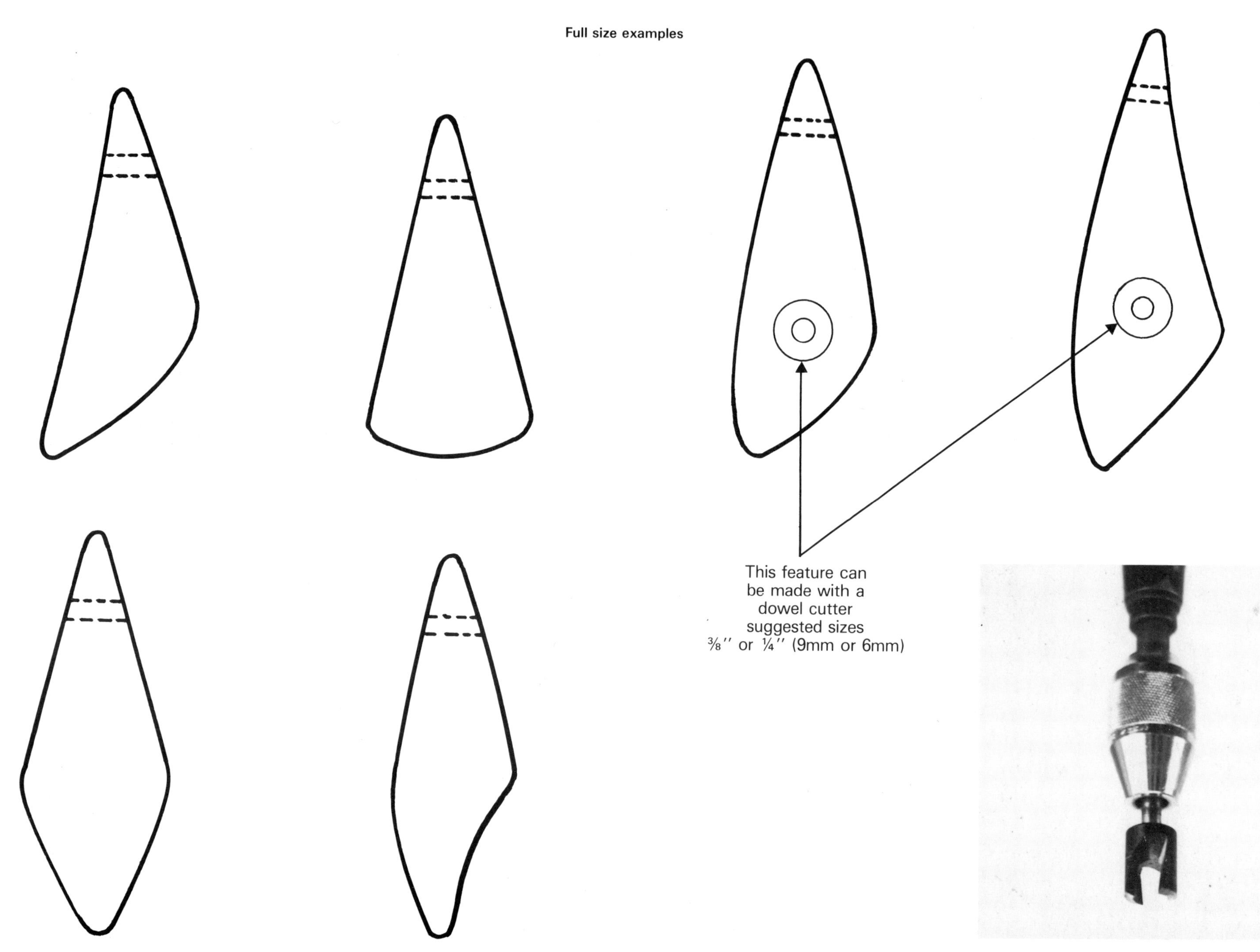

WORKING GUIDE

1
Trace a pattern from opposite page (or design a full size original). Then obtain and prepare a short length of appropriate material, Section 1⅜" x ½" (34mm x 12mm). Transfer pattern or make an original. Mark centre of thong or chain hole.

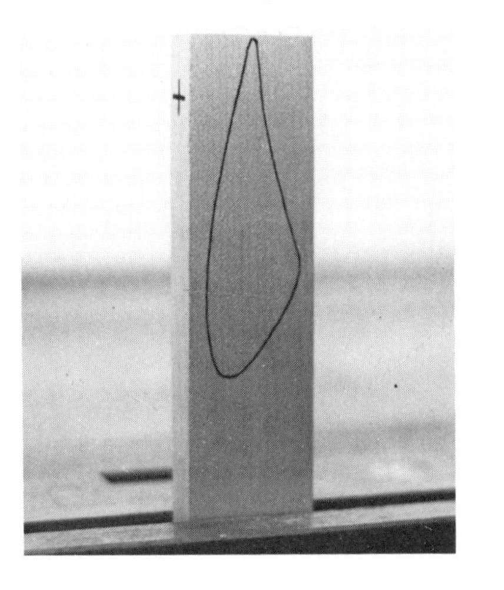

2
Test then bore for thong or chain.

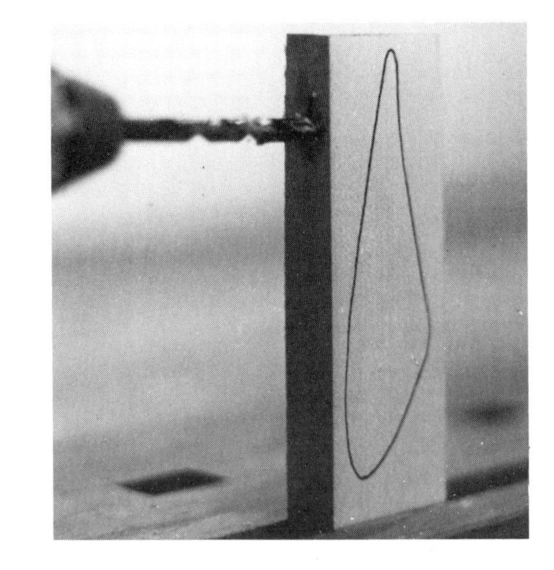

Note :
If you are to include a dowel cutter feature do this before the next process.

3
Saw off the waste and clean down to the lines with Wood Files.

4
Mark out back side 'rounding off lines'.

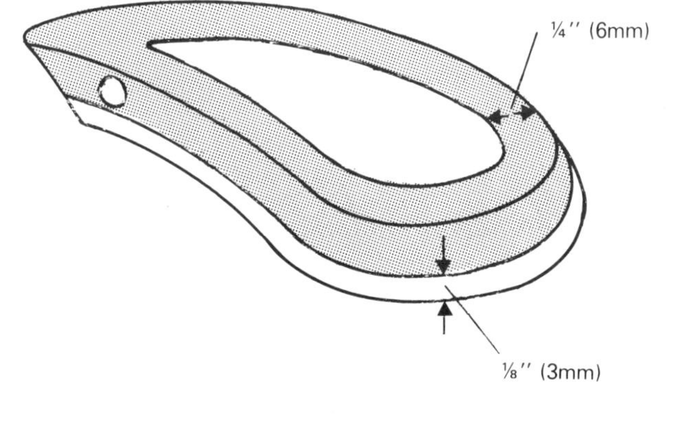

5
Round off the back with Wood Files. Clean up with abrasives. Test and fit thong or chain. Apply an appropriate finish.

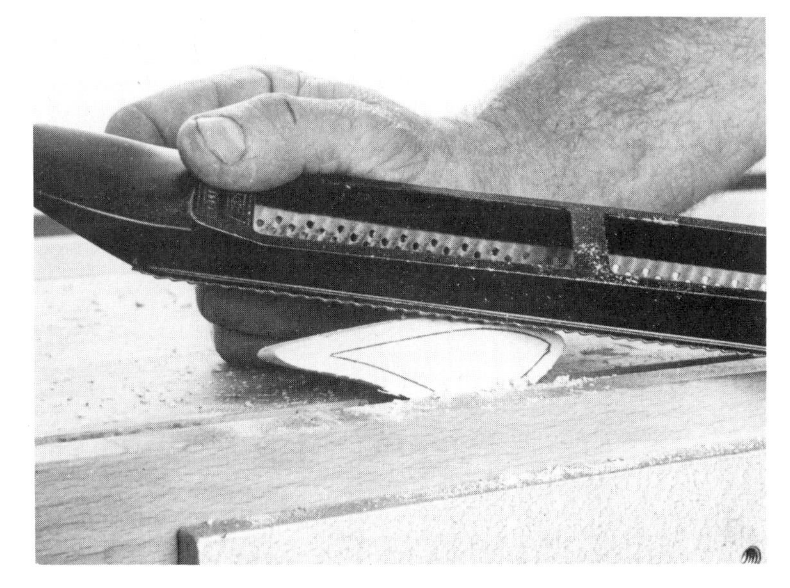

LAMINATED NECKLACES

A laminated necklace of varied presentation simply constructed with a fine chain and jump rings.

Chain length 30'' (762mm)

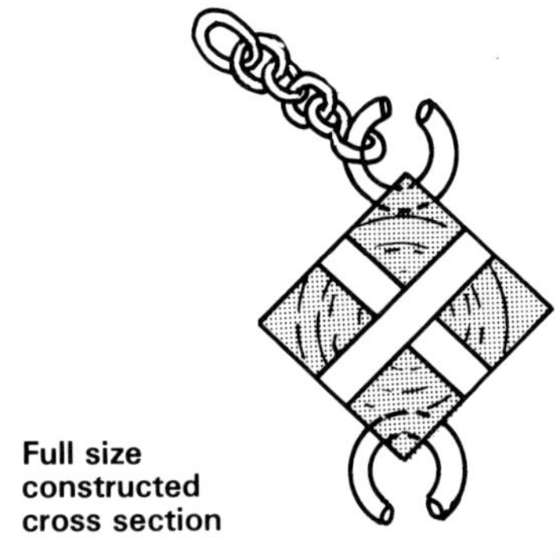

Jump rings ⅜'' dia. (9mm)

'The Countess' - Marian Elaine

Exploded sketch

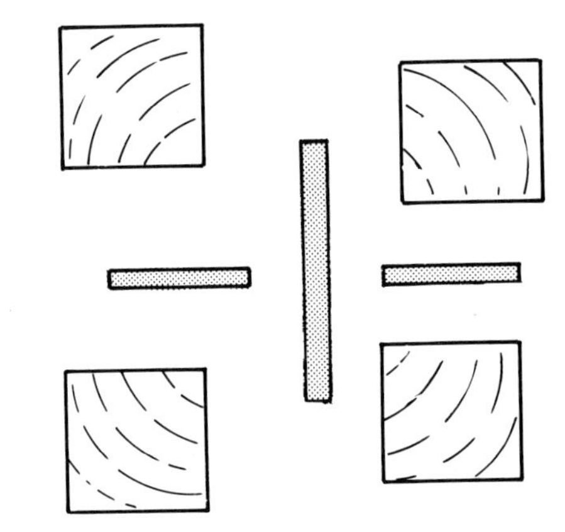

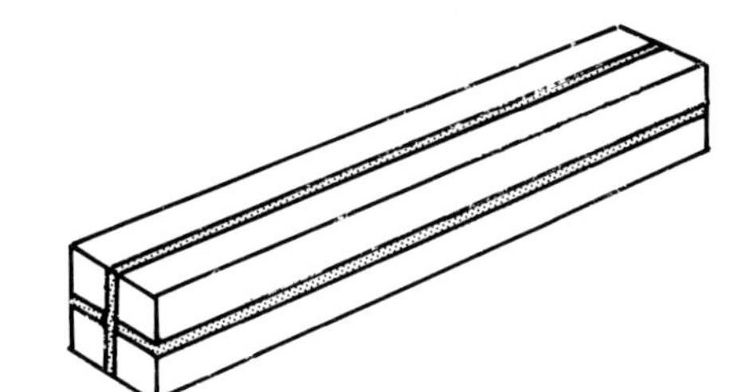

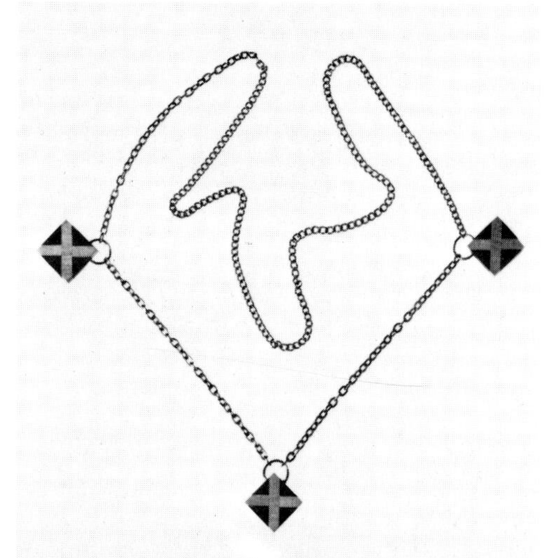

WORKING GUIDE

1
Obtain and prepare appropriate materials to size.
Note : Use the cross section below or design a full size cross section of your own.

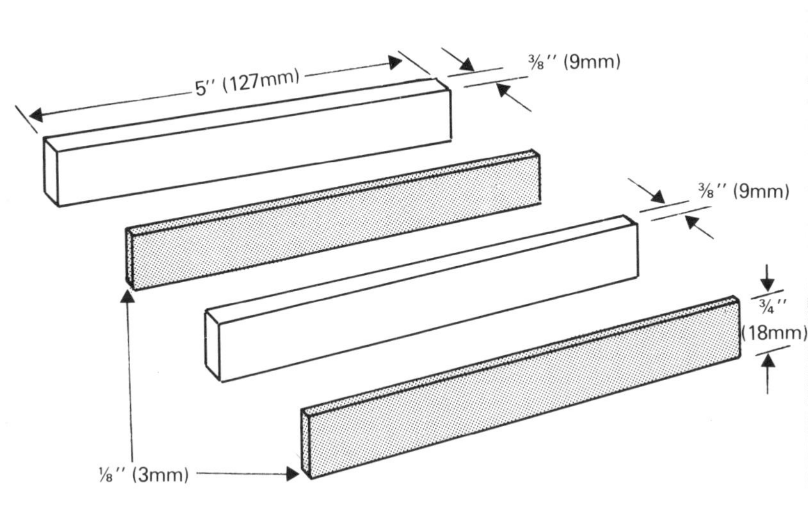

2
Apply a top quality appropriate adhesive. Suggest TIMBABOND No.636 to the three sections. Cramp and leave to set thoroughly.

3
Square the sides with a plane, then mark and saw down the middle of the block.

4
Square sawn surfaces.

5
Apply a top quality appropriate adhesive, suggest TIMBABOND No.636 to the three sections and leave to set thoroughly. Square the sides and ends, then mark out and saw 3/16″ (5mm) cross sections.

6
Clean up with abrasives. Mark, test and bore, then fit findings. Apply an appropriate finish.

LAMINATED BELTS

Julie

A highly decorative item for the young in heart. Laced together with strong duty leather thong.

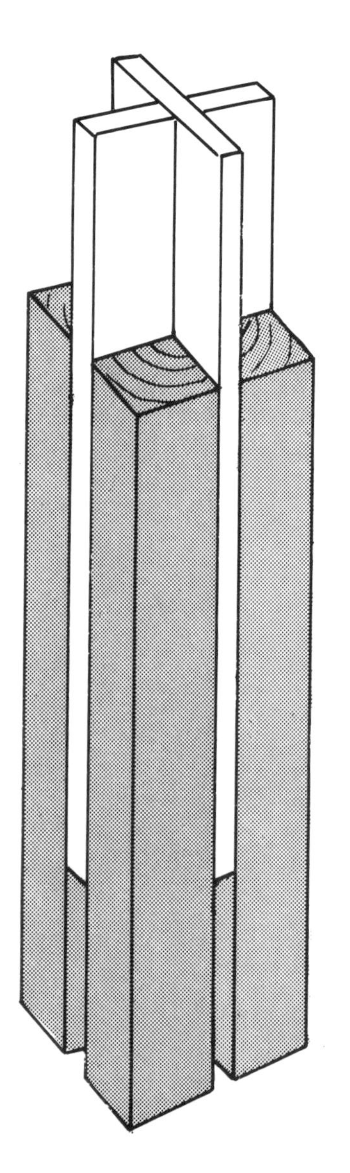

Burma Teak and English Sycamore.

WORKING GUIDE

1
Obtain and prepare appropriate material to size.
Use the cross section below or design a full size cross section of your own.

Cross section

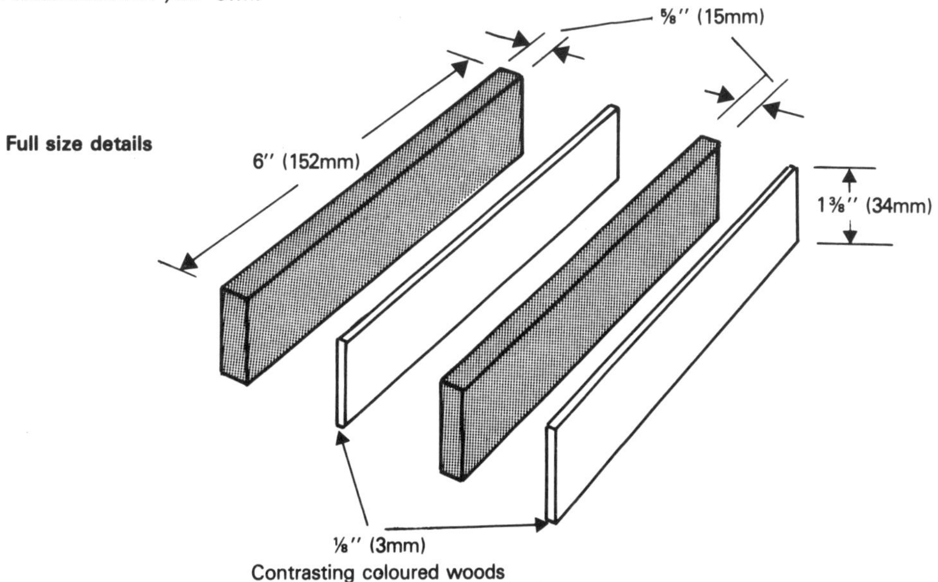

2
Apply a top quality appropriate adhesive, suggest TIMBABOND No.636 to the three sections. Cramp together and leave to set thoroughly.

Full size cross section

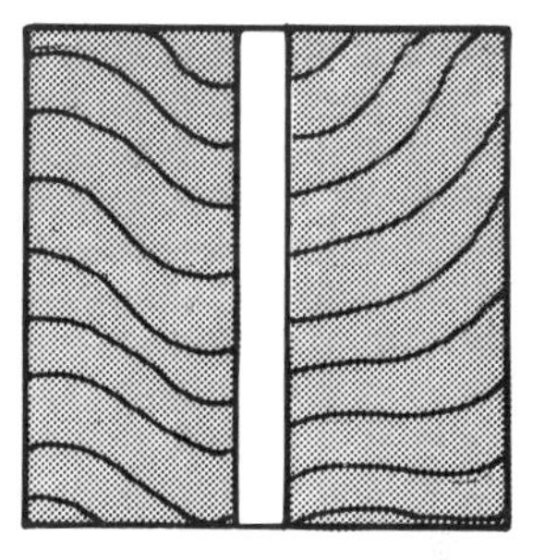

3
Square the sides with a plane then mark and saw down the middle of the block. Square sawn surfaces with a plane. Apply a top quality appropriate adhesive, suggest TIMBABOND No.636 to the three sections then leave to set thoroughly.

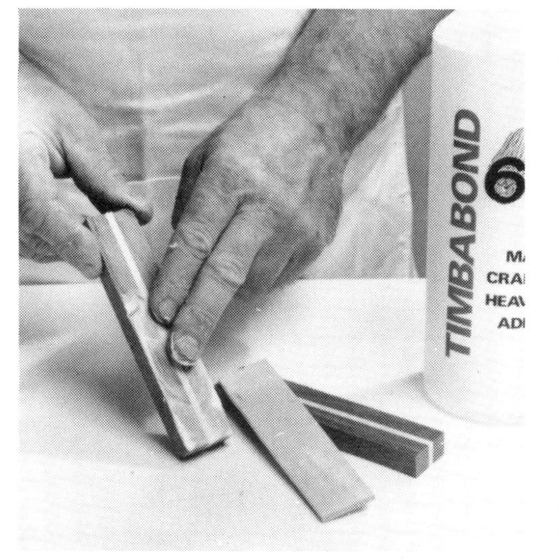

4
Square the sides and the ends. Mark out and saw ⅜'' (9mm) cross sections. (I use 14). Test, mark, then bore tight fitting thongs.

5
Clean up with abrasive. Apply an appropriate finish. Test and fit thong.

EAR RINGS

Care is needed to design tasteful appropriate shapes. Only use clean gold or silver findings because of the risk of infection from many other types of metal.

Anita

Woods Lacewood, Teak, English Sycamore, Sumach Cherry, Walnut.

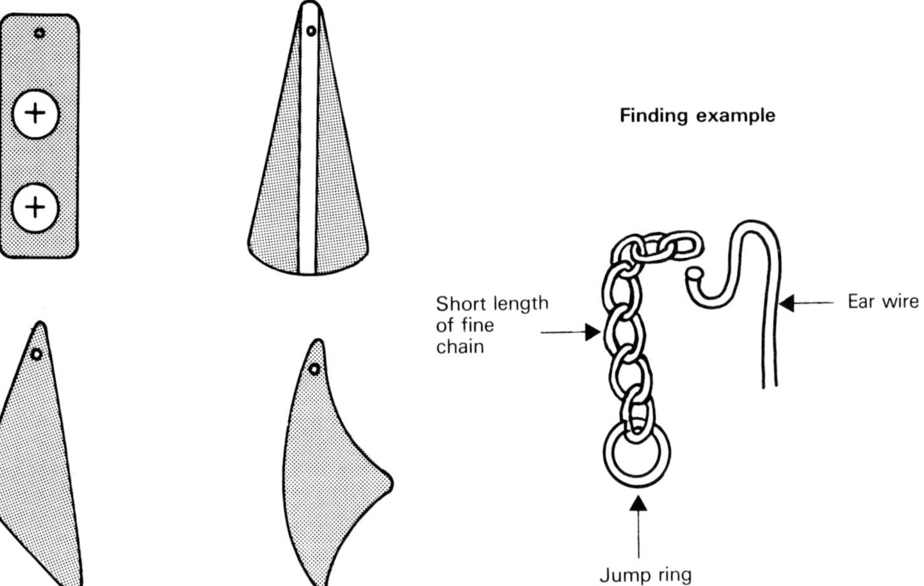

Full size examples

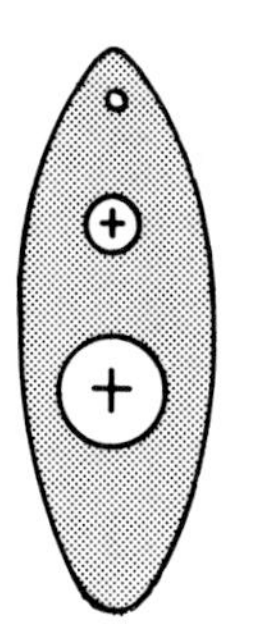

WORKING GUIDE

1
Trace the pattern from this page or design a full size original. Then obtain and prepare appropriate material and do any lamination necessary using ⅛" (3mm) thicknesses.

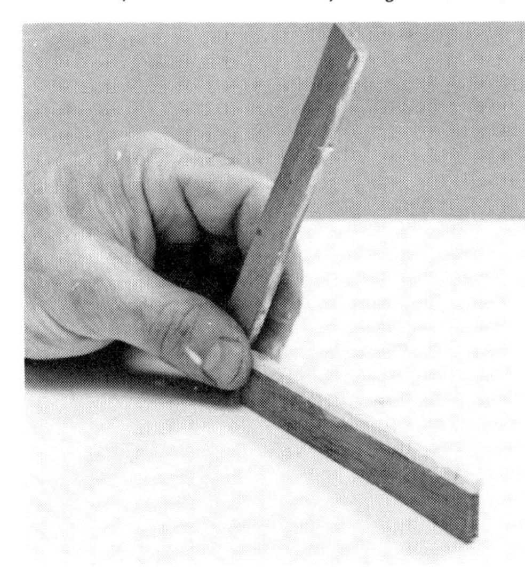

2
Transfer pattern onto material. Mark out the design. Bore any holes. Saw off the waste.

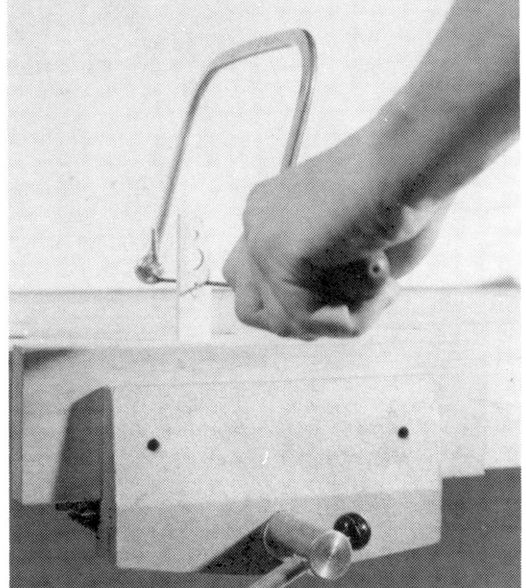

3
Carefully clean down to the lines with wood files. Clean up with abrasives.

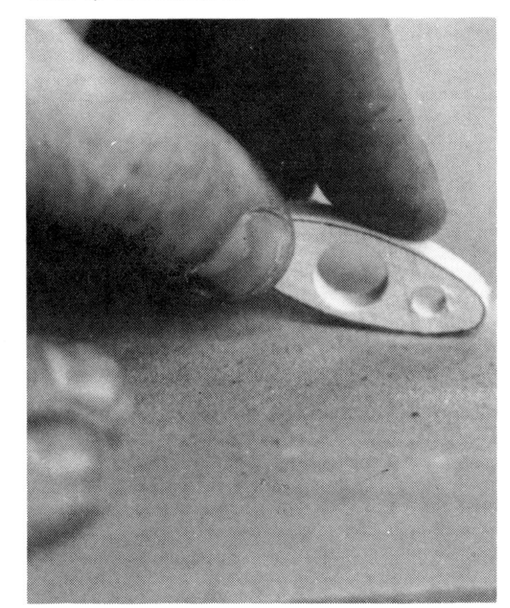

4
Test and fit findings. Apply an appropriate finish.

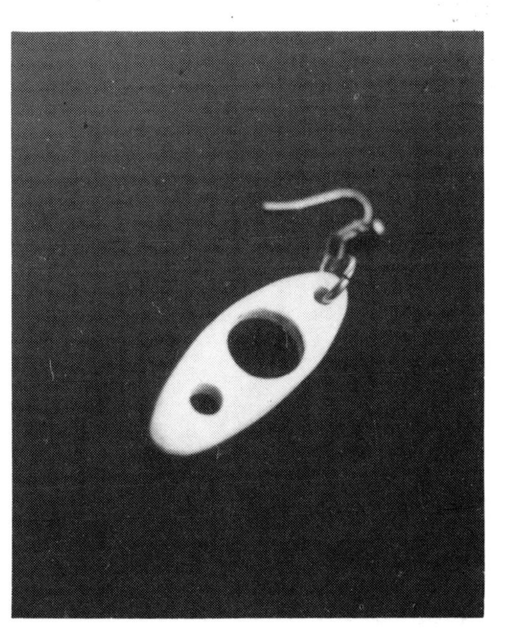

INTRODUCTION TO FURNITURE

To make a good piece of furniture is a wonderful experience and a treasure to use and a joy to behold. It can light up a room and give warmth and act as a stage for presenting other items of beauty and usefulness, e.g. porcelain, sculpture, books etc.

Each piece of furniture should be well designed, being constructionally sound, suitable for the work it has to do, well proportioned and not hard on the eye made of appropriate woods, used to the best effect of grain, colour and texture and coated with an appropriate finish. Any fitments such as handles, hinges etc. should be of good quality and in keeping with the design of the furniture. The best adhesive possible is also a very important issue in making any item of furniture, for it may have to withstand rigorous use and generally bond for life.

If you have the skill, there is a place for complex joints, e.g. decorative dovetail joints. These however, are very time consuming and often suffer from unequal shrinkage between end and side grain. Fortunately, modern top quality adhesives like TRETOBOND LIMITED manufacture, allow simple joints to be made very effectively, through the 'iron grip' of their adhesives, which will stand the test of time.

Note the use of simple dowel joints in making this attractive plate rack which takes a small amount of material and skill and is lightweight enough to hang successfully on any wall.

The design and each stage of preparation, marking out, jointing and constructing need to be approached very carefully and thoroughly in making any item of furniture. Accuracy, neatness and patience are essential - so are the right adhesives.

Wood English Sycamore.

Simple joints for different types of construction

Butt edge joint

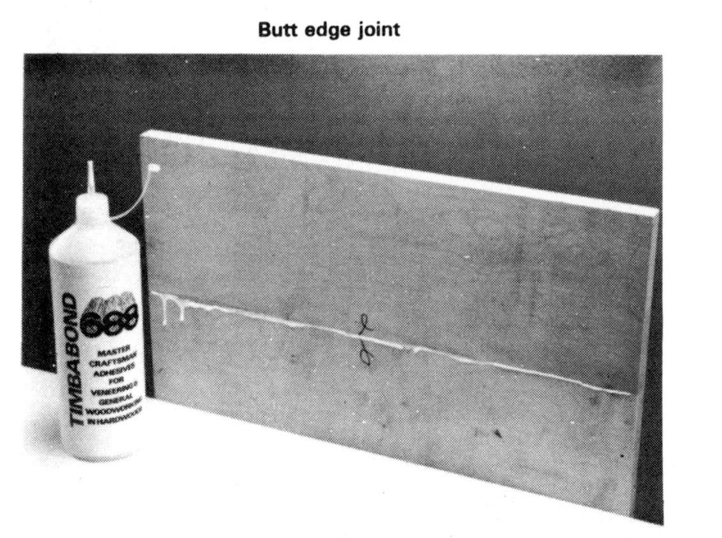

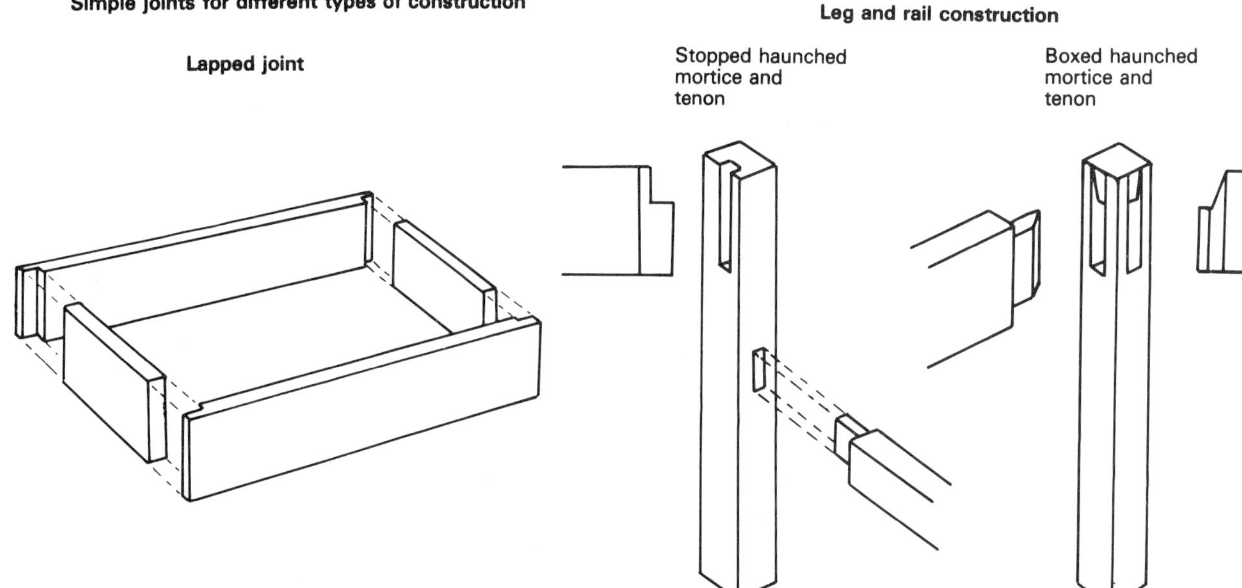

INTRODUCTION TO VENEERING

Veneering is not an easy process and it is very much an acquired skill. Care must always be taken, for so many things can go wrong whatever method you use.
One essential is a very thin sharp knife and so is a very flat surface (ground work) to lay your veneer on.
The adhesive you use should be easy to apply and have an ability to run evenly between surfaces.
Suggest TIMBABOND No.688 and there is no need to tooth groundwork to receive this excellent adhesive.
It is suggested that whenever veneer is being applied to one surface the under surface is also veneered to counterbalance and stabilise the board. Generally a simple press to lay veneer is much better than other methods.
Note the home made caul veneer press below.

ONE METHOD OF APPROACH

1

Cut veneer on a flat old board using a very sharp knife guided down an accurate straight edge. Always carefully 'STROKE' off the veneer rather than cut through by harsh pressure. Clear tape all joints together.

2

Spread evenly a top quality appropriate adhesive, suggest TIMBABOND No.688, on the groundwork and initially press down by hand oozing out the air bubbles and surplus glue. Then quickly place in a press and apply even area pressure and leave to set thoroughly.

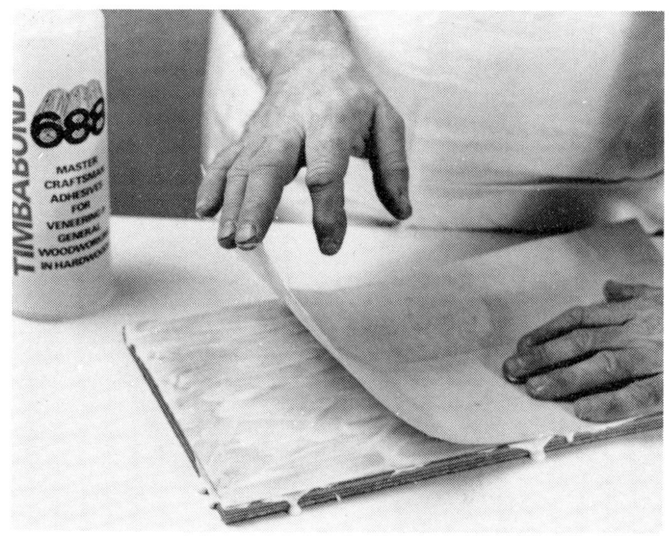

3
Home made caul veneer press

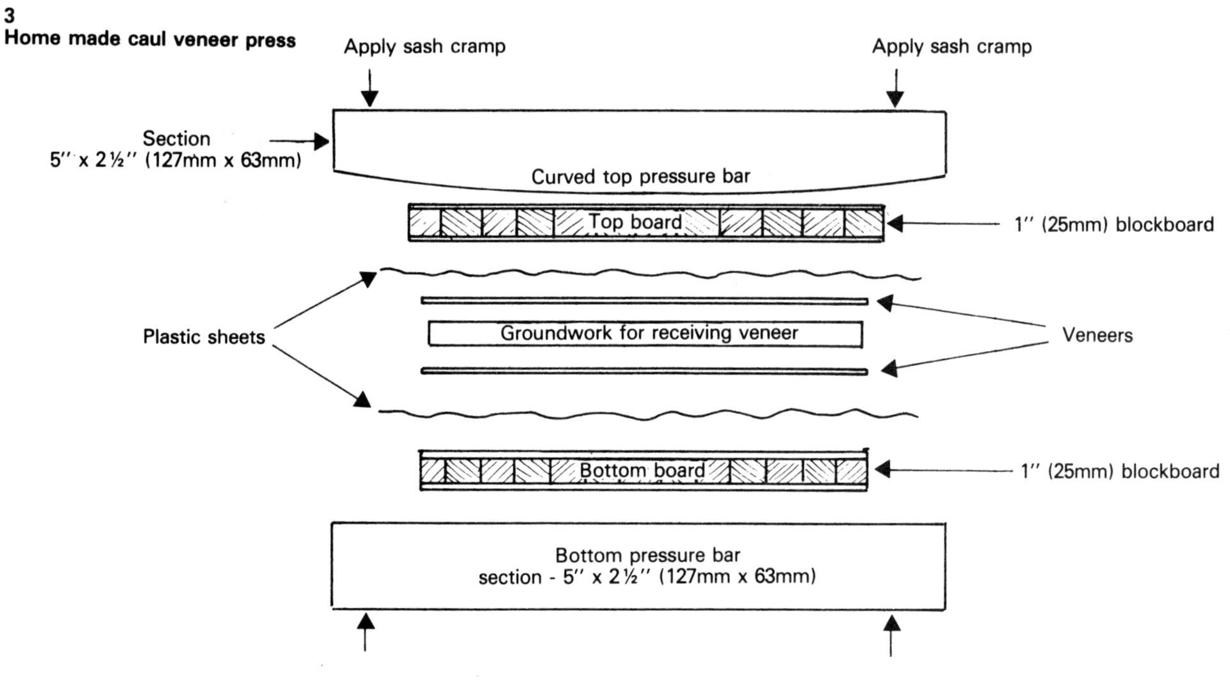

4

An excellent and convenient method for fastening on veneer edging (lipping) can be done with a top quality Contact Adhesive, suggest TRETOBOND NON FLAM CONTACT ADHESIVE.

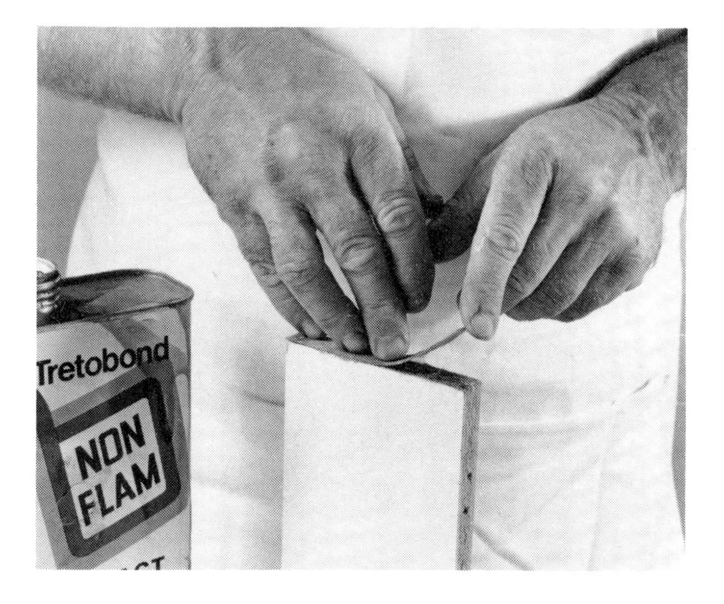

SMALL WALL CABINET

A small cabinet of simple construction utilising another framed material for a door. The cabinet is pivoted on a short length of piano hinge. The finish used is matt lacquer and wax.

WORKING GUIDE

1 *Obtain (or design and make) an appropriate sized framed painting, mural etc. for the door.*

2 *Obtain and prepare appropriate material to size for cabinet.*

3 *Mark out and cut joints.*

4 *Test fit and number joints.*

5 *Clean up with abrasives.*

6 *Apply a top quality appropriate adhesive, suggest TIMBABOND No.688 to all the joints.*

7 *Square and cramp framework together.*

8 *Wipe off any surplus adhesive with a clean damp cloth and leave to set thoroughly.*

9 *Fit and hang door etc.*

10 *Clean up with abrasives.*

11 *Apply an appropriate finish.*

12 *Fit and fix cabinet in the wall in a suitable position.*

Leather work by 'Hawk Hawkins' of Ogden, Utah, U.S.A.

Wood African Limba.

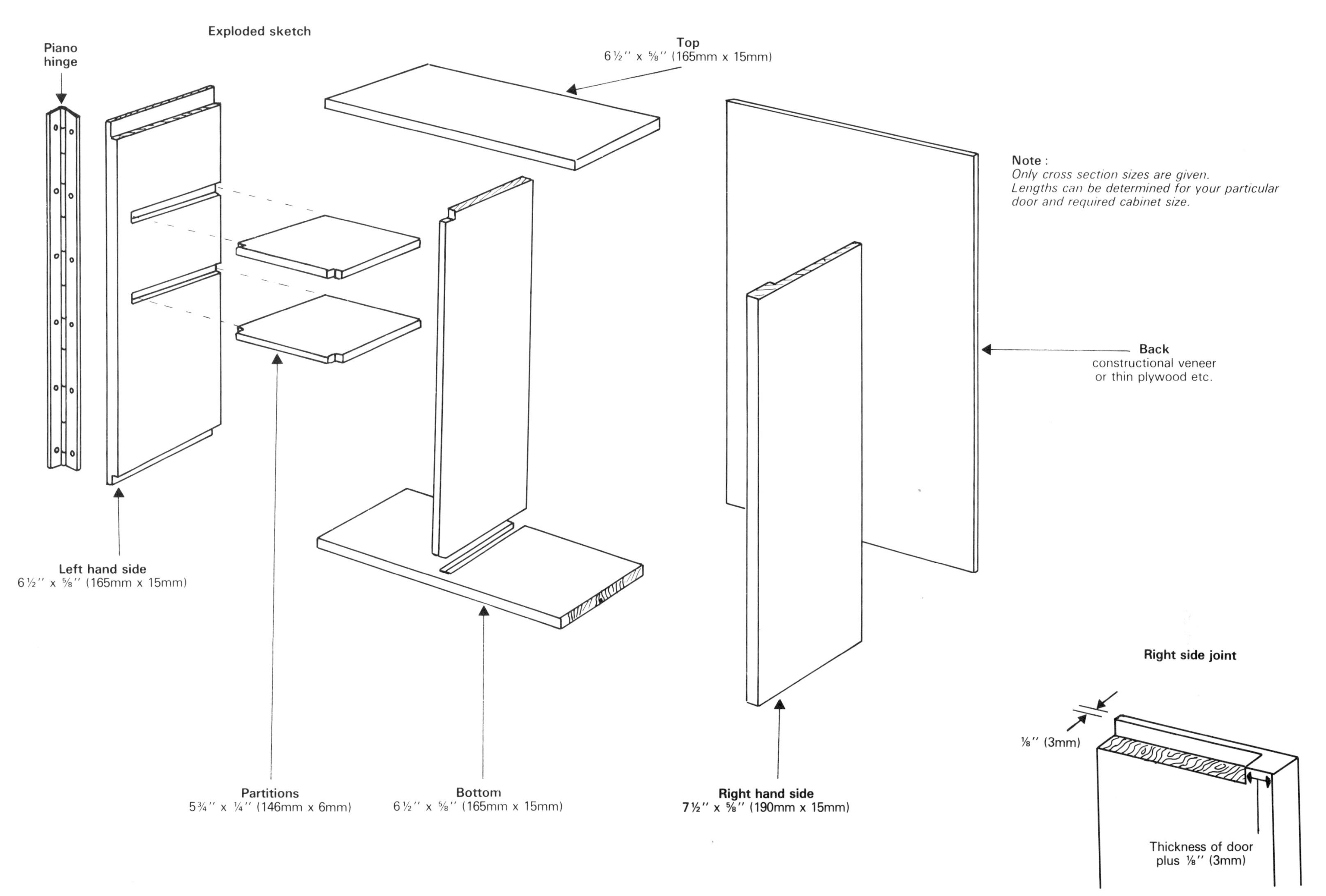
Exploded sketch
Piano hinge
Top
6½" x ⅝" (165mm x 15mm)
Note :
Only cross section sizes are given.
Lengths can be determined for your particular door and required cabinet size.
Back
constructional veneer
or thin plywood etc.
Left hand side
6½" x ⅝" (165mm x 15mm)
Right side joint
⅛" (3mm)
Partitions
5¾" x ¼" (146mm x 6mm)
Bottom
6½" x ⅝" (165mm x 15mm)
Right hand side
7½" x ⅝" (190mm x 15mm)
Thickness of door
plus ⅛" (3mm)

A TABLE FOR THE QUEEN

In June 1977 I was appointed by County Hall of Nottinghamshire to design and make a unique table and laminated sculpture for Her Majesty, Queen Elizabeth II as a Silver Jubilee Presentation from 'the people of Nottinghamshire'.

The framework of the table would be made mainly of Sherwood Wainscot Oak, so representative of the Shire of Nottingham and the theme of the table top would be appropriately veneered with many rare woods from the various Commonwealth Countries. This was in tasteful keeping with Her Majesty's Silver Jubilee Year.

I considered it a very great honour and pleasure to have been appointed to make such items and something very special to be in attendance at the presentation.

COMMONWEALTH WOODS USED FOR THE TOP

Birds Eye Maple (Canada)
Rock Elm (Canada)
Mahogany (Granada)
Kokrodua (Nigeria)
Walnut (Nigeria)
Makore (Sierra Leona)
Bubinga (Gambia)
Mountain Ash (New Zealand)
Queensland Walnut (Australia)
Black Bean (Australia)
Padauk (Papua New Guinea)
Oak (Tasmania)
Ebony (Lesotho)
Teak (Malaysia)
Lancewood (Jamaica)
Afromosia (Ghana)
Sapele (Ghana)

The presentation of the table and laminated sculpture to Her Majesty Queen Elizabeth II at County Hall, West Bridgford, Nottingham, England, U.K. - June 1977. (Permission for photographic inclusion finally granted in February 1980).

The Queen's Table.

TABLE DETAILS

As a personal choice I usually make a complicated top first, then the framework to suit. The finish used was a hard wearing gloss lacquer.

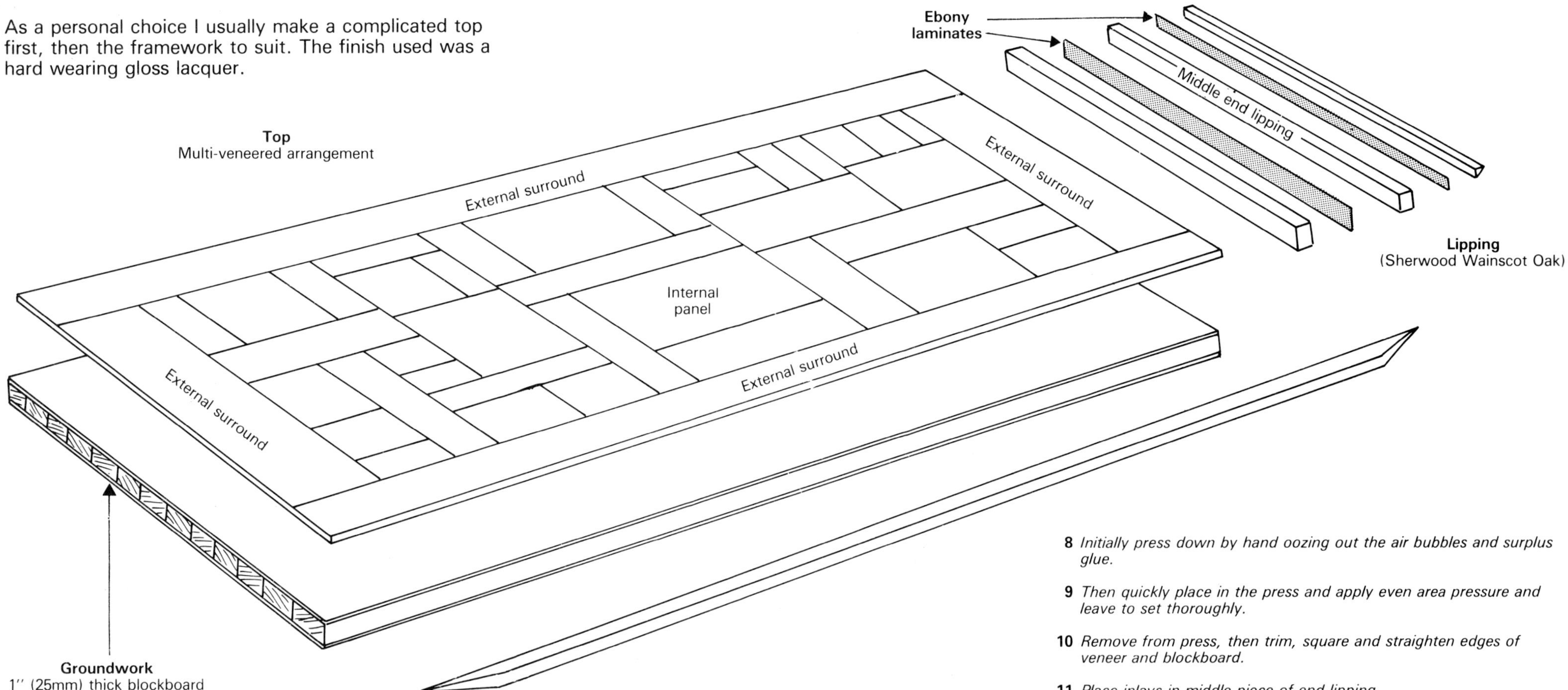

Note overall size of top
66″ x 22″ x 1″ (1676mm x 559mm x 25mm)

WORKING GUIDE FOR FRAMEWORK

1 *Obtain and prepare appropriate materials for top. (Size of blockboard 5′6″ x 1′10″ - 1675mm x 559mm). (Prepare lipping and laminates to suit the above sizes). (Gather numerous appropriate small leaves of veneer).*

2 *Cut each veneer carefully and develop a harmonious design.*

3 *Use clear tape to fasten each area of the internal panel together.*

4 *When satisfied with your internal panel arrangement, trim off the edges to size.*

5 *Cut, then tape on an appropriate external veneer surround.*

6 *Apply to the blockboard a top quality appropriate adhesive.*

7 *Lay veneer on blockboard after 15 minutes.*

8 *Initially press down by hand oozing out the air bubbles and surplus glue.*

9 *Then quickly place in the press and apply even area pressure and leave to set thoroughly.*

10 *Remove from press, then trim, square and straighten edges of veneer and blockboard.*

11 *Place inlays in middle piece of end lipping.*

12 *Apply a top quality appropriate adhesive to end lipping arrangements and cramp in position.*

13 *Leave to set thoroughly, then saw and plane ends of lipping, straight and square with sides of blockboard.*

14 *Apply an appropriate adhesive to the side lipping and blockboard, then cramp in position.*

15 *Leave to set thoroughly, then trim to length.*

16 *Plane lipping down to thickness of top.*

17 *Mark out level of lipping on underside of top.*

18 *Plane bevels with a plane.*

19 *Clean up surface of top and edges with a scraper and abrasives.*

20 *Apply an appropriate finish.*

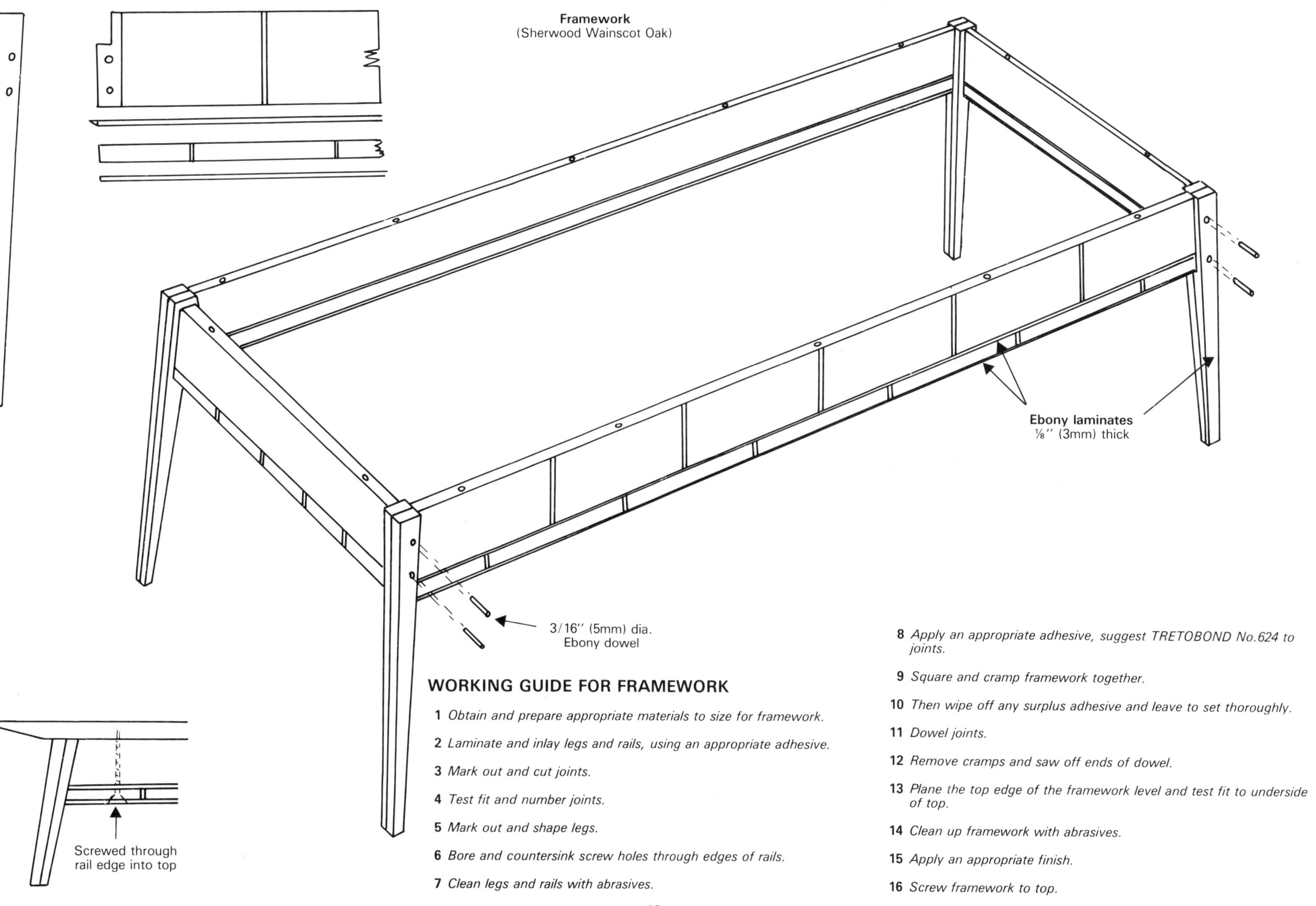

WORKING GUIDE FOR FRAMEWORK

1 *Obtain and prepare appropriate materials to size for framework.*

2 *Laminate and inlay legs and rails, using an appropriate adhesive.*

3 *Mark out and cut joints.*

4 *Test fit and number joints.*

5 *Mark out and shape legs.*

6 *Bore and countersink screw holes through edges of rails.*

7 *Clean legs and rails with abrasives.*

8 *Apply an appropriate adhesive, suggest TRETOBOND No.624 to joints.*

9 *Square and cramp framework together.*

10 *Then wipe off any surplus adhesive and leave to set thoroughly.*

11 *Dowel joints.*

12 *Remove cramps and saw off ends of dowel.*

13 *Plane the top edge of the framework level and test fit to underside of top.*

14 *Clean up framework with abrasives.*

15 *Apply an appropriate finish.*

16 *Screw framework to top.*

SLIM LINE BENCH TABLE

This simple bench type of construction is a slender useful occasional table appropriate for most rooms or the hall.

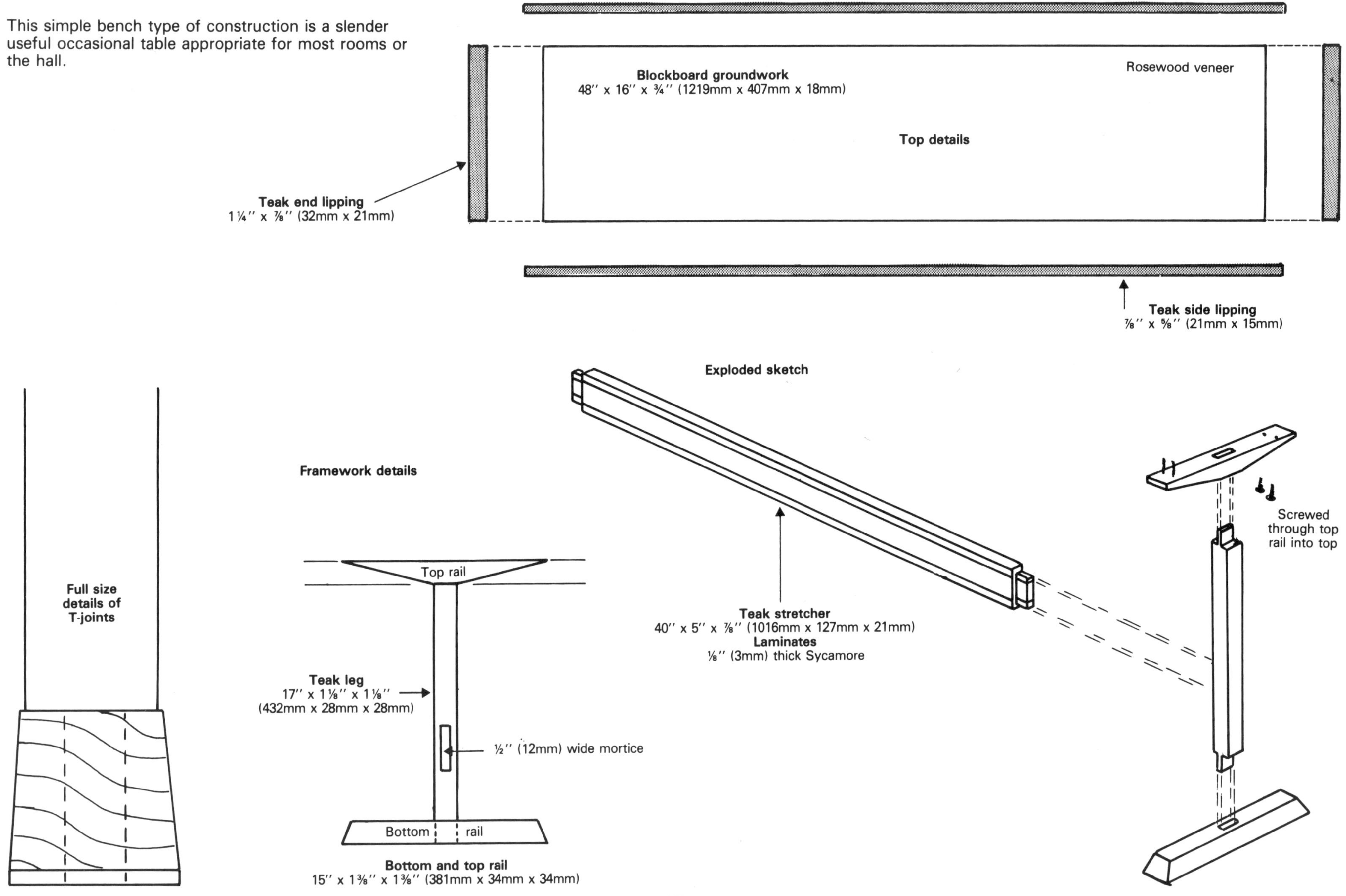

Top Rio de Janeiro Rosewood, lipped with Burma Teak. **Framework** Burma Teak. **Laminate** English Sycamore.

LARGE PLATE RACK

A simple large plate rack suitable for the kitchen or lounge to house and display every day, or occasionally used items. The wood used is top quality Pine, and finished with a hard wearing high gloss lacquer.

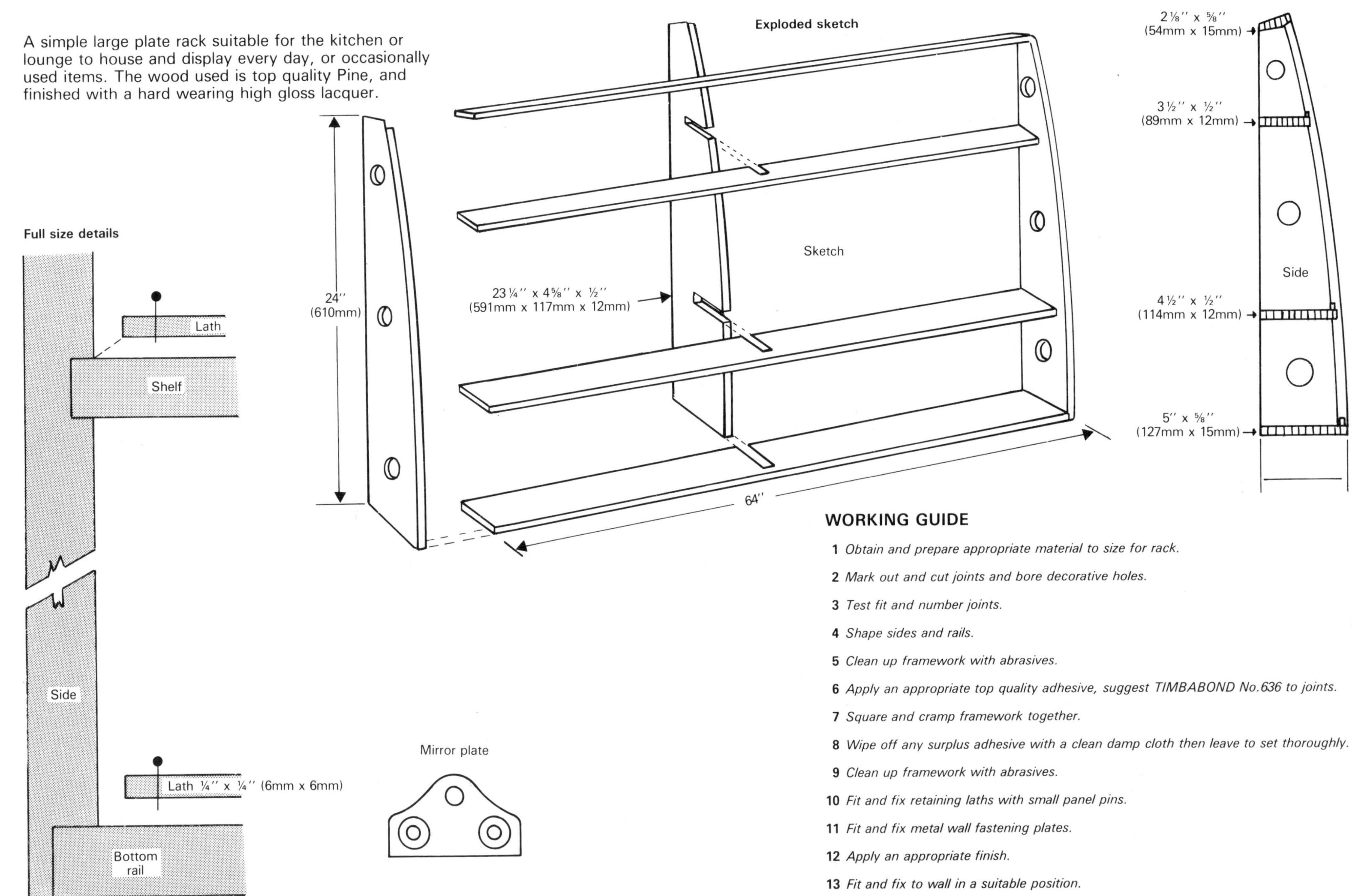

WORKING GUIDE

1 *Obtain and prepare appropriate material to size for rack.*

2 *Mark out and cut joints and bore decorative holes.*

3 *Test fit and number joints.*

4 *Shape sides and rails.*

5 *Clean up framework with abrasives.*

6 *Apply an appropriate top quality adhesive, suggest TIMBABOND No.636 to joints.*

7 *Square and cramp framework together.*

8 *Wipe off any surplus adhesive with a clean damp cloth then leave to set thoroughly.*

9 *Clean up framework with abrasives.*

10 *Fit and fix retaining laths with small panel pins.*

11 *Fit and fix metal wall fastening plates.*

12 *Apply an appropriate finish.*

13 *Fit and fix to wall in a suitable position.*

Wood Red Deal.

SLIM LINE TEA TROLLEY

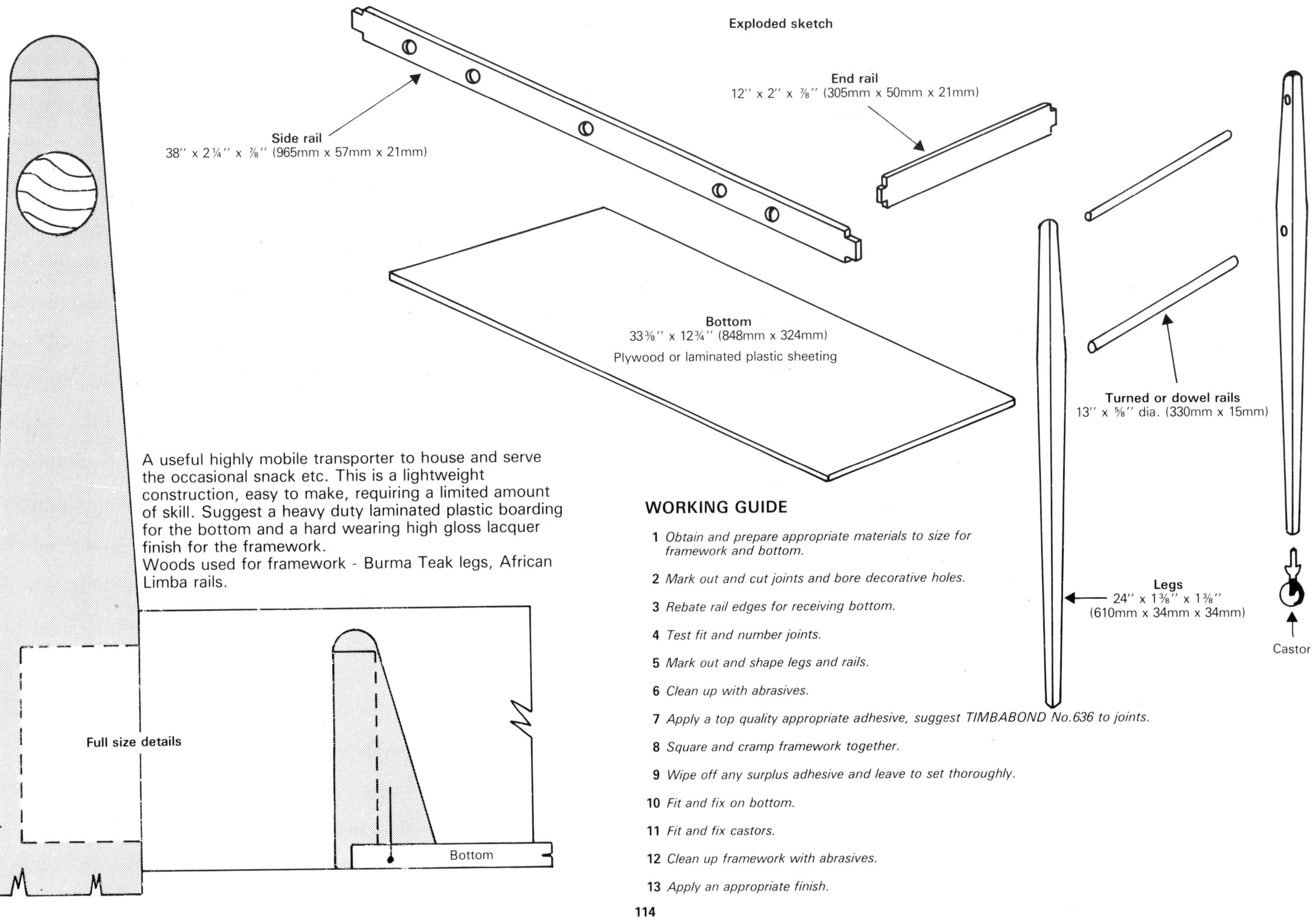

A useful highly mobile transporter to house and serve the occasional snack etc. This is a lightweight construction, easy to make, requiring a limited amount of skill. Suggest a heavy duty laminated plastic boarding for the bottom and a hard wearing high gloss lacquer finish for the framework.
Woods used for framework - Burma Teak legs, African Limba rails.

WORKING GUIDE

1. *Obtain and prepare appropriate materials to size for framework and bottom.*
2. *Mark out and cut joints and bore decorative holes.*
3. *Rebate rail edges for receiving bottom.*
4. *Test fit and number joints.*
5. *Mark out and shape legs and rails.*
6. *Clean up with abrasives.*
7. *Apply a top quality appropriate adhesive, suggest TIMBABOND No.636 to joints.*
8. *Square and cramp framework together.*
9. *Wipe off any surplus adhesive and leave to set thoroughly.*
10. *Fit and fix on bottom.*
11. *Fit and fix castors.*
12. *Clean up framework with abrasives.*
13. *Apply an appropriate finish.*

Woods Burma Teak and African Limba.

ORGAN OR NEEDLEWORK STOOL

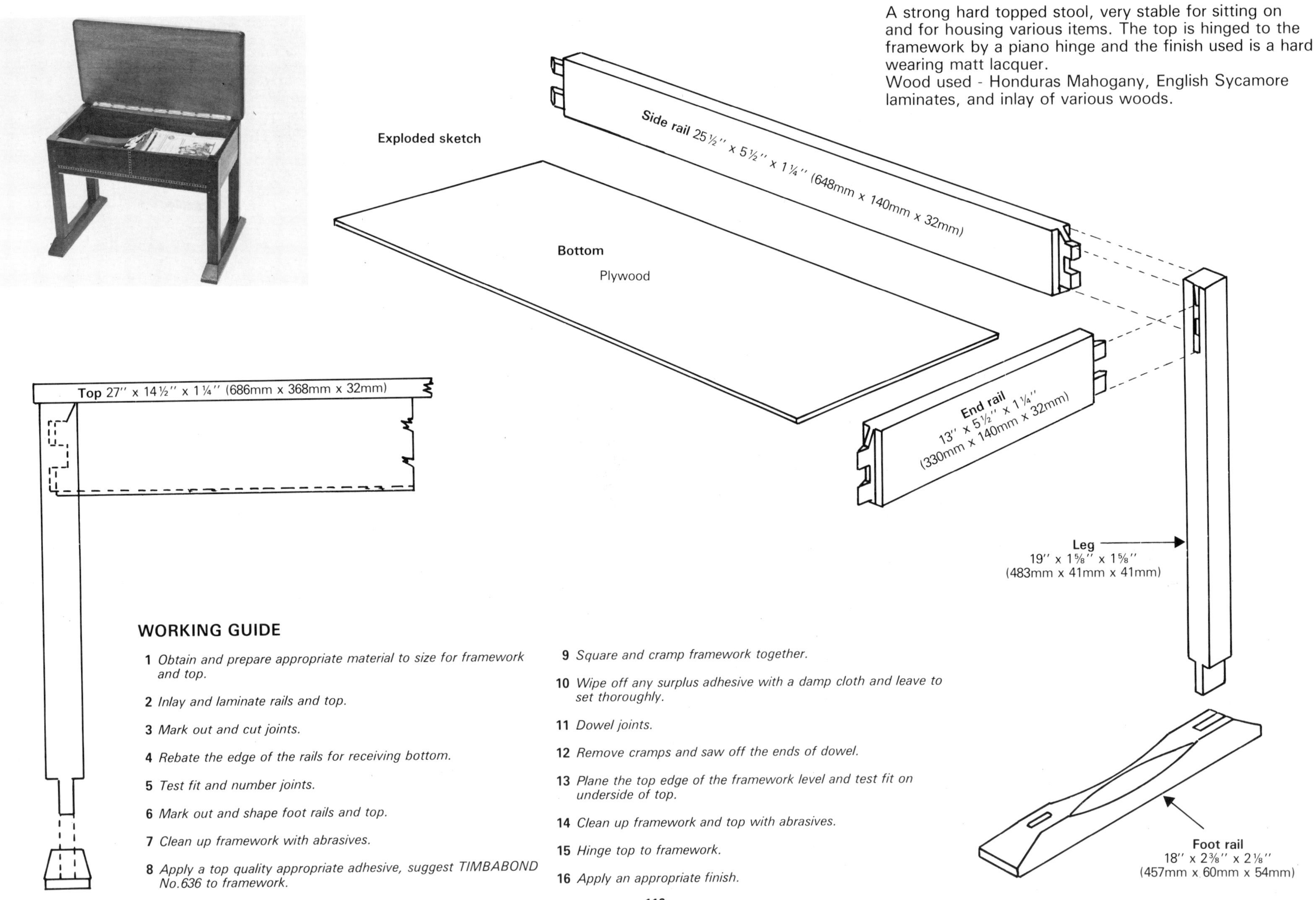

A strong hard topped stool, very stable for sitting on and for housing various items. The top is hinged to the framework by a piano hinge and the finish used is a hard wearing matt lacquer.
Wood used - Honduras Mahogany, English Sycamore laminates, and inlay of various woods.

WORKING GUIDE

1 *Obtain and prepare appropriate material to size for framework and top.*

2 *Inlay and laminate rails and top.*

3 *Mark out and cut joints.*

4 *Rebate the edge of the rails for receiving bottom.*

5 *Test fit and number joints.*

6 *Mark out and shape foot rails and top.*

7 *Clean up framework with abrasives.*

8 *Apply a top quality appropriate adhesive, suggest TIMBABOND No.636 to framework.*

9 *Square and cramp framework together.*

10 *Wipe off any surplus adhesive with a damp cloth and leave to set thoroughly.*

11 *Dowel joints.*

12 *Remove cramps and saw off the ends of dowel.*

13 *Plane the top edge of the framework level and test fit on underside of top.*

14 *Clean up framework and top with abrasives.*

15 *Hinge top to framework.*

16 *Apply an appropriate finish.*

Part of the John Matthews collection.

Wood African Limba.

Woods Rio de Janeiro Rosewood and Burma Teak. **Inlays** Various Woods.

CARVER CHAIRS

Framework Burma Teak. **Laminate** English Sycamore. **Inlay** Various Woods.

ROCKING CHAIR

Wood Honduras Mahogany. **Laminate** Indian Rosewood.

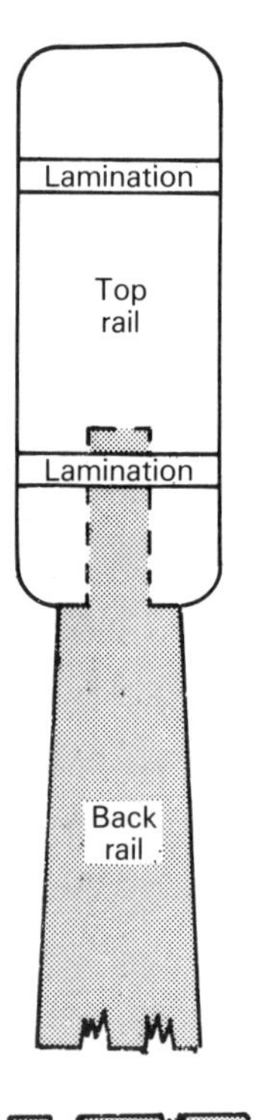

A complex structure requiring a good deal of time and skill but well worthy of the effort.

Note :
Round off the bottom rails around which the woven material will be situated to prevent fraying.

WORKING GUIDE

1. *Obtain and prepare appropriate material to size.*
2. *Inlay and laminate top rails and mullions.*
3. *Mark out and shape runners.*
4. *Mark out and cut joints.*
5. *Test fit and number joints.*
6. *Shape legs and rails etc.*
7. *Clean up with abrasives.*
8. *Apply a top quality appropriate adhesive, suggest TIMBABOND No.636 to the joints.*
9. *Square and cramp framework together.*
10. *Wipe off any surplus adhesive with a clean damp cloth and leave to set thoroughly.*
11. *Dowel joints.*
12. *Consider and obtain appropriate materials for woven bottom.*
13. *Weave seat bottom.*
14. *Clean up framework with abrasives.*
15. *Apply an appropriate finish.*

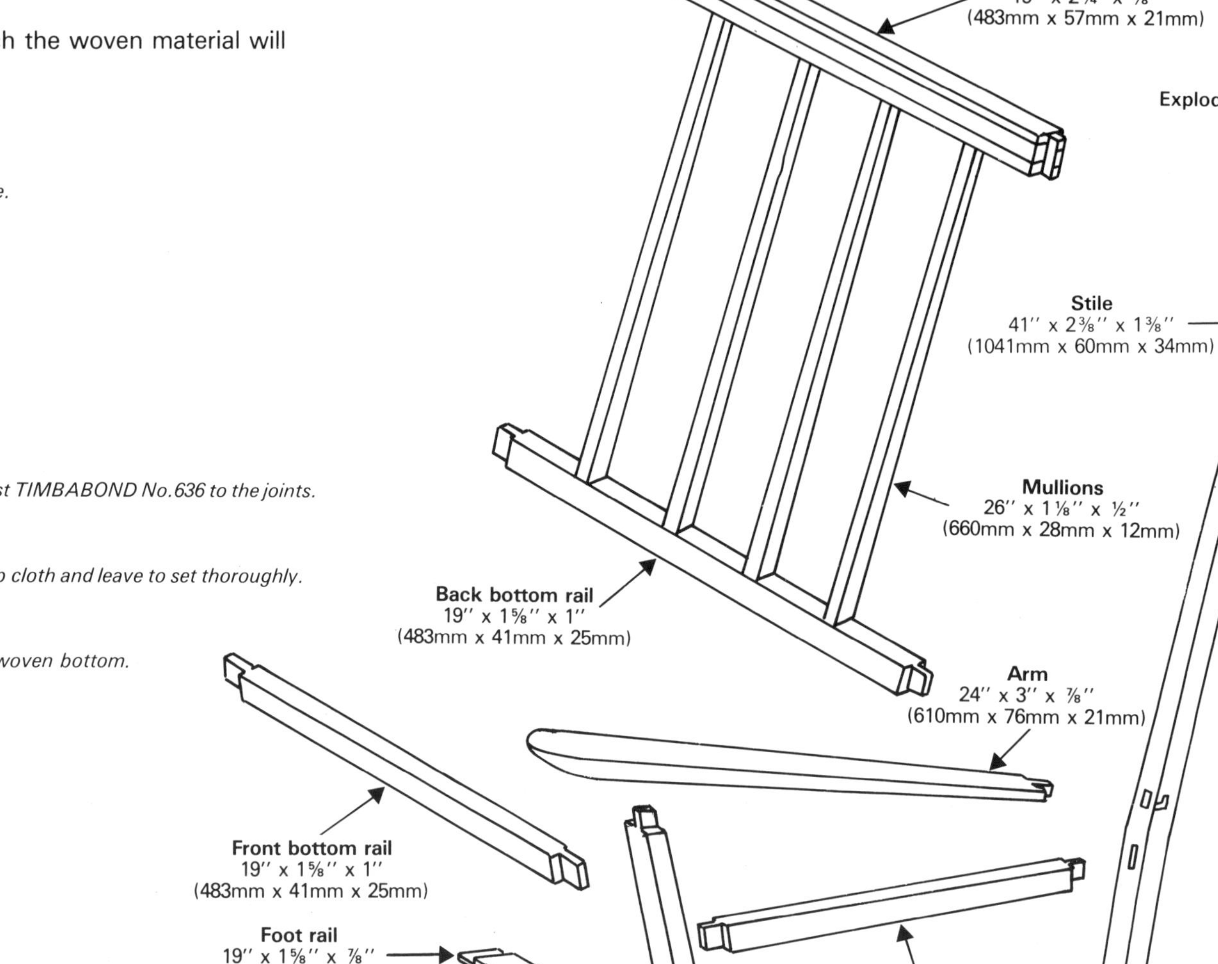

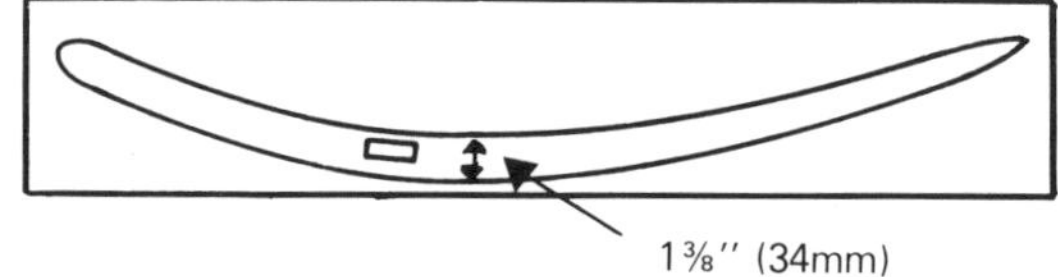

INTRODUCTION TO THE OLD ENGLISH LONGBOW

I first became interested in making Longbows when I was approached to make one for permanent display at Chatsworth House in Derbyshire, England. First of all I delved into the background through various sources, e.g. Museums, books, old manuscripts etc. and from the knowledge gained, and practical trial and error made various test bows. Finally I was able to produce one of quality for Chatsworth from English Yew supplied by the Duke of Devonshire through the good offices of his excellent Forestry Officer, Mr. John Hughes.

This old traditional bow bends as gracefully as a ballet dancer and is a fine mobile piece of functional sculpture. It is not expensive to make one, requiring no elaborate sites or lamination, but it does need care in making for accuracy in shooting requires accuracy in making, and a steady well practised strong arm. Also an eagle eye and the will after every shot - to do better - as with everything we design, make and use.

Various woods can be used to make this traditional bow, e.g. Yew, Lemon Wood, Dagama, Witch Elm, Ash etc. Only use the best quality piece available with a straight grain, and well seasoned.

There is something very special about this bow, whose shaft tapers elegantly, is well balanced and bends to a lovely elliptical shape.

The history of the bow is most intriguing and I have taken the liberty to include brief details below for readers who enjoy learning about the past which is so important to understand the present and future.

BRIEF HISTORICAL BACKGROUND

The English first became aware of the power of the Longbow on the receiving end in the Pundit Wars in Wales during the 12th century. During this early awakening period the Welshmen made Longbows from roughly hewn Witch Elm and developed a high degree of skill in using this bow in warfare.

Through this bitter experience Edward I realised the potential of this weapon and set about equipping and training his subjects. He brought about a law 'that all who earned less than 100 pence per annum should attend and practise regularly at the numerous target butts and earth mounds, conveniently situated in each village, town and city throughout the land'. This concerned 95 per cent of the population, and the weekly practice established a very large trained unit of skilled bowmen throughout the land, ready to serve King and Country whenever the occasion was required.

At these training sessions all had to be fully alert of the dangers of beginners and rash characters, for should anybody get injured or killed because of the importance of this training, no action would be taken. It was just a question of taking practice very seriously and being alert at all times.

THE BOW

The bow stave was often made of Yew grown around the Mediterranean and Central Europe. Yew from these areas is straight grained and of a finer and more even texture than of English Yew which is often coarse and twisted with many natural defects, generally unsuitable for producing good straight grained sections for bow staves.

It is best to cut a section from Yew which comprises of part white Sapwood which is resilient for the back and for the inside, the belly, red Heartwood which resists compression. Such a section should be cleft off the log very carefully with wedges not to cause any internal defective checks which can occur from vigorous splitting with wedges.

The length of the bow varied from 5'10" to 6'6" with a pull up to 100lbs according to the stature and strength of the archer. Horn ends were sometimes fitted but generally notches were cut directly into the wood. The arrow rested above the hand and on a bare stake with no ornate handle in the middle. The string was kept well waxed when strung the shape of the bow was an attractive ellipse bending directly from the handle down the tapered limbs. Ancient longbows can be seen in the Tower of London and the British Museum. The cost of a bow in those days varied from 4 to 7 pence.

THE ARROWS

Arrows were made from strong flexible grained Ash split down the natural line of the grain with wedges and axes to ensure that any weak defect in grain structure would immediately be revealed for the particular shaft to be discarded. At the business end of the arrow was a barbed sharp edged V type of metal blade or for armour piercing a long solid slender bodkin type of blade. The flights were made from grey goose feathers and a guide to arrow length was half the length of the bowstring.

THE BOWMEN

The bowman was a yeoman, a freeman, no one's slave, and got paid the princely sum in those days of between one to two pence per day. He was the best of his kind who through Royal Decree from the age of seven spent long hours regularly at the village butts acquiring the skill which developed him into a piece of deadly artillery which was mainly responsible for England's devastatingly continual victories against the French in the 100 years War, setting a foundation from which the future Empire was developed.

So feared and hated was the English Longbowman by the French that no mercy was given at the hands of his captives. For example, when the garrison of Soissens fell to the French they hung every archer, 300 all told. Their dress was simple, surmounted by a white surcoat on which was enblazened the Red Lion of St. George, clearly and proudly worn. Besides the bow they carried a shooting glove and leather case containing a sheath of arrows, 24 in all and often a dagger, sword and maul for close combat fighting.

THE BOWMEN IN BATTLE

In the 100 years war in France, the English whenever possible set up their battle station at the top of a hill with a good view down the approaching slope on which the French would attack with heavy armed knights on horses, numerous infantry and often Genoese Mercenary Crossbow men. At the centre of the English line would be foot soldiers. Behind these arrayed the Cavalry who where flanked on each wing by archers. In front of the archers in order to repel any direct attack by charging horsemen were strong sharp pointed staves, about 8' long driven into the ground at a wicked sloping angle pointing towards the enemy. Behind this porcupine defence the archers sat gazing down the slope at their adversaries.

When the French started to move up the slope the archers would remove their steel skull caps in which two bow strings were kept safe from rain. They'd select one, fitted it into the bow nocks, added a little wax to the string and elegantly took up a sideway stance waiting for their enemies to come into range. The arrows would be stuck into the ground within comfortable reach of the archer. The first arrows he would select would be the flight arrows, about eight in number which could reach greater distance than the normal battle arrow, being slightly longer and narrower of flight. Through experience they knew when the opposition had come into range, back went the strings right to the nose and on the word 'loose' hundreds of ash shafts leapt into the air humming their way, climbing up, up, then ploughing down onto and into the charging foe. Many arrows would find their mark in the joints of Knights armour, through his eye visor, and all the parts of the unprotected foot soldier. The horses were often hit. These caused more damage, mad with pain charging recklessly about, turning backwards and ploughing death to all behind on foot. Still the French charged on. The Genoese crossbow mercenaries laboured to wind up their arbalests, a slow process during which many were slain by longbow arrows and charging horses. They could not match the rapid fire of the longbows and struggled with their heavy weapons to find a suitable area to aim and discharge their bows. The Longbow men powered between eight and twelve arrows per minute, if one did not find flesh, another one would. Their weapon cost little compared to the cost of a fully armed knight on horse but they decimated the flower of the French Army often before they had chance to reply. Eventually some reached the English positions. At this the bowmen put their bows to one side and joined in the hand to hand combat, strong at hand and light of feet, mobile as tigers, they fought with unmatched agility alongside the men at arms.

Let us look quickly at two actual battles, one on land and one at sea which give a clear picture of the Longbowman's skill and quality in battle.

VICTORY AT SLUYS

The English longbowmen were mainly responsible for the victory at sea against the French at Sluys in 1340. Edward engaged the French Fleet in the harbour. His ships contained around 12,000 archers and from their decks they fired remorselessly into the French Fleet. Their arrows descended like locusts into every part of the French vessels leaving no place to hide. If they jumped over the side it meant sudden death by drowning in their heavy weighted armour. It is thought that over 30,000 French were killed in this sea battle, mainly by longbowmen.

VICTORY AT AGINCOURT

Probably the best known victory which the English fought was at this famous battle named after and near Agincourt Castle. There, on the 25th October, 1415 the Feast of St. Crispin, Henry V with a small band of tired, many ill and near starvation, defeated the French well fed troups. The English Army consisted of 5,000 archers and 1,000 men at arms. These were totally outnumbered by the 25,000 French. The archers were mainly responsible through rapid fire and deadly aim for killing 10,000 French and winning the day. Only a high degree of skill, the right temperament and a noble spirit could have won against such tremendous odds.

Probably the last time the longbow was used in battle was during the retreat of the British to Dunkirk not many years ago. Then, a young English Officer aimed and shot from a longbow an arrow which hit a German soldier - let us hope there will be no need to use any kind of weapon ever again against any man.

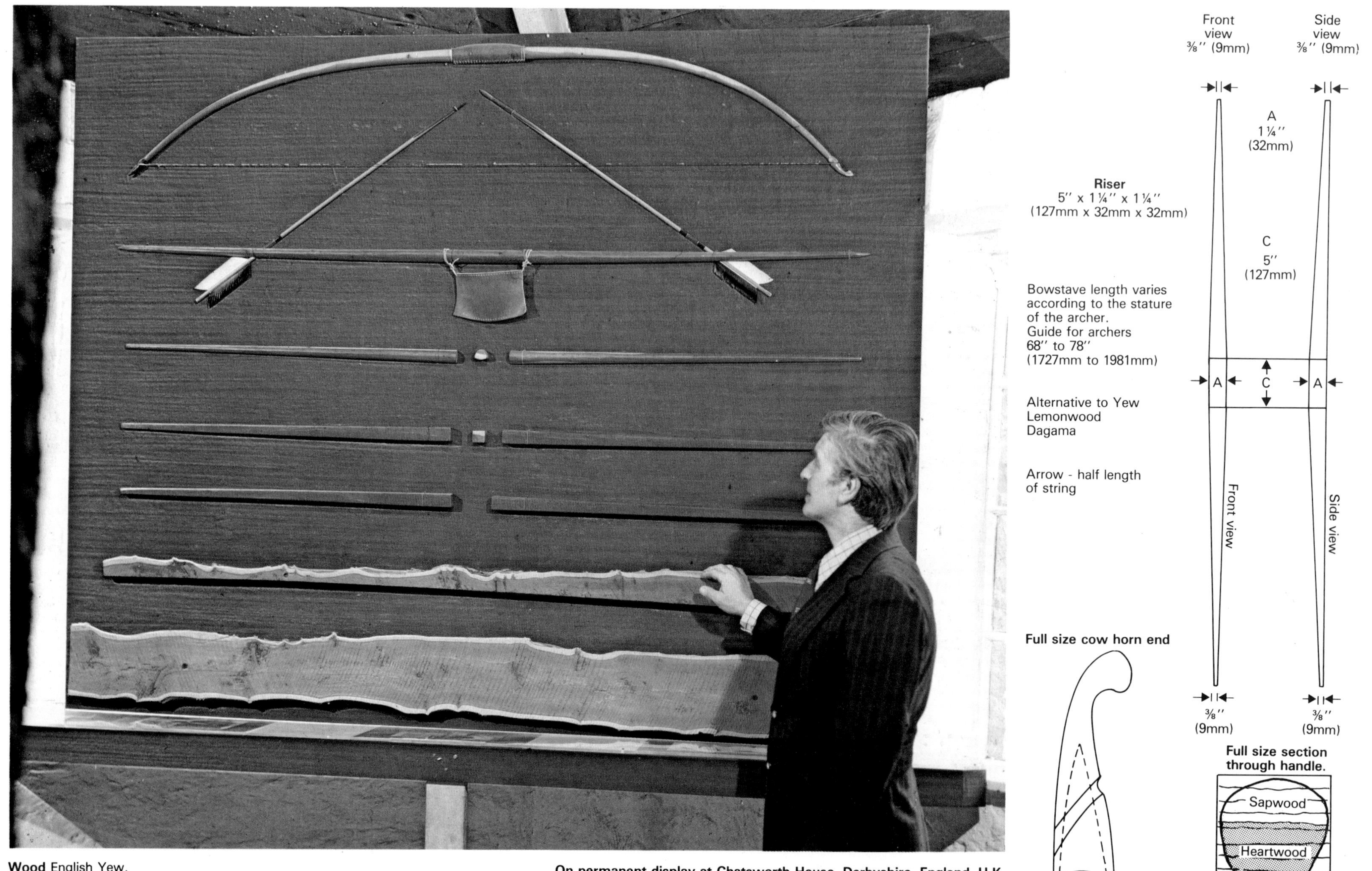

Wood English Yew.

On permanent display at Chatsworth House, Derbyshire, England, U.K.
Owners - Their Graces The Duke and Duchess of Devonshire.

MODERN CROSSBOW

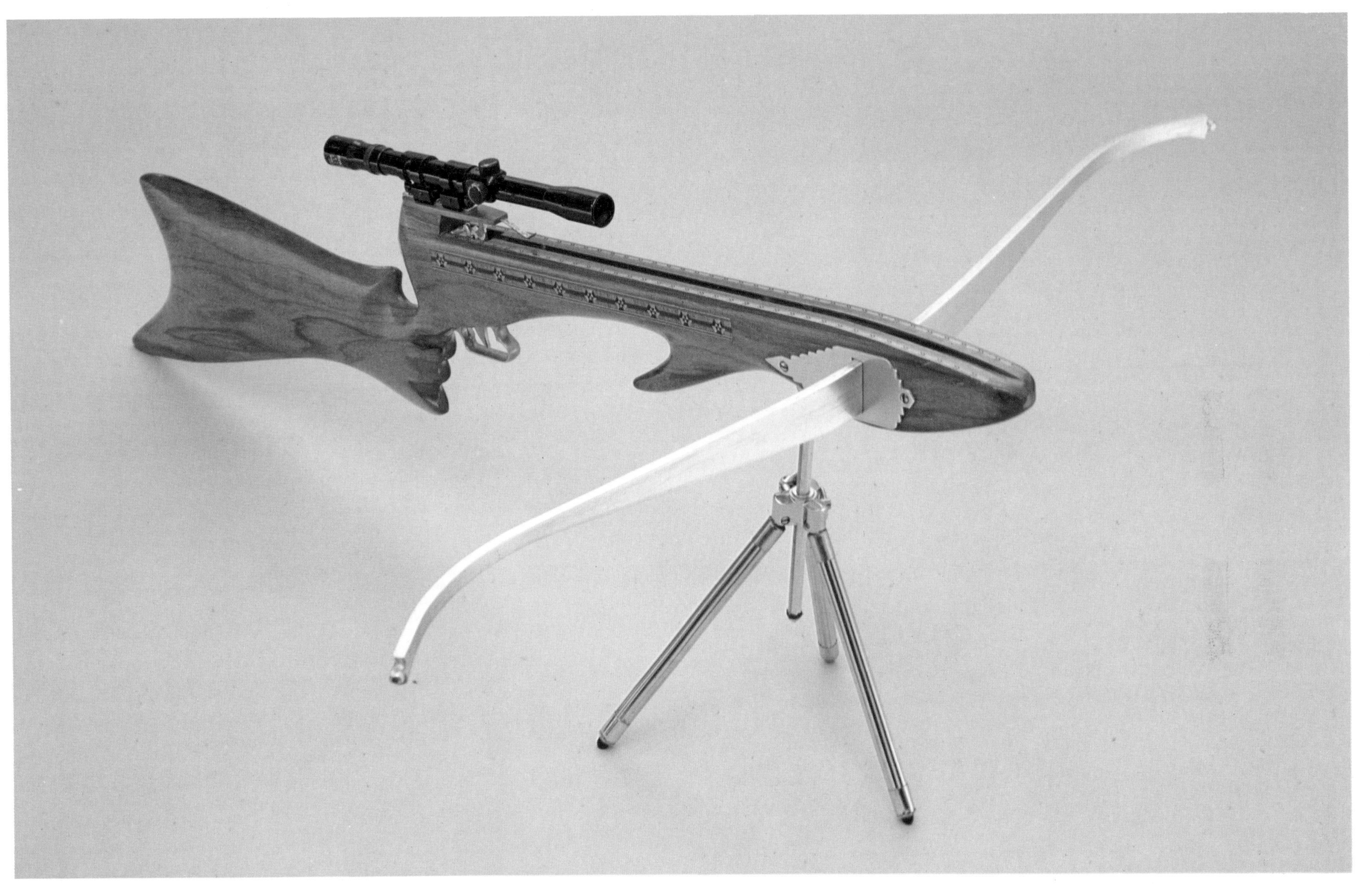

Stock African Limba. **Central Laminate** English Sycamore. **Inlay** Various Woods. **Part of the John Matthews collection.**

WORKING GUIDE FOR MAKING AN OLD ENGLISH LONGBOW

1
Select a straight grained piece of appropriate wood, if possible containing Heartwood and Sapwood, then carefully wedge off a section 1½" x 1½" (38mm x 38mm).

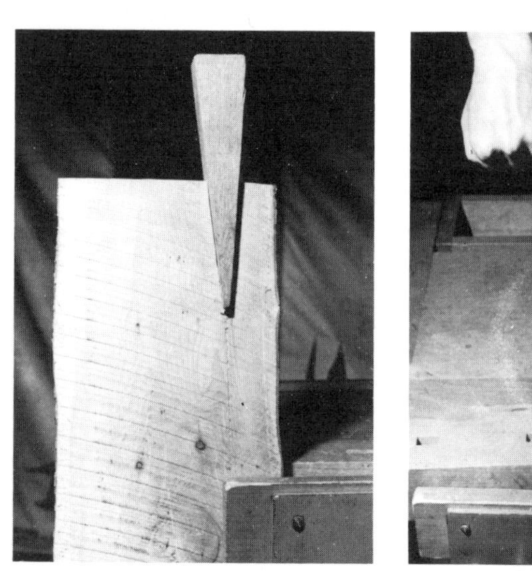

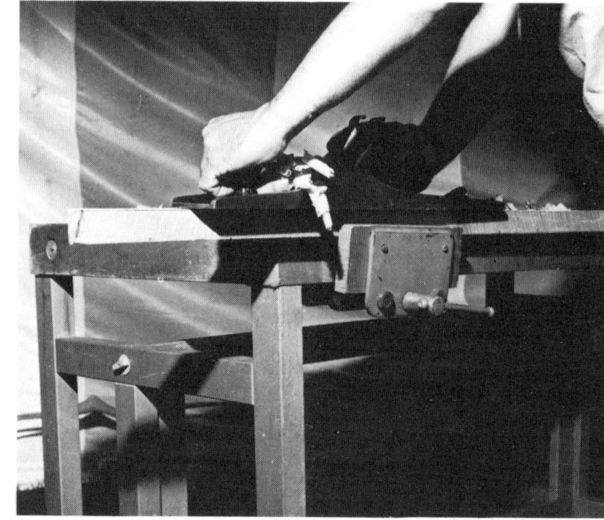

2
Plane straight and square to a finished size of 1¼" x 1¼" (32mm x 32mm).

3
Mark out tapers on front and remove the waste.

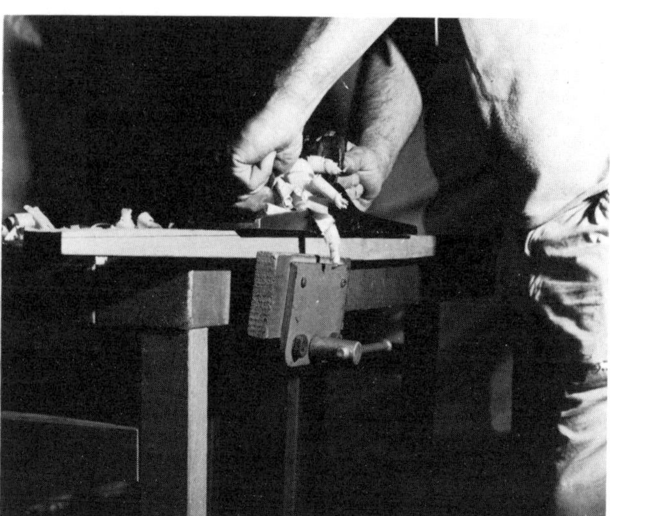

4
Mark out tapers on side. Remove the waste.

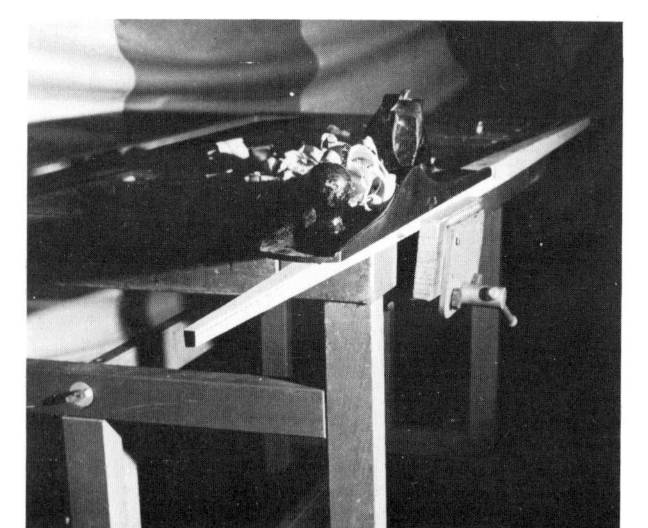

Note final shape of section.

5
Mark out rounding off lines and remove the waste evenly with Surform Tools then Cabinet Files.

6
Cut string notches, or fit and fix on horn ends with a top quality appropriate adhesive, suggest TRETOBOND NON FLAM CONTACT ADHESIVE.

7
Wedge in a simple framework and apply a loose string, then bend and note whether both arms work evenly.

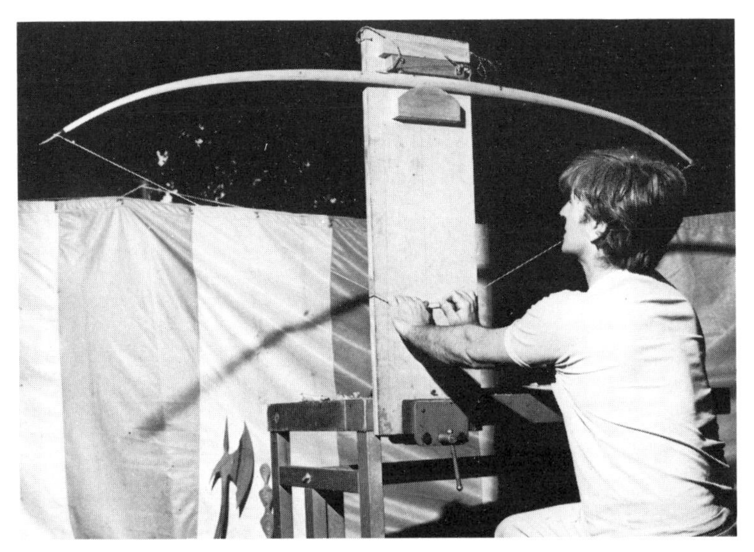

8
Adjust where necessary by removing any 'hard spots'. Finally bend back to arrow length.
The test draw weight can be calculated by placing a spring balance at the centre of the string and pulling downwards, to arrow length.

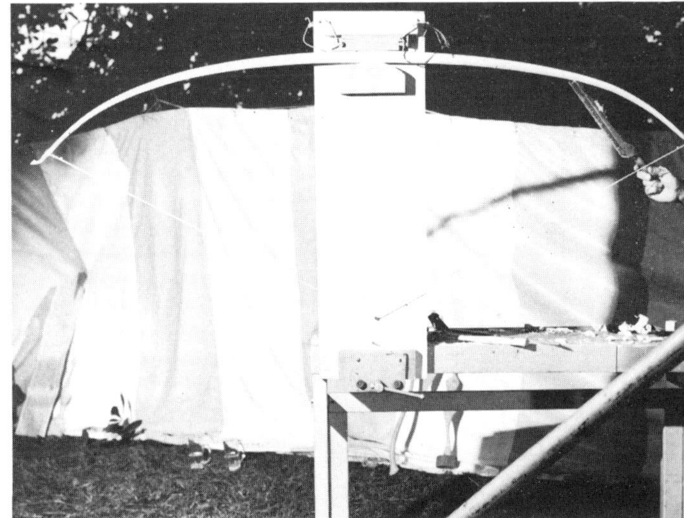

9
Clean up with abrasives.

10
Make a riser for the centre 5" x 1¼" x 1¼" (127mm x 32mm x 32mm). This will help from a comfortable grip.

11
Hollow out the inside of the riser and round off the outside.

12
Lace riser to stave.

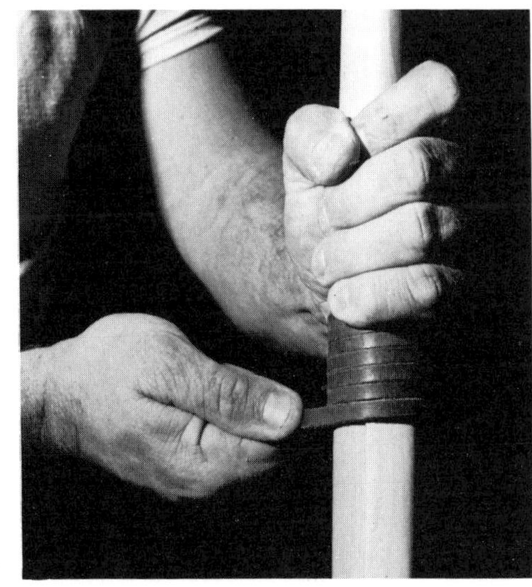

13
Use with total care at all times.

ANCIENT CROSSBOW EXAMPLE

Note :
In 1975 I had the pleasure of making this ancient type of crossbow to go alongside the Longbow at Chatsworth. It proved to be a very interesting project and was made from local Chatsworth Yew.

INTRODUCTION TO CROSSBOWS

Crossbows, because of their power and accuracy have been described as 'the ultimate primitive weapon'. Care should be taken at all times in using this type of apparatus. They have lightning release and sometimes trigger happy fiddlers from time to time, and the child drawing power must never be overlooked.

It is suggested that crossbow men join a club which has a well organised safety range.

Always check any metal prods for metal fatigue before and after a firing session. Also strings and all working parts. Load very carefully and enjoy hitting GOLD only. Leave nature for all to see, alive in it's natural surroundings - not with it's head on the wall.

BRIEF HISTORICAL NOTES

Crossbows have been used for hundreds of years, examples from many cultures are to be found in museums throughout the World, e.g. there are examples of ancient Chinese Crossbows in the New York Metropolitan Museum, some of which are complexed repeaters, very advanced in design.

William the Conqueror made good use of crossbows in his conquest of England in 1066.

In 1134 Pope Innocent III forbad the use of the crossbow and so did Conrad III of Germany because of the terrible injuries caused in medieval warfare.

Richard I of England developed a unique Corps of crossbow men and in 1307 died from being hit by a bolt from a crossbow - from which side no-one knows.

Henry VII chartered 'no man shall shoot a crossbow without the King's licence, excepting he be a Lord or have 200 Marks of Land' - not too many in those days.

Today, in the U.S.A. 40 states have anti crossbow laws of one sort or another. Mainly a legacy from their Colonial past.

On target in Cincinnati, Ohio, U.S.A. 1976.

MODERN CROSSBOW EXAMPLE

Part of the John Matthews collection.

CROSSBOW Mk.1

Woods Stock, African Limba. **Central Laminate** English Sycamore. **Inlays** Various Woods.

This bow is for firing one arrow at a time and can readily be fitted with a telescopic site and adjustable stabilising tripod.

Stock details :
Laminate the stock with a top quality appropriate adhesive, suggest TIMBABOND No.636. The lamination adds strength and durability to the structure, and also adds an attractive decorative feature. Use a wood which is straight grained and mild working, and one which is 'middle weight', e.g. African Limba, Honduras Mahogany, Japanese Elm, Walnut, etc. with a Sycamore ⅛″ (3mm) laminate.

Sketch of laminated vertical cross section

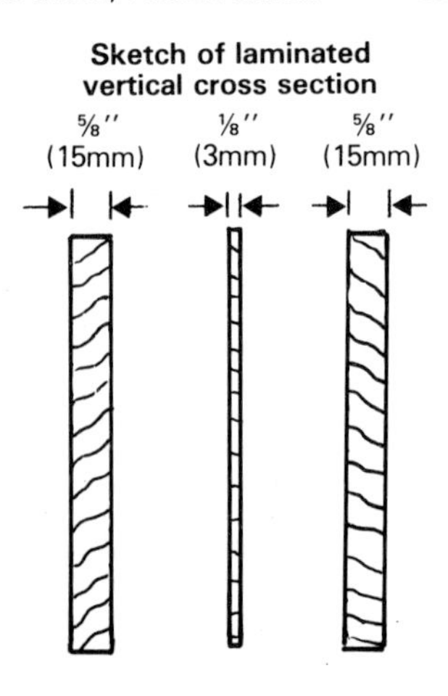

Overall size of Stock 40″ x 8½″ x 1⅜″ (1016mm x 216mm x 34mm)

Marking out grid for Stock
(use 2″ (5mm) squares)

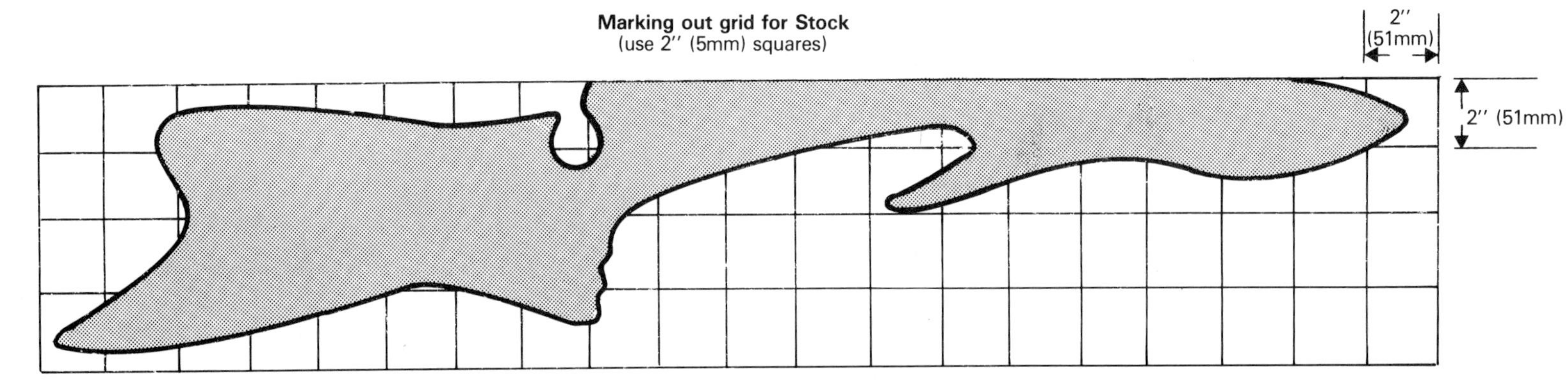

Full size details of front view

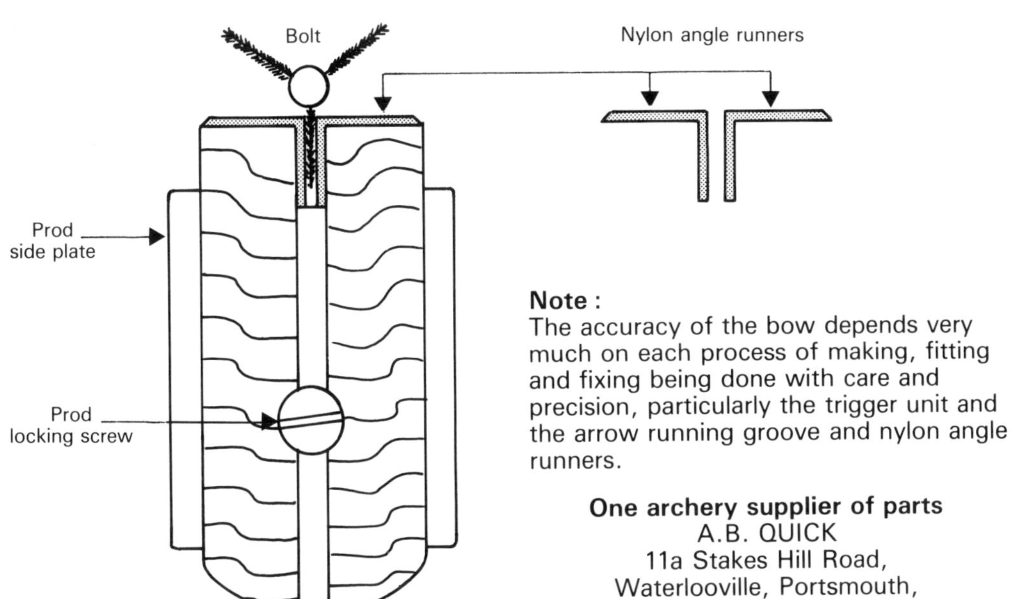

Note :
The accuracy of the bow depends very much on each process of making, fitting and fixing being done with care and precision, particularly the trigger unit and the arrow running groove and nylon angle runners.

One archery supplier of parts
A.B. QUICK
11a Stakes Hill Road,
Waterlooville, Portsmouth,
England, U.K.

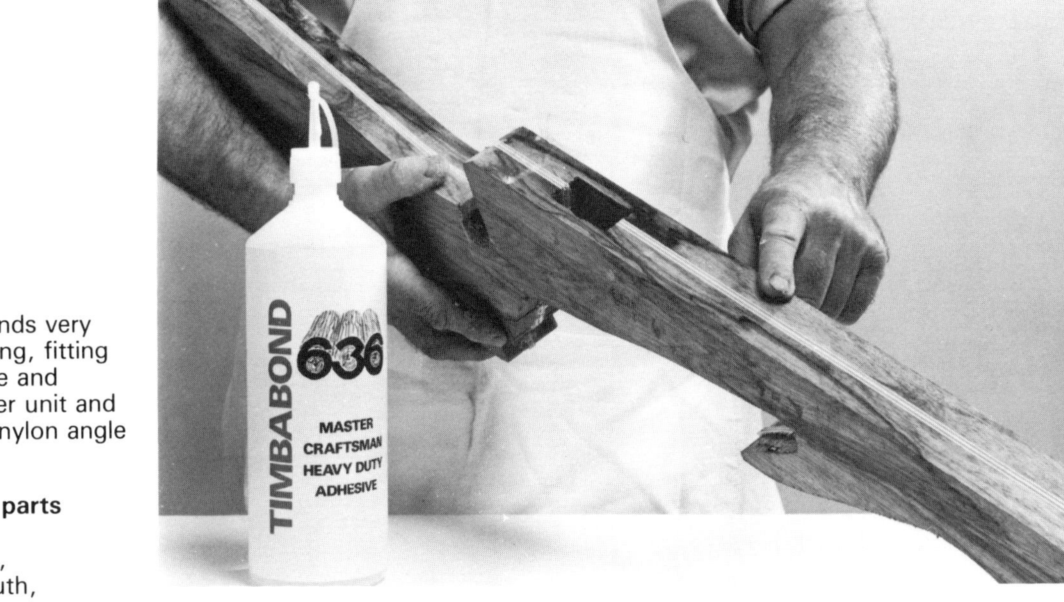

Laminated Stock.

Prod details
Material - normal 75st extruded alloy bar 36″ x 1½″ x 5/16″ (914mm x 38mm x 8mm)

Strong to match 75lbs draw weight made of dacron

Bolt elevation retaining spring
(made from spring steel)

Full size details of aluminium alloy bracket

Full size details

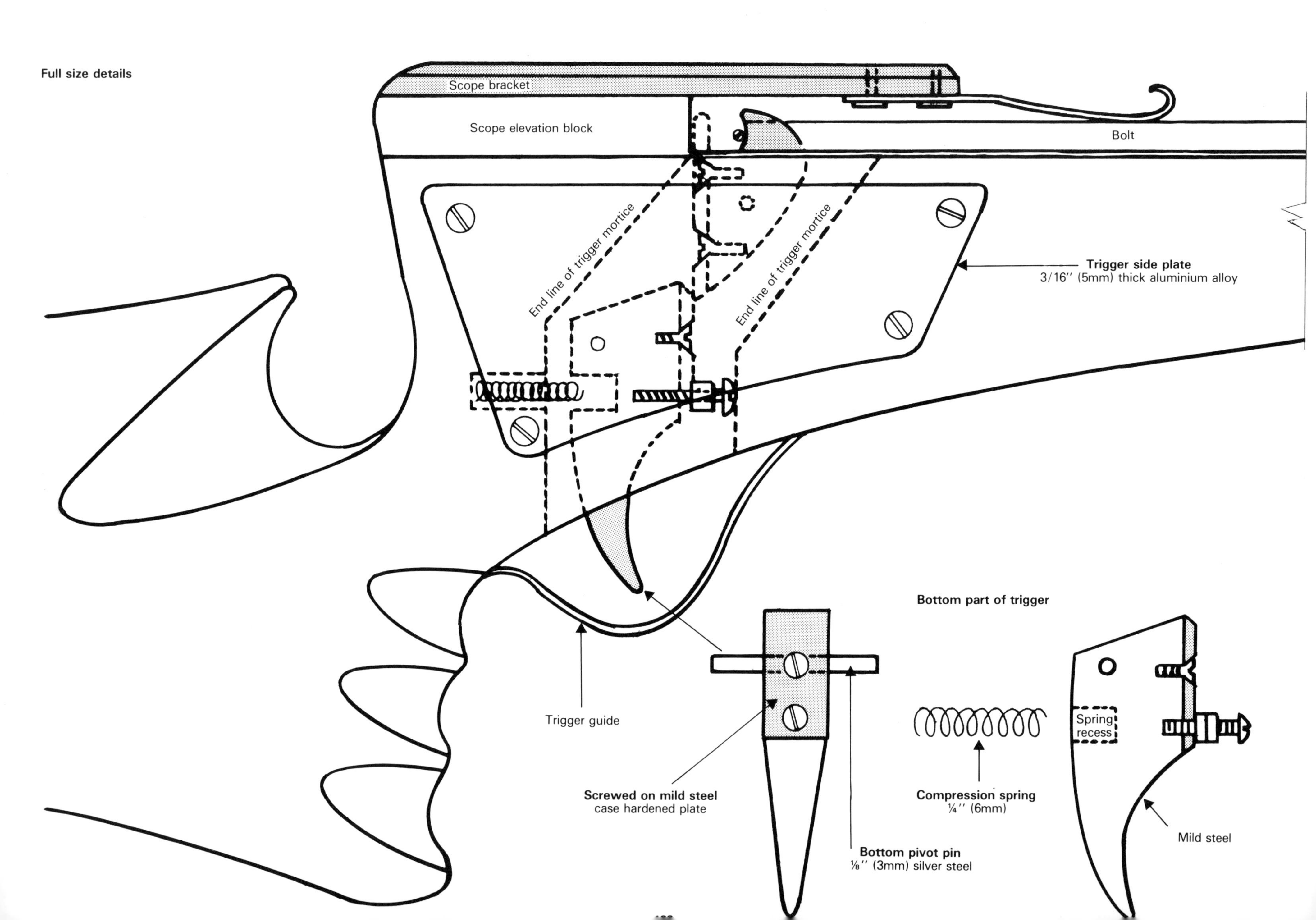

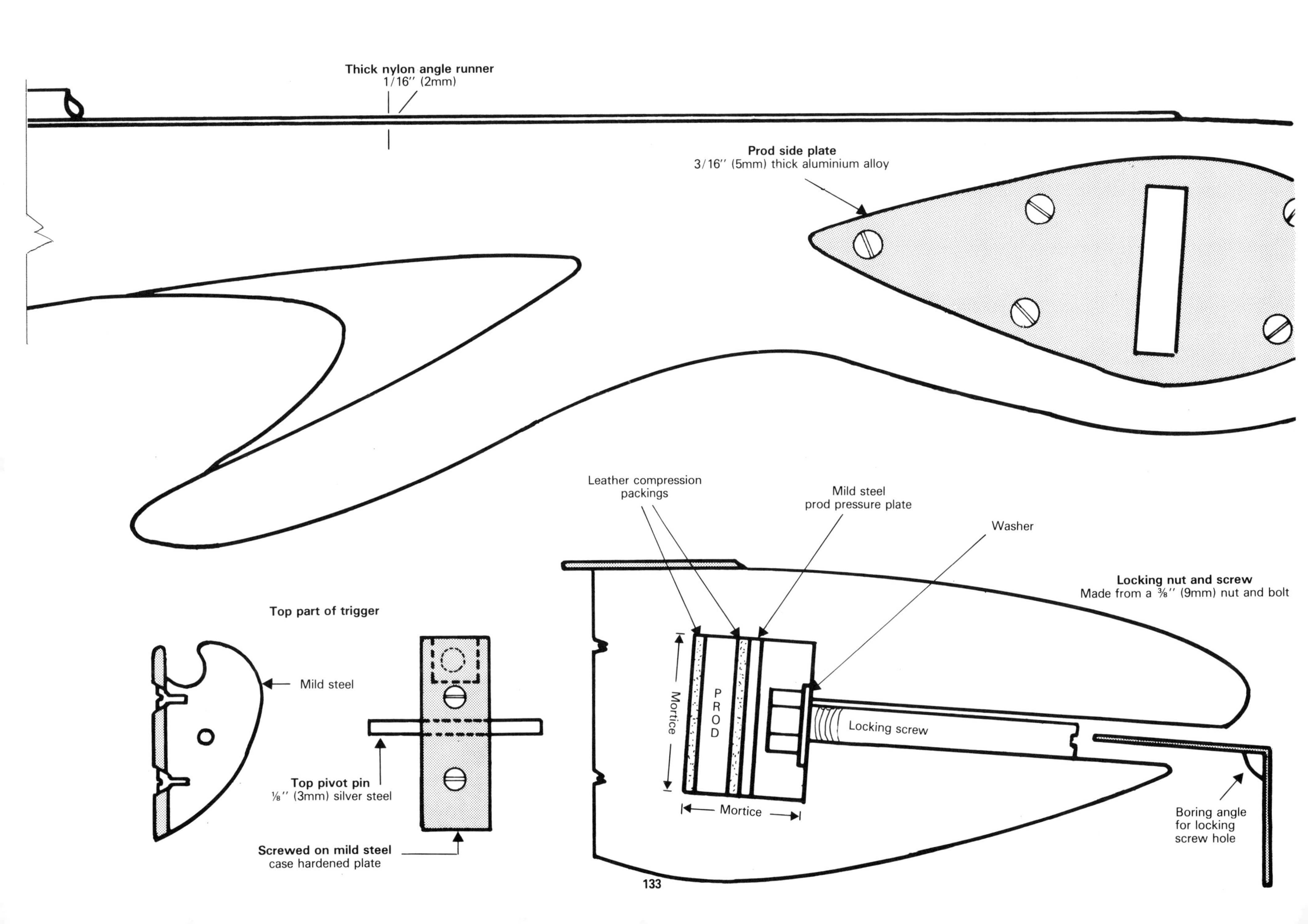
Thick nylon angle runner
1/16'' (2mm)
Prod side plate
3/16'' (5mm) thick aluminium alloy
Leather compression packings
Mild steel prod pressure plate
Washer
Locking nut and screw
Made from a ⅜'' (9mm) nut and bolt
Top part of trigger
Mild steel
Mortice
PROD
Locking screw
Top pivot pin
⅛'' (3mm) silver steel
Mortice
Boring angle for locking screw hole
Screwed on mild steel
case hardened plate

WORKING GUIDE

1
Obtain and prepare appropriate materials for the stock. Then laminate sections together with a top quality appropriate adhesive, suggest TIMBABOND No.636. Then plane top edge straight and square.

2
Mark out the profile of the stock.

3
At front end mark centre of locking screw hole and mark on side boring angle guide.

4
Then bore ⅜″ (9mm) dia. hole, 4¼″ deep (108mm).

5
Trace, then mark out mortice position. Bore and chop out mortice.

6
Saw off waste and clean down to lines with Surform Tools.

7
Make trigger unit and guard. Mark out trigger mortice and mortice end guide lines.

8
Bore, then chop out mortice.

9
Fit trigger unit and guard.

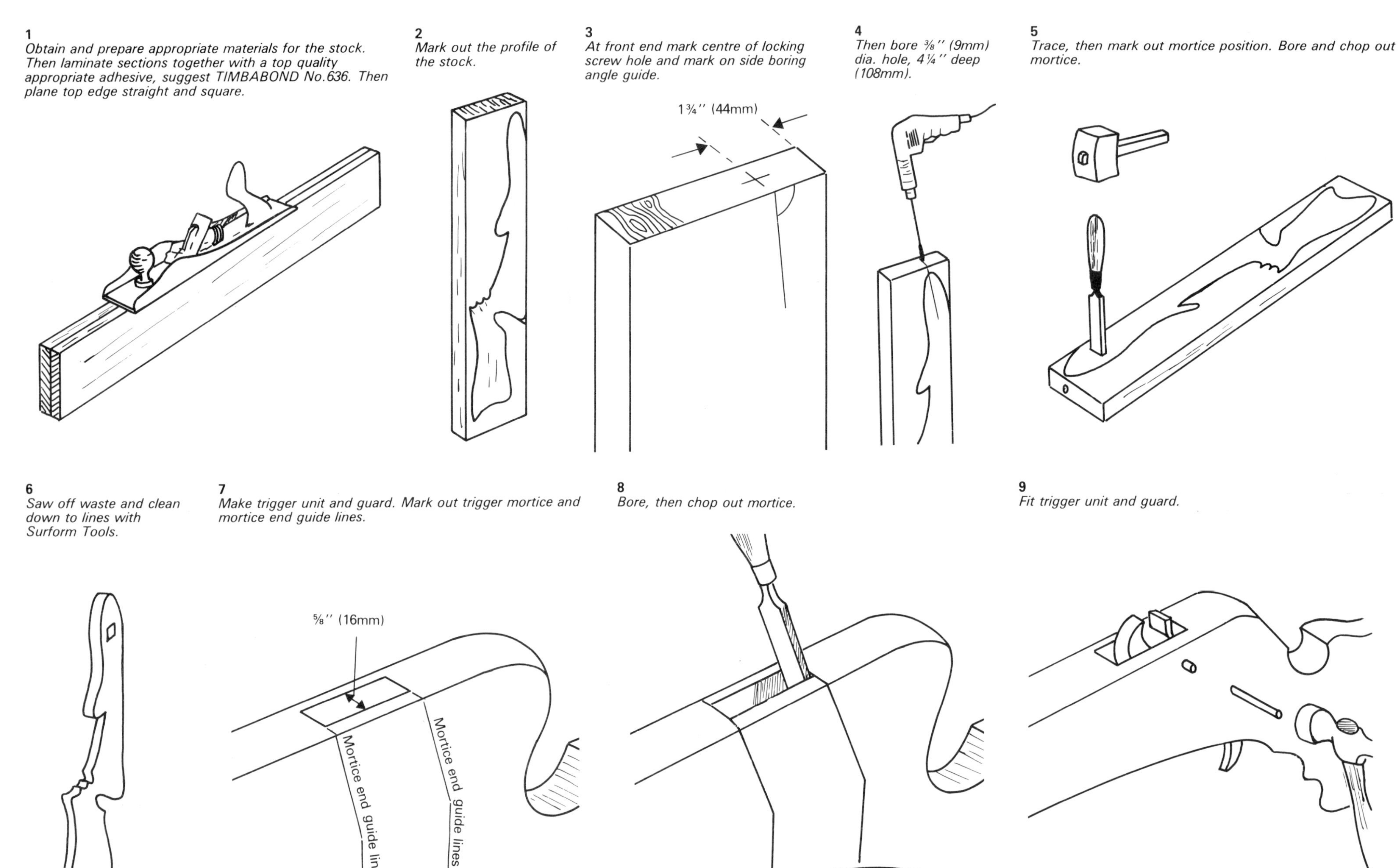

10
Remove trigger assembly and cut flight groove up to trigger mortice.

Flight groove

11
Do any inlaying at this stage.

12
Fit and fix scope elevation block with a top quality appropriate adhesive, suggest TIMBABOND No.636.

Scope elevation block

13
Fit and fix nylon angle runners with a top quality appropriate adhesive, suggest TRETOBOND NON FLAM CONTACT ADHESIVE.

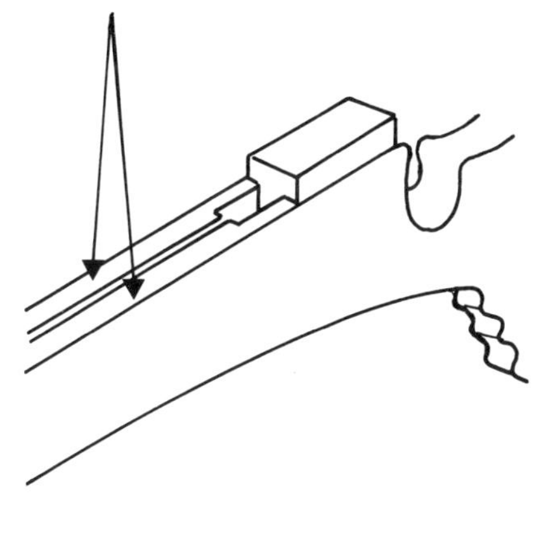

14
Make, fit and fix with screws, scope bracket, trigger side plates, and prod.

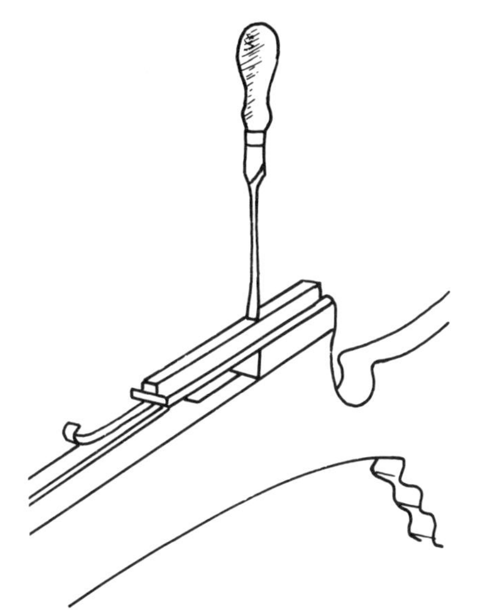

15
Round off all sharp corners and form finger grips with Surform Tools. Clean up with abrasives.

Butt section shape

16

FIT AND FIX

TRIGGER ASSEMBLY AND GUARD

PROD AND TRIGGER SIDE PLATES

PROD LOCKING SCREW

TRIPOD

STRING

SCOPE

CALIBRATE ON A RANGE

APPLY A HARD WEARING WATERPROOF FINISH

ALWAYS BE VERY CAREFUL

CROSSBOW Mk.2

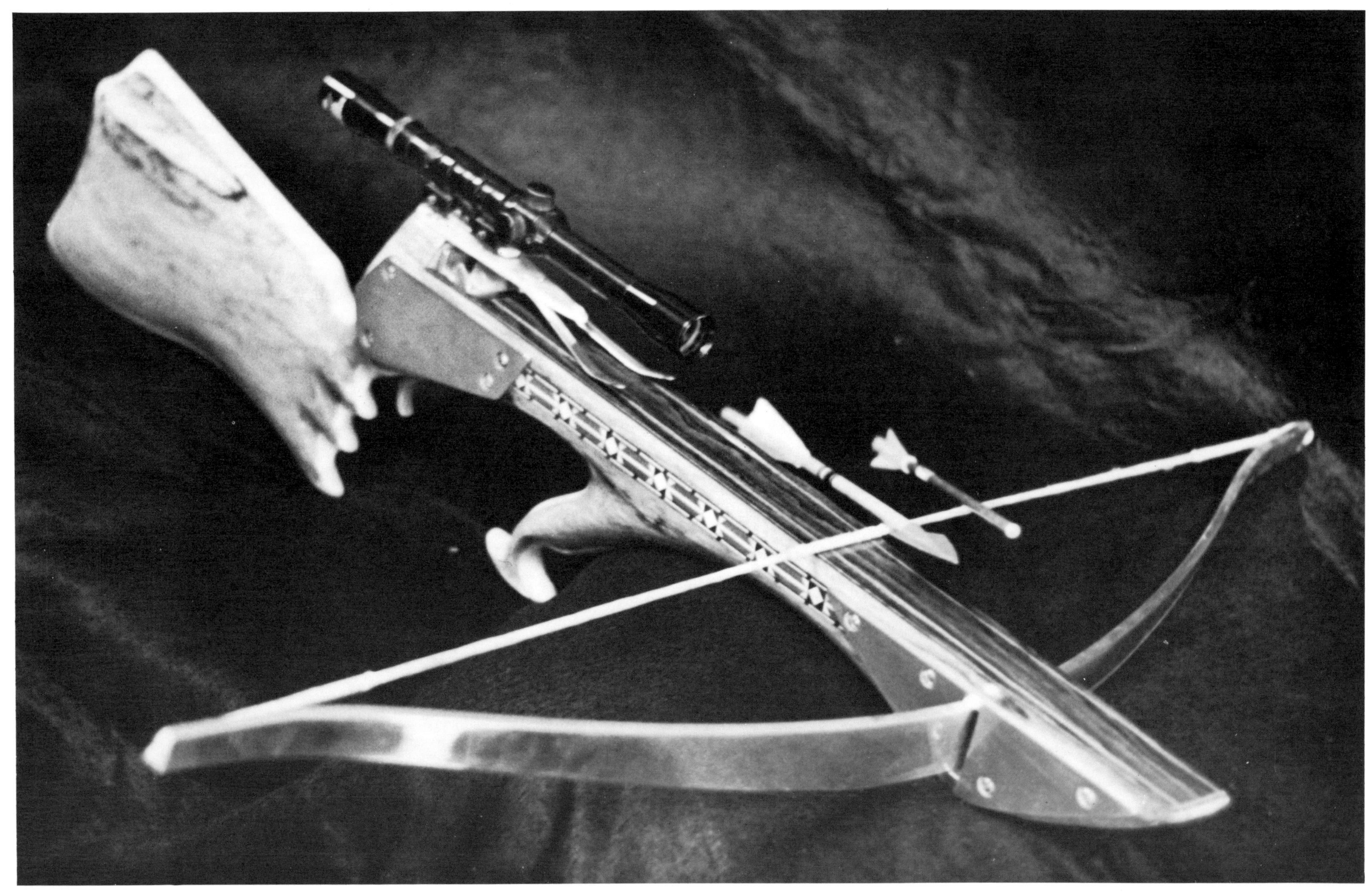

Woods Stock, African Limba. **Central Laminate** English Sycamore. **Inlay** Various Woods. **Owner - Old N°9 Museum, Davenport, Iowa, U.S.A.**

This bow will fire two arrows both at the same time and can be fitted with telescopic sights and stabilising tripod.

The trigger mechanism is not easy to make and fit but the working model well made is a splendid piece of equipment and one which will give pleasure to the user and stimulate the onlooker.

Note :
Details of special features are on this page and for other features see details of Mk.1 for general materials, prod, string, stock length etc. and working guide.

SPECIAL FEATURES

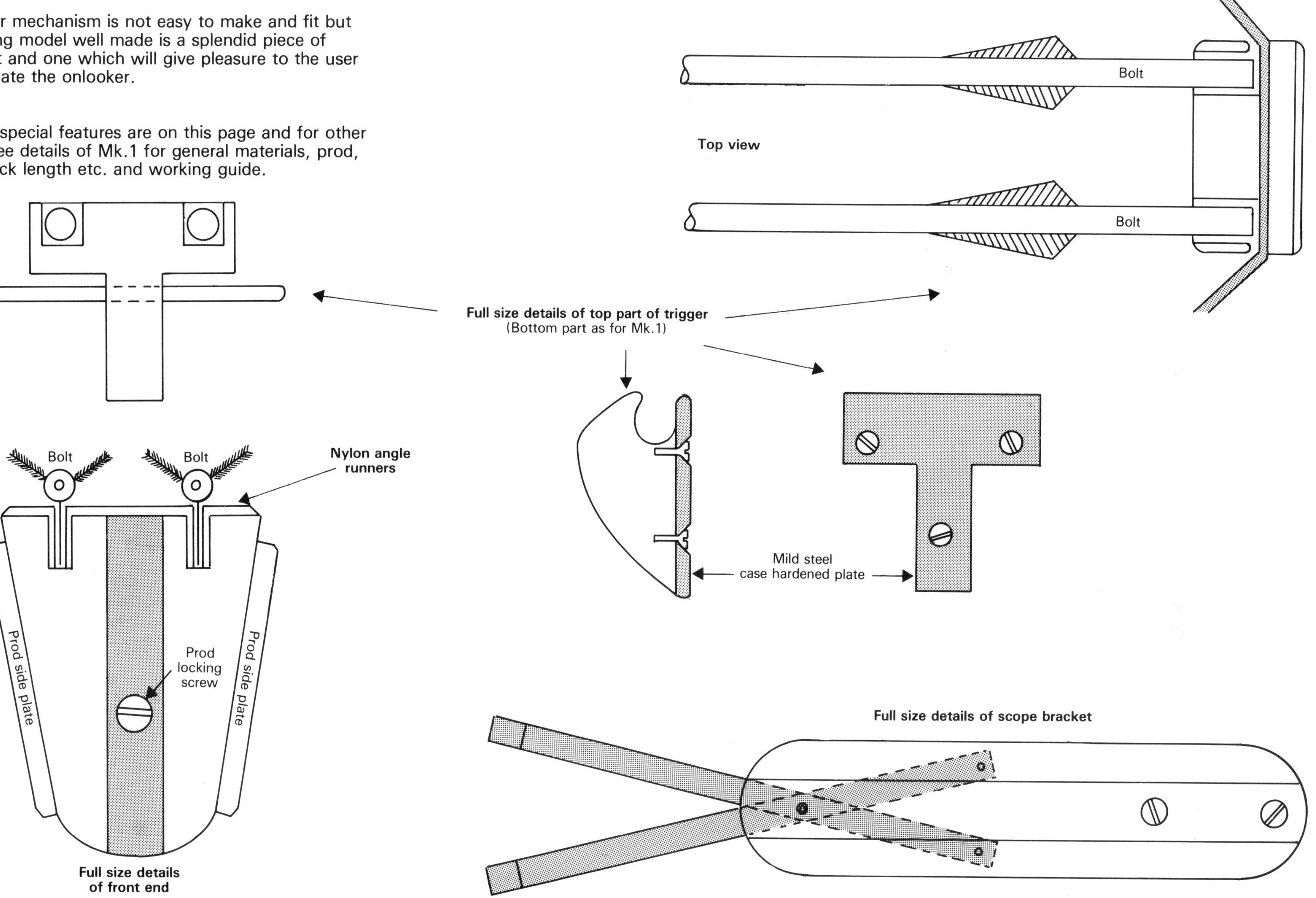

VARIOUS EXAMPLES OF WALKING STICKS

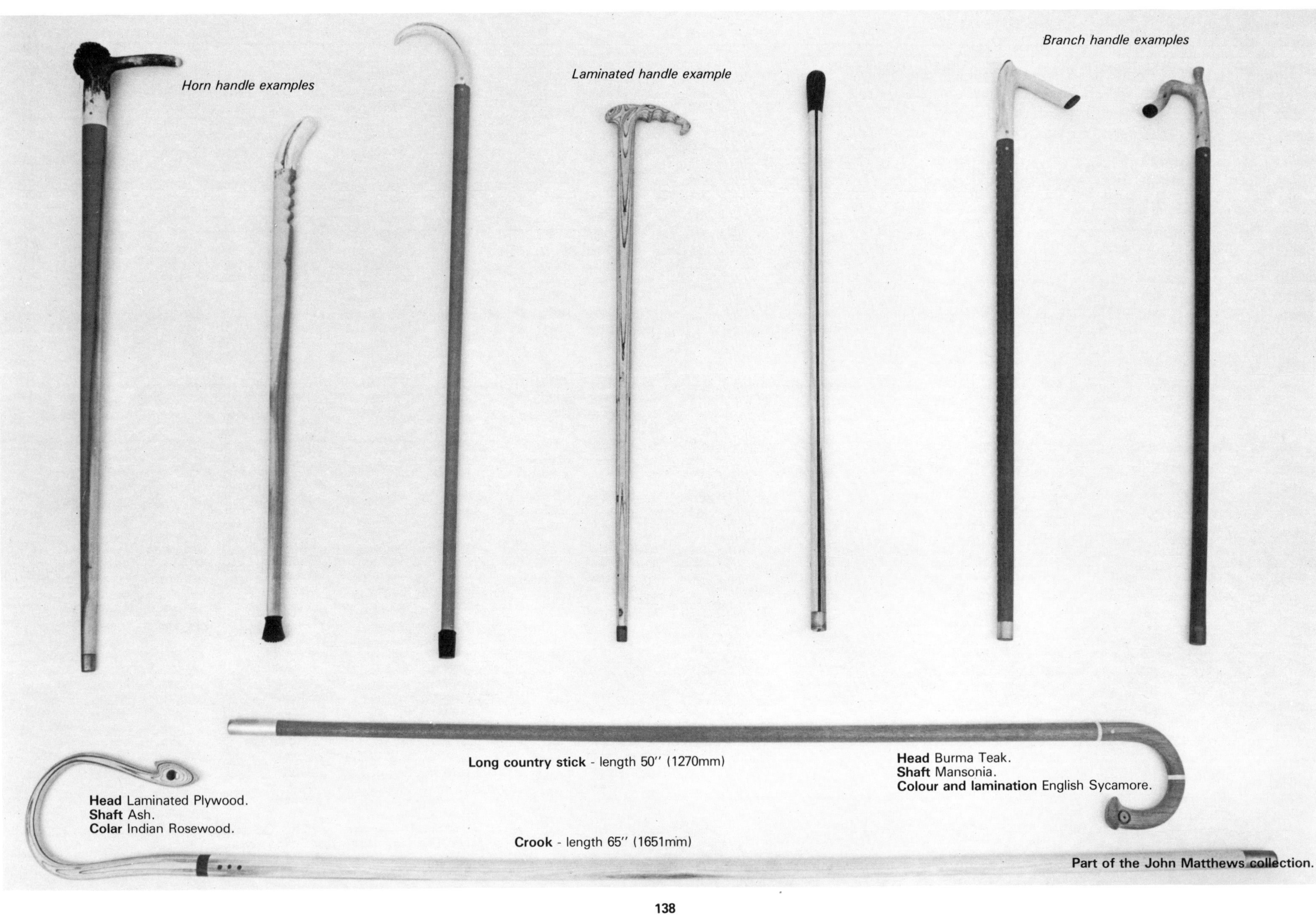

AND CROOKS

For those who indulge in evening or weekend walks a stick is a true and trustworthy partner and a pleasurable and useful companion. It can also be an extra helping 'hand' for injured legs etc. If, like myself, you have a dog a walking stick can act as a useful barrier between the unwelcome attentions of dog to dog. Walking sticks can also be a decorative feature for the wall or stand at home, and should the occasion arise, a repellent of evil intent.

For the shaft, use strong medium weight straight grained hardwoods, e.g. Ash, Dogwood, Chestnut, Hazel etc. and for the handle an overall durable and strong, nice to hold warmth retaining material.

Lamination can often add another degree of strength and attractive features, especially if a slimline stick is required.

Note :
An excellent strong 'natural' handle can be developed from an appropriate sized branch shape.

Example below

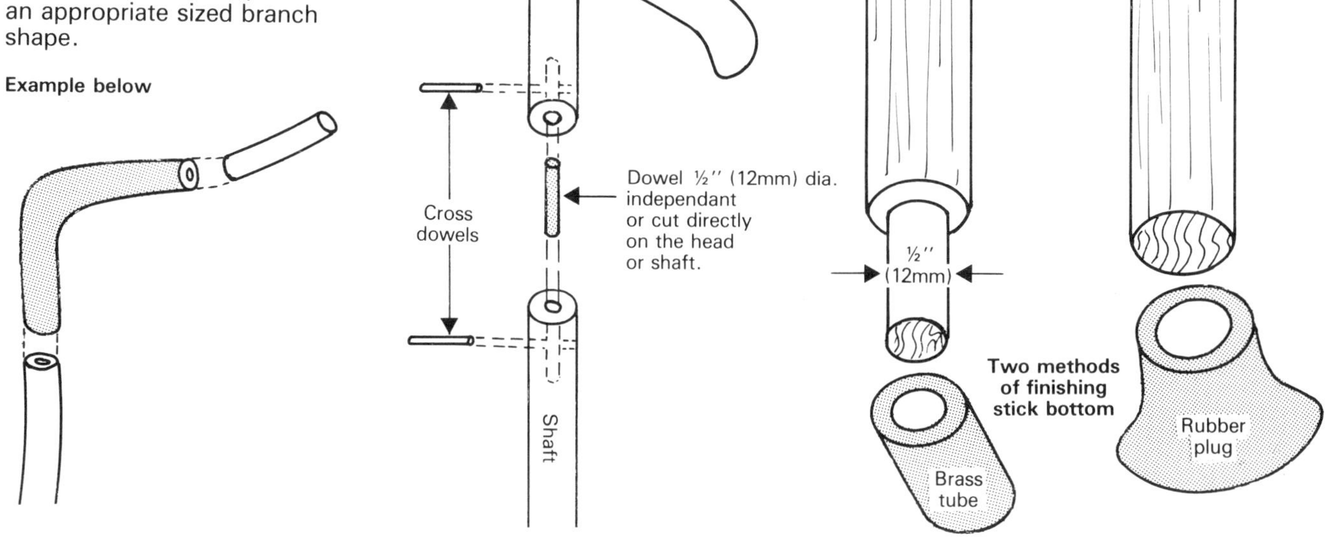

WORKING GUIDE

1
Obtain and prepare appropriate material to size, laminate, if and where desired. Cut dowel and fit head to shaft.
Note : It is suggested that you generally work in a traditional manner directly from the raw material.

2
Shape head and shaft. Test fit brass ends at foot of stick.

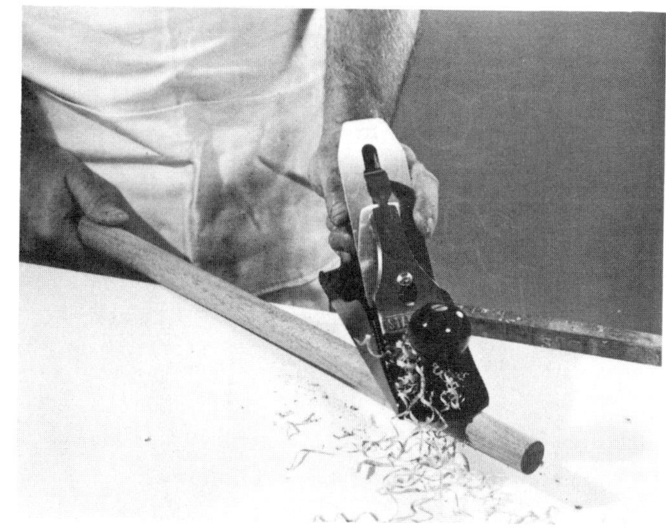

3
Apply a top quality appropriate adhesive, suggest TIMBABOND No.636 to joints and fitments. Construct and leave to set thoroughly. Clean up with abrasives, then apply appropriate finish.

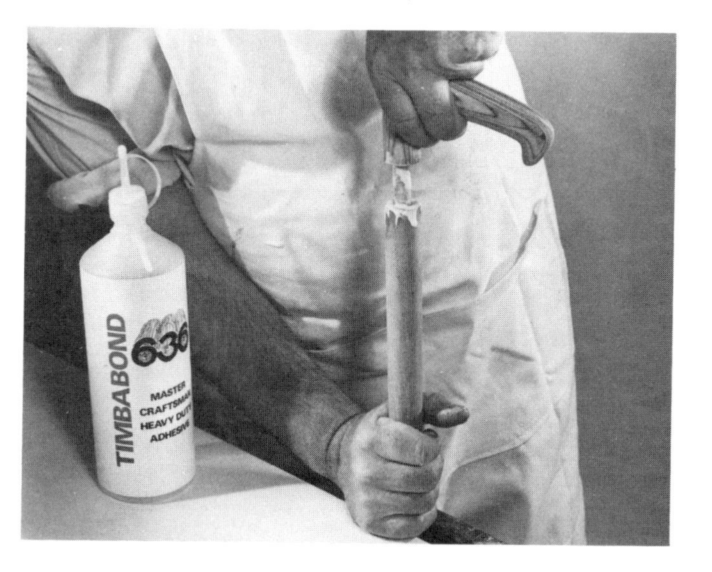

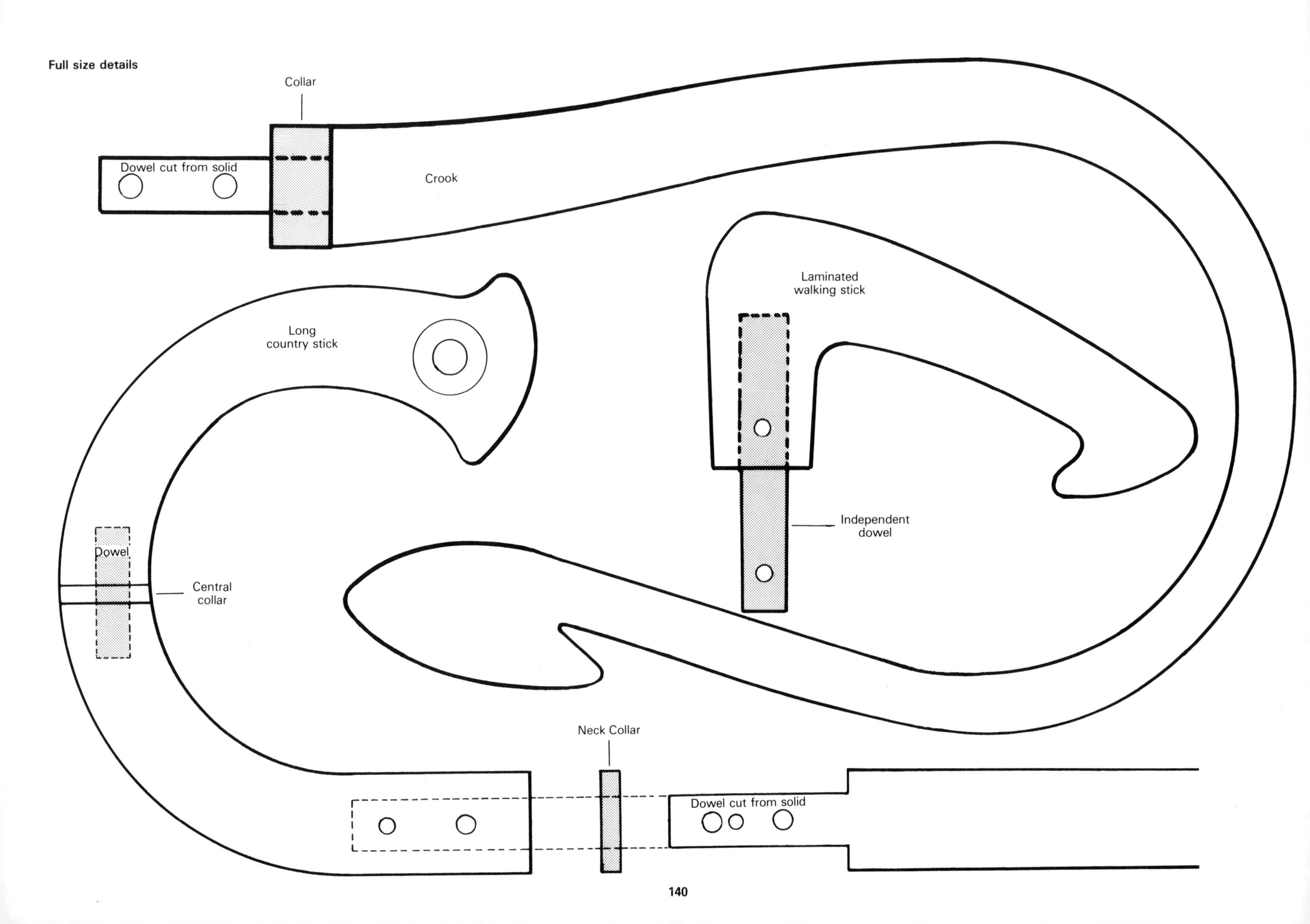
Full size details
Collar
Dowel cut from solid
Crook
Laminated
walking stick
Long
country stick
Independent
dowel
Dowel
Central
collar
Neck Collar
Dowel cut from solid

MISCELLANEOUS SECTION

This section contains various items generally done with dowel construction.

This is one of the simplest forms of jointing. If clean cut tight fitting holes are bored, and a top quality appropriate adhesive is applied correctly, much can be achieved within a short space of time with limited skill and tools. If a pedestal drill is available this can prove an added bonus.

Note :
Always fasten work down firmly during boring processes - better safe than sorry.
Also test bore and fit dowel in a waste piece of wood before boring the 'real thing'.

Wood African Limba. **Dowel** Honduras Mahogany.

Note :
The simple and effective use of dowel in these two useful everyday items.

Woods Framework African Limba. **Dowel** African Limba.
Bottom Plywood veneered with Rio de Janiro Rosewood.

CANDLE STICKS

An attractive highly decorative twin candle holder to act as a display unit for the table etc.

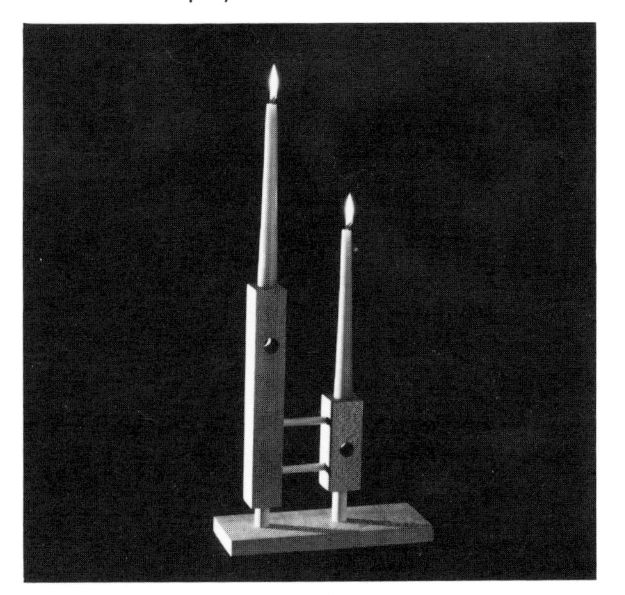

Wood Lacewood.

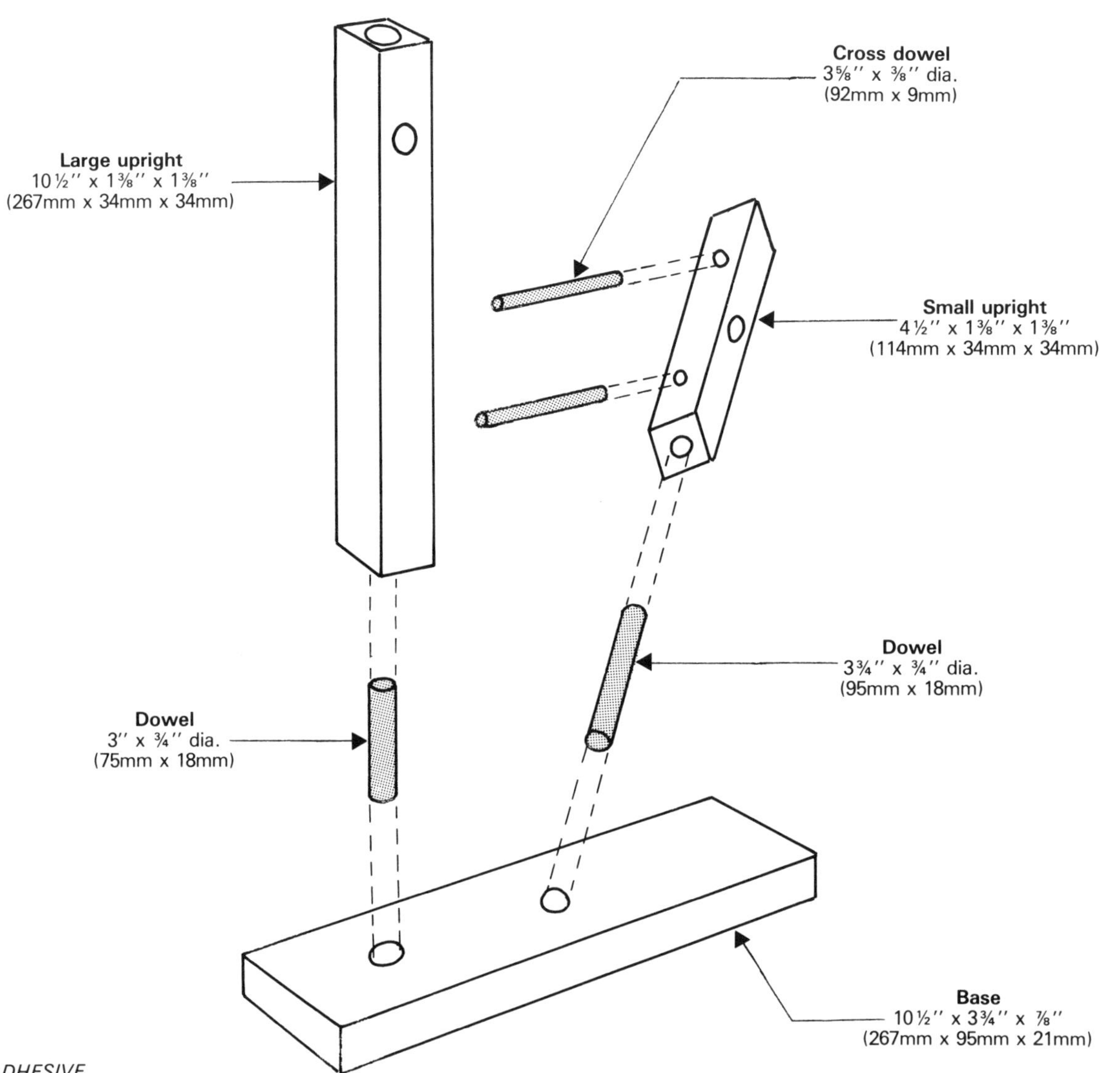

WORKING GUIDE

1 *Obtain and prepare appropriate materials to size.*

2 *Mark out centre of dowel holes and decorative and candle holes.*

3 *Bore decorative holes.*

4 *Test, then bore tight fitting holes for dowels and candles.*

5 *Test fit together.*

6 *Clean up with abrasives.*

7 *Apply a top quality appropriate adhesive, suggest TIMBABOND No.636 to dowel holes.*

8 *Tap fit together.*

9 *Wipe off any surplus adhesive with a clean damp cloth.*

10 *Leave to set thoroughly.*

11 *Fit and fix a furniture protective pad (leather or felt) to underside of base. Use a top quality appropriate adhesive, suggest TRETOBOND NON FLAM CONTACT ADHESIVE.*

12 *Clean up with abrasives.*

13 *Apply an appropriate finish.*

TABLE LAMP

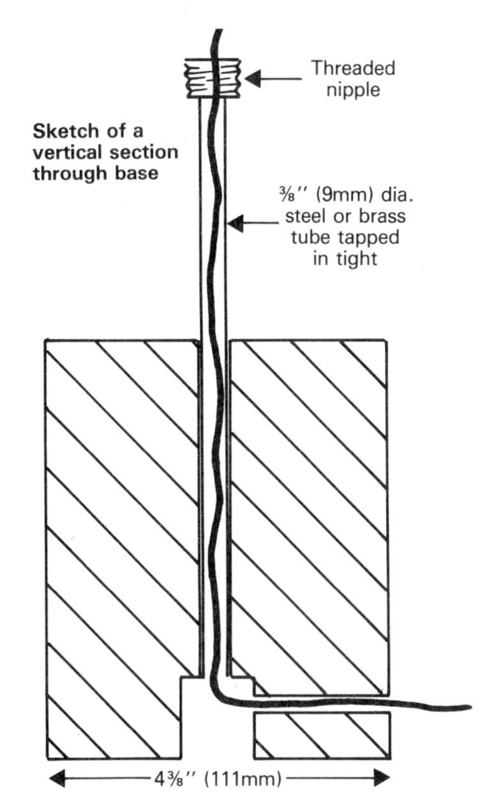

Cut decorative grooves with a tank cutter in a pedestal drill. Fasten the work down firmly and use the slowest speed possible. Fit and fix on bottom of base a furniture protective pad (leather or felt).

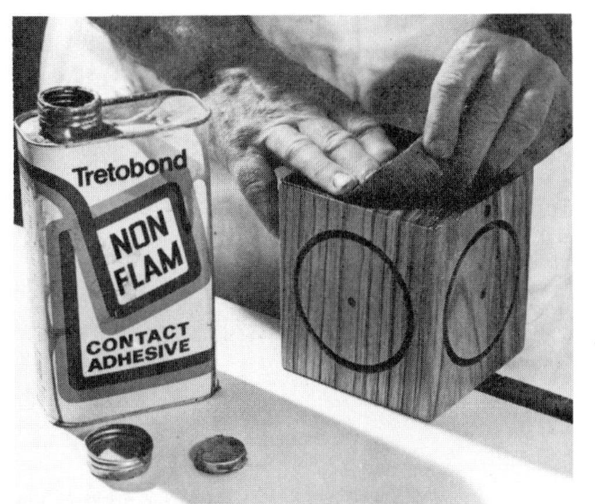

A heavy based attractive table lamp for service throughout the house. Simple to make and will stand heavy duty use.

Note :
Take great care in wiring up the plug and bulb holder. If you are not totally sure let an experienced person do the wiring - be sure!

WORKING GUIDE

1 *Obtain and prepare appropriate materials to size.*

2 *Mark out tube and wire hole centre.*

3 *Test, then bore tight fitting tube hole and side hole for wire.*

4 *Mark out centre of decorative circular grooves.*

5 *Form decorative grooves and be very careful cutting these with a tank cutter.*

6 *Clean up with abrasives.*

7 *Fit and fix nipple to tube end and tap fit into base.*

8 *Fit in wire.*

9 *Fit and fix a furniture protective pad (leather or felt etc.) to underside of base. Use a top quality appropriate adhesive, suggest TRETOBOND NON FLAM CONTACT ADHESIVE.*

10 *Clean up with abrasives.*

11 *Apply an appropriate finish.*

12 *Correctly wire up plug and bulb holder, and test carefully.*

Wood Pitch Pine.

CARVED HORS-D'OEUVRES TRAY

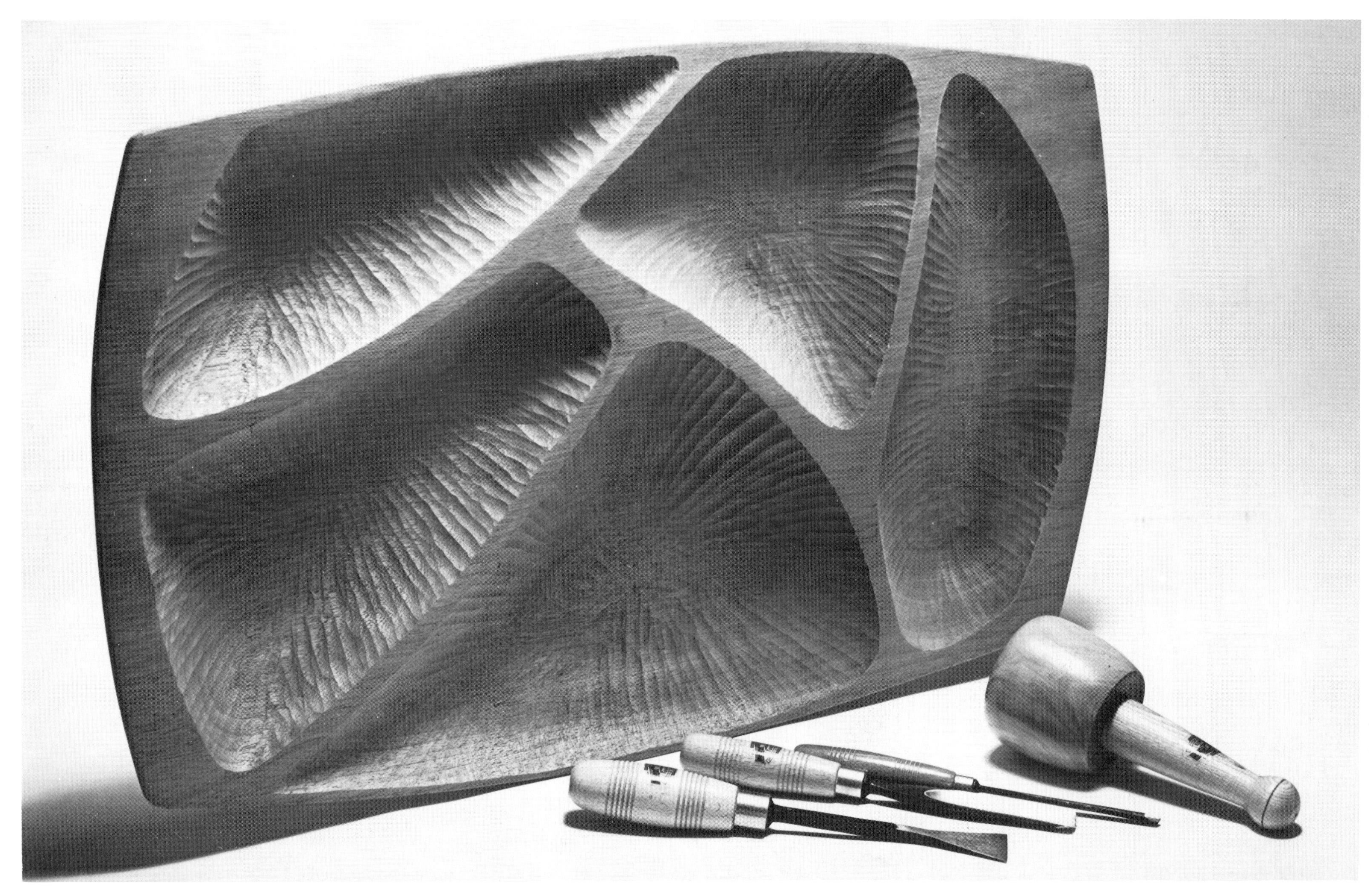

Wood Honduras Mahogany.

Part of the John Matthews collection.

CARVED LAMINATED BOWL

In these two miscellaneous examples note the excellent concrete bond achieved by TIMBABOND No.688 along the centre of the Carved Hors-d'oeuvres Hardwood Tray and by TIMBABOND No.636 in laminating the very porous carved round bowl in Pine Plywood.

Only appropriate top quality adhesives would hold joints together during the heavy gouging and hammering necessary to make such items - a tribute to modern adhesive technology.

Wood Laminated Pine Plywood.

Part of the John Matthews collection.

SPECIAL LARGE PROJECTS

In recent years it has been my pleasure and privilege to take part in many varied and unique projects, e.g. designing original and special items and restoration work, films, T.V. organising, International Exhibitions and visits on both sides of the Atlantic. Some I feel will be of interest to the readers and are worthy of inclusion in this section.

Art and craft to me has become a passport to developments of many kinds. It has also been the vehicle to promote excellent relationships over a wide area between different Nationalities, a theme so important if this World is to exist in future harmony for the benefit of all mankind.

Such a lot can be achieved through willingness and skilled hands if only goodwill is fervent and prevalent between all men.

Y.M.C.A. ALTAR

There is something special about making items for the House of God and I consider it a privilege and a necessary part of any designer's experience and work. This altar on the right was one I made in the early 1960's during my student residency at the Y.M.C.A. Nottingham for it's internal Chapel.

The design of the central panel I sketched direct from the random stone arrangement of different hues and sizes in the front of the altar in the sanctuary of The Old Cathedral Church of St. Michael's in Coventry, England.

This design, developed in various veneers, I thought would be appropriate and attractive for the central feature of the Y.M.C.A. Altar.

Details of the Altar :
Surround English Oak.
Crosses English Sycamore.
Vertical side panels Rio de Janeiro Rosewood.
Central panel numerous varied woods, including East Indian Satinwood, Ebony, Birds Eye Maple, Zebrano, Bubinga, Indian Laurel, Burma Teak, Padauk, African Mansonia, Australian Walnut, Silky Oak, Indian Rosewood, Avodire, Afromosia.

Owners - **Y.M.C.A., Nottingham, England.**

SCULPTING FILMS MADE IN NEW YORK CITY, U.S.A.

In the late sixties I was taken to New York City to make a number of 16mm films and concept loops on Creative Sculpting, sponsored by Stanley Tools of New Britain, Connecticut for educational and television release.

The studio was in the heart of the City and the director and owner Mr. Victor Kayfetz did all the camera work and much of the script. It was a very instructive experience to work under such a talented man, alongside Stanleys' very able Educational Adviser, Mr. Bob Campbell of Somera, Connecticut. The final results were well worth the effort of shipping and packing 200 fragile sculptures from England to the U.S.A. and of five weeks studio work in the centre of New York City.

The filming experience I gained under Victor and Bob have been invaluable in all the recent T.V. and film work I have done in this Country.

Studio Contact Sheets of some of the Film Sets for Creative Sculpting. Note the excellent use of super-imposed background subject matter.

CHURCH FURNITURE FOR THE U.S.A.

For many years I have had the pleasure and instructive experience of attending the American International Wood Carving Exhibition held at The Great Mississippi Valley Fair Grounds in Davenport, Iowa. This is a most wonderful Exhibition of it's kind and is staged tastefully in a modern well-lit dome at the centre of the general Exhibition ground. The man who developed it, and is second to none in his field, is the Secretary Chester D. Salter. He is always well ahead of his 'craft' in promoting entertainments of quality, and has done more than any other man to promote Wood Carving Exhibitions on an International Scale. His Exhibition has been the stimulant and model for many others to learn from and develop over it's many successful years.

Although it is an International Exhibition the nucleus is a true family affair with many of the best people in carving helping and attending in the development of each Exhibition.

There is always an excellent Banquet held in Davenport on the first Saturday of the ten day event, which is the highlight of the Woodcarving Calendar.

To win any ribbon at Davenport is truly a prize to cherish and be proud of - the competition is of such quality!

The Show always starts the first Thursday in August, and is well attended for the ten day duration. Often as many as 500 carvers make the trip to visit this unique spectacle.

In 1971 and 1972 Chester arranged for me to demonstrate and make during the Exhibition a communion table and a lectern for the Inter Denominational Chapel in St. Luke's Hospital, Davenport. The wood was to be cut from old Oak pews covered with thick varnish, dated 1876. These pews were salvaged from Trinity Cathedral, Davenport. The results can be seen on this page and I cannot think of anything more engaging and important than making for the House of God.

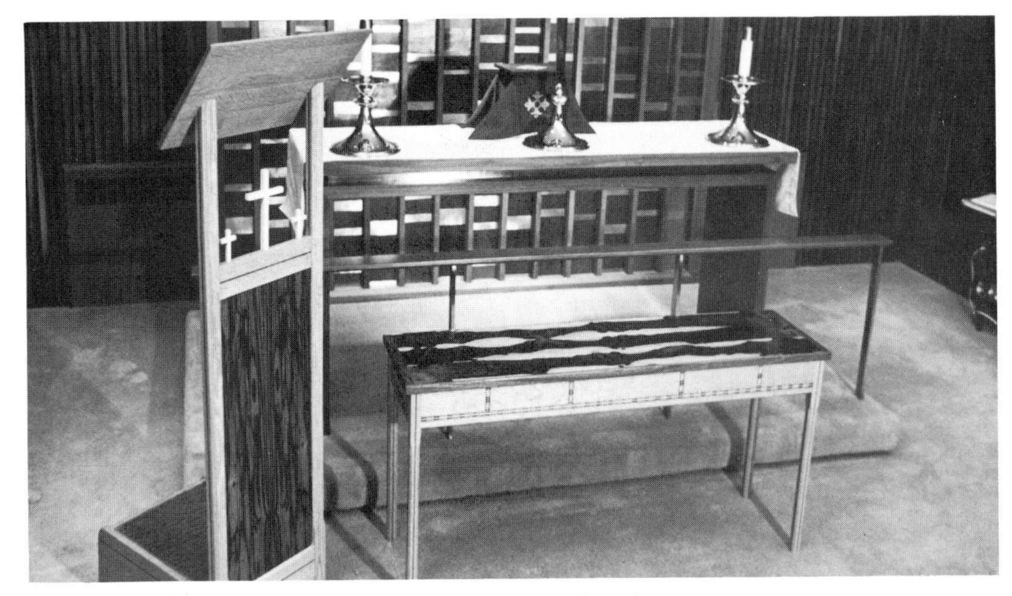

Woods for frameworks American Oak and Indian Rosewood Laminates.
Table top Rio de Janeiro Rosewood. **Inlays** Various Woods.
Lecturn front Ebony. **Crosses** English Sycamore.

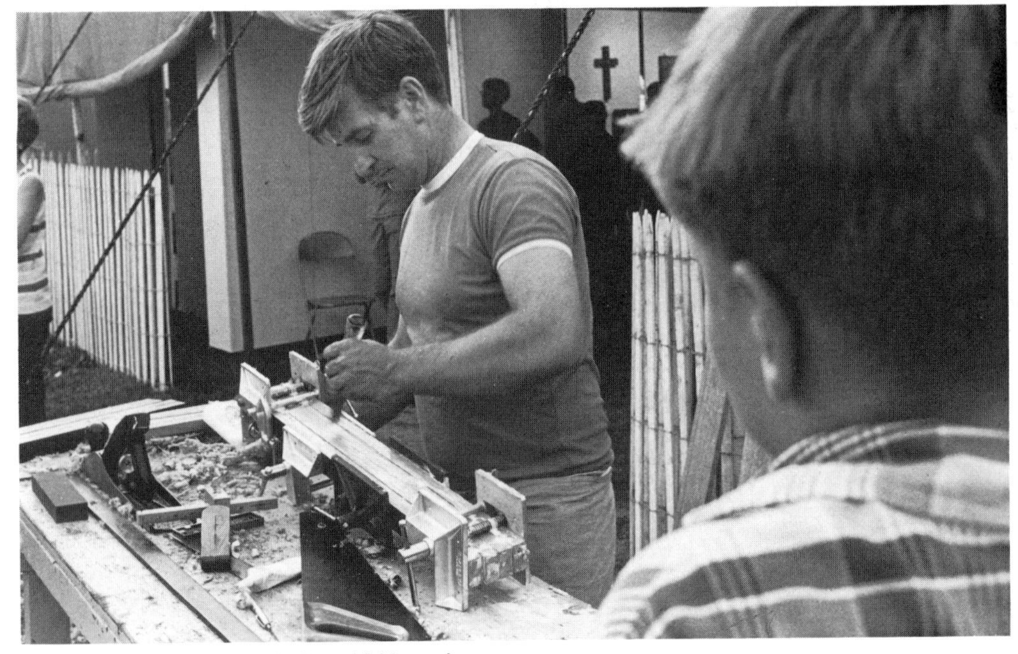

Laminating table legs outside the exhibition exit.

Polishing communion table.

The Chaplain, Author and Chester Salter.
Presentation at St. Lukes in August 1971.

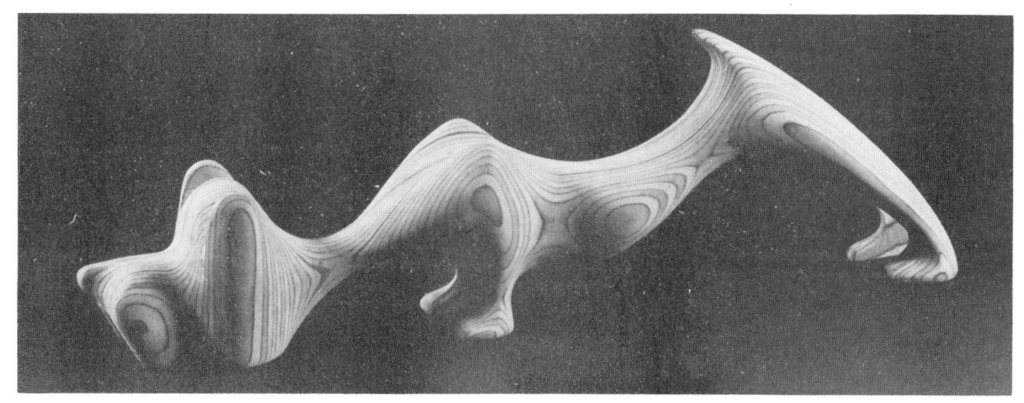

King Sniffer (carved at Davenport by the author). **Laminated Birch Plywood.**

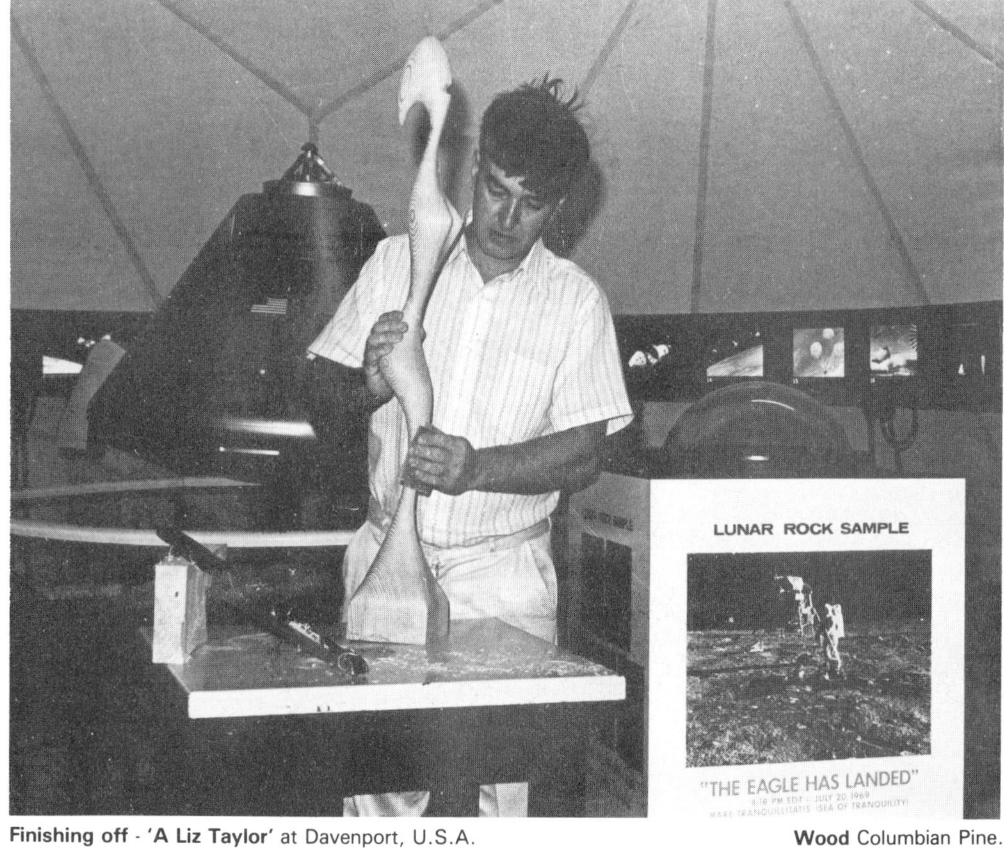

Finishing off - **'A Liz Taylor'** at Davenport, U.S.A. **Wood** Columbian Pine.
Owner - **Sam Cooper of Davenport, Iowa, U.S.A.**

'The Buffalo Hunter'
One of the many excellent carvings displayed at the Davenport Show. Carved by the wonderful artist Dixie Lea Muir of Oak Grove, Missouri, U.S.A.
Wood American Black Walnut.

THE CANADIAN NATIONAL EXHIBITION (C.N.E.)

In 1976 I was demonstrating sculpture at the American International Exhibition in Davenport, Iowa, when Mr. Douglas Palmer, a Director and Past President of the Canadian National Exhibition asked me if I would travel to his pending Exhibition in Toronto to discuss the possibility of developing an International Wood Carving Exhibition at the C.N.E.

Within one week I crossed the border into Canada, had initial discussions on the subject and was appointed Developer/Adviser to design and promote an International Wood Carving Exhibition for 1977 and 1978 of work from North American and other parts of the World.

The Exhibition had to be closely linked with agriculture, as this was the Branch of the C.N.E. which would sponsor and stage woodcarving in their East Annex Hall.

First I got down to the business of writing a total show programme, apart from the Decoy Section where I relied totally on Paul Burdette of Orton, Ontario to develop this section. He did so much in this area to make it a success and this Exhibition will always be in his debt.

In writing the programme I included a large general section of carving classes, something for every type of approach and technique, a beginners section, and very important - a section for youth. Also I included an introduction to the aims of the show, details of how to enter and entry forms, lists of awards, general rules and regulations, details of accommodation, demonstrations, sales, introduction to classification - in total a complete comprehensive booklet. This complete layout was forwarded to Toronto where I journeyed in the New Year to discuss the design of the Show Area.

During this development period I visited old friends, Henry Taylor Tools, William Marples Tools, Stanley Tools, Black and Decker, Ashley Illis to inquire direct if and where they would support the show and present their products as awards. They all gave generously and provided excellent demonstration staff at the C.N.E. Booths the following years. I visited all the judges I appointed, mainly from the U.S.A. and all did a first class job in what is always a very difficult task. They included Mike de Nike, Richard Belcher, Huber King, Herbert Siegel, Benoi Deschenes, Robert Campbell, and Bob Butler.

I also got in touch with leathercrafters and included the initial section in the 1978 Exhibition, appointing one of the leading lights in this field to judge the classes, Mr. Monty Higgins of Port Wayne, Indiana, U.S.A.

The printed programme were forwarded to many appropriate addresses of well known carvers throughout the World and I travelled to many Countries to meet various Carving Chapters to inform them about the Exhibition and encourage them to enter. Also I wrote Introductory Articles in various magazines on the Show Prospectus and Ed. Gallenstein did an excellent job in Chip Chats throughout the wide membership. Altogether I travelled over 80,000 miles promoting this woodcarving programme. Details of one travel itinery is included in this page.

For the first two Exhibitions I encourage and obtained the first hand help at the Show of many experienced carvers, e.g. Huber King, Dick Belcher, Ed. Gallenstein, Buddy Palmer, Steve Torda, who did so much to present and make those first two shows highly successful then, and for the future. We also had a great deal of help from the Davenport end by Chester D. Salter, who gave his experience, help and accommodation for carvings and to C.N.E. officials in a very generous manner and in the spirit of co-operation between the Shows.

The C.N.E. Show lasts 21 days and over 4 million attend the complete Show. It is a long duration for an exhibition and requires a great deal of work and much credit must go to the administrators Ross and Marian Farr and members of the permanent and occasional staff. All helped towards making a success.

Through such Exhibitions many of the general public become aware for the first time of the popularity of woodcarving and some good number take up the tools - the art is flourishing. What more could be asked!

Three wonderful helpers and the exhibition. Sam Cherone of Malden Mass U.S.A., Buddy Palmer of Pampa Texas U.S.A., Dick Belcher of Dayton Ohio U.S.A.

The Booklets

The Gold Award Winner for the Silver Jubilee. Display of work done by my pupils at Westbourne School, Nottinghamshire, England. Displayed at the 1977 C.N.E.

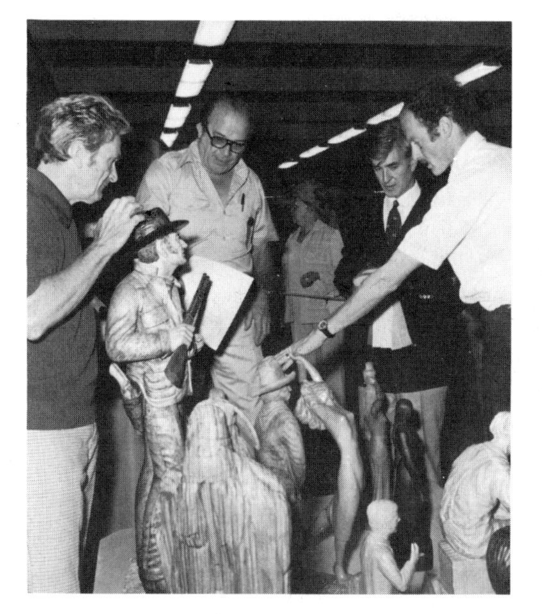

Judging duties with Professor Robert L. Butler, Michael de Nike, Benoi Deschenes.

Benoi Deschenes on St-Jean-Port-Joli, Quebec, Canada, magnificant best of show 1978. 'Les Voyageurs' (in basswood).

Presenting best of show trophy to Benoi at the Toronto banquet in 1978.

Huber the King of Windham Ohio, Great Award winning Carlsberg relief.
Wood Basswood.

An award winning realistic bird by a leading artist - Bob Ptasnick of Toronto, Canada.

Buddy Palmer of Pampa Texas, Wonderful Award winning complexed Buffalo Hunt entitled 'Buffalo Falls'.

TRANSATLANTIC PROJECT FOR THE SOUTHWELL MINSTER RESTORATION APPEAL 1978

My extensive travels for the Canadian National Exhibition throughout North America brought me in contact with a whole spectrum of top quality characters and artists who work creatively in wood, stone and leather. I fervently wanted to bring a large group of these over to England, and if possible for a good cause, as a worthy theme to display and demonstrate their skills and arts, and to entertain and help educate the general public in the wonderful hand work being created in North America. The programme would also have to combine work with pleasure, so they could enjoy a part holiday in our lovely Countryside and get to know the people.

The good cause was on my doorstep - for 1978 was a special restoration appeal year for the local Southwell Minster, the stone jewel of Nottinghamshire, 1,004 years old. A building of exceptional grace and devotion over the Centuries, and the mother Church of the Shire. The very amiable Provost, The Very Revd. J.F. Pratt liked the idea of Americans and Canadians coming over and helping by putting on demonstrations of their work for the benefit of the Appeal Fund. So the seed of the idea began to flourish early in 1977. We got together with various members of the Minster Staff and congregation who would provide the accommodation on a guest basis, and help with many other arrangements.

Initially I sent off invitations to 50 North Americans, right across the Continent and set about lining up an appropriate interesting itinerary, a mixture of work and holiday for our guests. I also visited the B.B.C. television studios at Pebble Mill to see an old friend who I had worked with before on television, the very able Producer, Roger Casstles, to see whether he would be interested in filming this event. He was, and produced an excellent unique film which has been screened several times, and no doubt through this has made many more people aware of Southwell Minster's Appeal and of the wonderful characters who helped from North America. The film was entitled very aptly 'THE PILGRIM CARVERS' which sums up the spirit of the programme.

NAMES OF NORTH AMERICAN ARTISTS

Edward F. GALLENSTEIN of Cincinatti, Ohio, U.S.A.
Herbert and Margaret SIEGEL of New York City, N.Y., U.S.A.
Michael and Jane DE NIKE of New Jersey, U.S.A.
Eugene and Ruth LANGHAUSER of Los Angeles, California, U.S.A.
Erwin and Dorothy CALDWELL of Gainsville, Texas, U.S.A.
John GARTON of Smith Falls, Ontario, Canada.
Paul and Dorothy BURDETTE of Orton, Ontario, Canada.
Bob and Jeanette CAMPBELL of Stafford Springs, Connecticut, U.S.A.
Bob and Heather PTASNIK of Toronto, Ontario, Canada.
Don and Edith MUELLER of Stretton, Illinois, U.S.A.
Richard and Barbara BELCHER of Dayton, Ohio, U.S.A.
George VANDER HEYDEN of St. Louis, Missouri, U.S.A.
Thomas CASSIDY of Morris, Illinois, U.S.A.
Louis ROTH of California, U.S.A.
Tony and Josephine SBLENDORIO and their son Mark, of New Jersey, U.S.A.
Robert and Norma HIBLE of Danville, Illinois, U.S.A.
William and Margaret BASSWOOD FISHER of Mercer, Montana, U.S.A.
Ross and Marian FARR of Toronto, Ontario, Canada.
Steve and Helen TORDA of Toledo, Ohio, U.S.A.
Monty and Carol HIGGINS of Fort Wayne, Indiana, U.S.A.
Sam and Alice COOPER of Davenport, Iowa, U.S.A.
Bob and Leola BINGHAM of Spring, Texas, U.S.A.
Professor Robert BUTLER and his wife of State College, Pennsylvania, U.S.A.
Arnold MIKELSON of White Rock, British Columbia.
Emile and Celia BOROS of Wayne, New Jersey, U.S.A.
Joseph and Pamela AVERSO of West Paterson, New Jersey, U.S.A.
Dale and Bea BERKE of Mountain Home, Arkansas.

ITINERARY OF VISIT

Wednesday 24th May
0800 Meet in London and travel North for lunch at Hardwick Hall, Derbyshire.
1800 Arrive at Southwell Minster, for hosts and guests to meet, and proceed to unpack at the various homes.
2030 Reception and Dinner at Saracen's Head given by Henry Taylor Tools of Sheffield.

Thursday 25th May
0915 Depart Southwell for Newstead Abbey Nottinghamshire for a tour of House and Gardens.
1200 Depart for lunch and tour of Marples Tools Dronfield near Sheffield.
1700 Travel back to Southwell and in the evening depart for Banquet at the Master Cutler's Hall at Sheffield provided by Marples Tools.
2400 Arrive back at Southwell.

Friday 26th May
0915 Depart Southwell for lunch and tour of Josiah Wedgwood Works, Stoke-on-Trent.
1630 Leave for dinner at the Castleton Hotel, Derbyshire.
2315 Return Southwell.

Saturday 27th May
1030 Depart Southwell for Felley Priory, Nottinghamshire, there to demonstrate and exhibit work.
1200 Lunch.
1330 to 1800 Exhibition.
1930 Late Dinner/Dance at Shoulder of Mutton.
2300 Back at Southwell.

Sunday 28th May
1800 Depart for Chatsworth for Exhibitions and Demonstrations all day. Packed lunch provided and evening meal at the Devonshire Arms, Baslow.
2315 Arrive Southwell.

Monday 29th May
0900 Depart Southwell for Chatsworth to put on demonstrations and exhibitions all day.
1700 Leave Chatsworth for an early dinner and Jazz Concert at The Blue Boar, Hucknall.
2300 Arrive Southwell.

Tuesday 30th May
0915 Depart Southwell.
1015 Arrive Edwinstowe, the centre of Sherwood Forest for demonstrations and exhibitions all day. Packed lunch, and dinner in the evening at The Blue Boar Inn, Hucknall. Evening Exhibition at The Blue Boar.
2330 Depart for Southwell.

Wednesday 31st May
0930 Depart Southwell for Bakewell, Derbyshire, for lunch. Depart Bakewell and arrive at Teversal Miner's Welfare for high tea, followed by demonstrations and exhibitions, a cricket match, brass band and marching displays and evening dance.
2330 Depart for Southwell.

Thursday 1st June
1020 Meet in Southwell Minster for Grand Tour.
1215 Lunch in Trebeck Hall.
1400 Working Exhibitions in Nave of Minster.
1930 Concert of American Music in the Minster and late dinner at Saracen's Head.

Friday 2nd June
Early morning visit to Nottingham and lunch at Trent Bridge Cricket Ground.
1930 Reception by Nottinghamshire County Council at County Hall.

Saturday 3rd June
1015 Leave Southwell for Thoresby Hall, Nottinghamshire to put on exhibitions and demonstrations all day. Return in the evening for farewell buffet supper at The Great Hall, Southwell Minster.

Sunday 4th June
0930 Visitors attend Service in the Minster, then leave for working demonstrations at Thoresby Hall, all day.

Monday 5th June
0900 North Americans depart for London by coach.

FOOTNOTE

Arising out of all this has come long standing friendships, founded between different Nationalities over a wide area. Awareness was focused on many important issues, and certainly 'Hands Across the Sea' became a living reality through this project. The issue of help between Nations is so important if the World in the future is to get over the International escalating problems. The Minster project was a marathon of a task, was complex and relied on so many people to help in different ways. I can't help but wonder if behind all this there was not a wonderful Guiding Hand.

Just off the bus for the initial reception by the provost and hosts at Southwell with the Minster in the background.

A good will and transatlantic friendship occasion at the United States Embassy in Grovesnor Square London during the presentation of a carving from Orange County court judge Eugene Langhauser of California to a British counterpart justice.

Two of the many happy characters

Count S. Torda of Toledo, Ohio, U.S.A.

Norm Davies of Tacoma, U.S.A. (specialist in carving toilet seats)

A working demonstration by a true 'Master' of relief carving Benoi Deschenes of Quebec, Canada, at the lovely Felley Prior home of those fine hosts, Major and the Hon. Mrs. Chaworth Muster.

RESTORATION PROJECT - THE VENICE SIMPLON ORIENT EXPRESS - GRANDS EXPRESS EUROPEANS

The Venice Simplon Orient Express which is scheduled for running in 1982 is to provide a twice-weekly luxury Waggons-Lits and Pullman Service on the London/Paris/Lucerne/Miland/Venice Route.

Some of the World's finest unique first class carriages of the 1920's vintage will be very carefully and lovingly restored to their full splendour. The whole project is unique to the World of working restoration and travel and it is a great pleasure and privilege to be working on such a venture to put the best of the past aright for future generations to admire and enjoy.

The Company behind this massive project is 'The Sea Containers Group'. My involvement came about through a chance meeting with the very amiable and dedicated Project Consultant, Mr. William Devitt early in 1979. Shortly after this meeting I was engaged to restore the marquetry panels on several carriages of the V.S.O.E. To restore these panels required a good deal of experimenting, plus technical advice in replacing areas of damage to exotic veneers and inlays. TRETOBOND LIMITED PRODUCTS and Staff proved extremely helpful in approaching and mastering this difficult task.

To restore this train is a courageous and giant enterprise, requiring a great deal of skill in design, engineering application, travel log and other skills of a wide spectrum and a massive investment. The Captain behind this unique project is the President of Sea Containers, Mr. J.B. Sherwood, under whose patronage all has been possible to once more 'steam' a train and 1920 carriages of unique refinement from London, through France, Germany, Austria, Switzerland, over the Alps into glorious Venice - what an undertaking! It has been my pleasure to have taken part in this restoration and present to the readers of this book a stimulating glimpse of some of the panels. The carriages I was mainly concerned with were AGATHA, ZENA, IBIS and IONE, all containing different marquetry designs in varying exotic woods. Their panels which thoroughly line the interiors required a great deal of restoration work to bring them back to their initial glory. Damp, frost, fire and sun had all taken their toll of them and resulted in peeling and bubbling of the veneer and inlay from their blockboard groundwork, in some cases complete panels were missing and large strips were absent.

All the panels were originally polished by the old fashioned traditional method - layers and layers of French Polish and this was largely responsible, for preserving most of the panelling in a condition where it was still possible to restore. The adhesives originally used were the old fashioned 'Slab Horse Glue' which in many areas had decayed under damp conditions and sometimes through the heat generated by scalding hot steam pipes. My task was a formidable one to clean down and strip where necessary and replace with matching veneer and inlay. It was quite a task just obtaining appropriate grained exotic woods of matching texture, e.g. Ebony, Satinwood, Yew etc. and finding the most appropriate adhesives were initially quite a task. I found difficult positioning and injecting of the adhesives was best done with a veterinary syringe with a large bore needle. Cramping was a problem solved by trial and error and led to home-made wooden G Cramps to solve, but after attending a meeting in London at Sea Containers Headquarters I realised that mine were but a few of the problems, but small, compared to the overall project's development, e.g. engineering, air conditioning travelling, administration etc.

Restoration is often more difficult than originating, and it should never be frowned upon in any way. We must preserve our heritage for the future, otherwise even more glass and concrete office blocks will obscure and totally blind all horizons, take us over, cold and insipid reflecting in their blatant glare cold comfort, void of artistry and craftsmanship which have inspired man in all cultures throughout the Centuries to produce the very best possible within minds and materials.

Creative Work is so important for it is the opposite of the scourge of mankind, destructivity, which should be totally alien to the existence of sensible civilisations.

Work on a Panel of Carriage IONE (English Yew).
Fitting a new area of veneer, then - cramping in position a new area and also cleaning up a lower solid kicking board.

A renovated panel of Ebony and Satinwood from carriage - AGATHA.

HOME MADE CRAMPS

I needed a great many cramps and because of the possibility of not requiring so many ever again and the expense of purchasing such a large number of factory made ones, I made with wood threads and taps simple and easy to manufacture and apply wooden ones using odd pieces of hardwood and plywood. The handle and shoe ends are adhered to the dowel and so is the plywood to the solid frame. Such cramps may prove economical to make and useful to the readers.

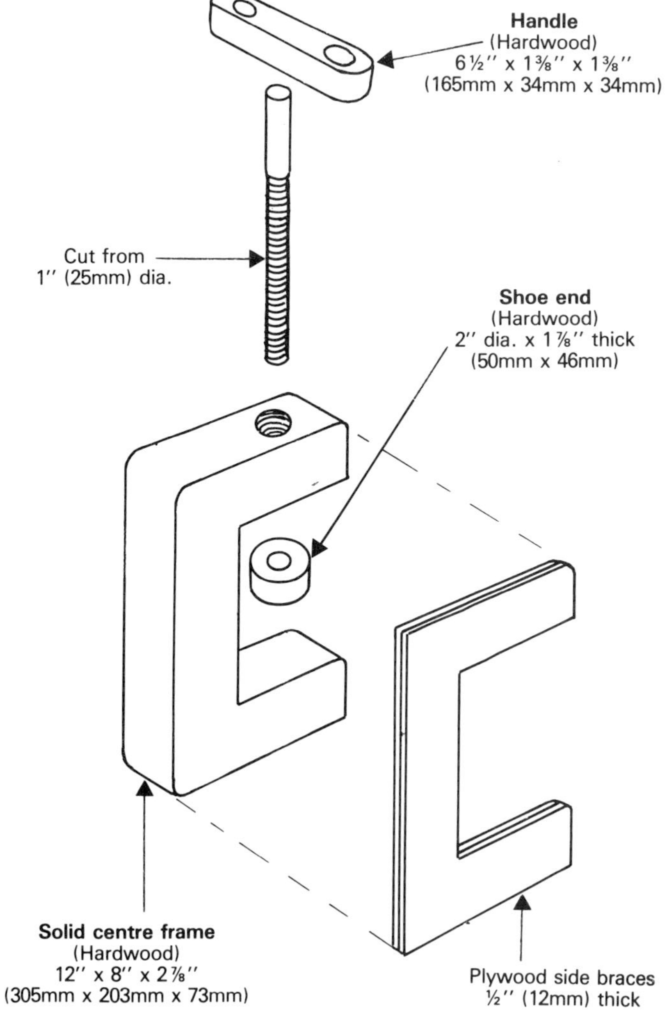

A good thread box and appropriate taps if applied with care and lubricated with linseed oil during cutting produces excellent results.
The CONOVER system of THREAD BOX AND TAPS is the best one I have come across - so many systems just do not work efficiently.
Address for enquiries: CONOVER WOODCRAFT SPECIALISTS INC., 18125 Madison Road, Parkman, Ohio 44080, U.S.A.

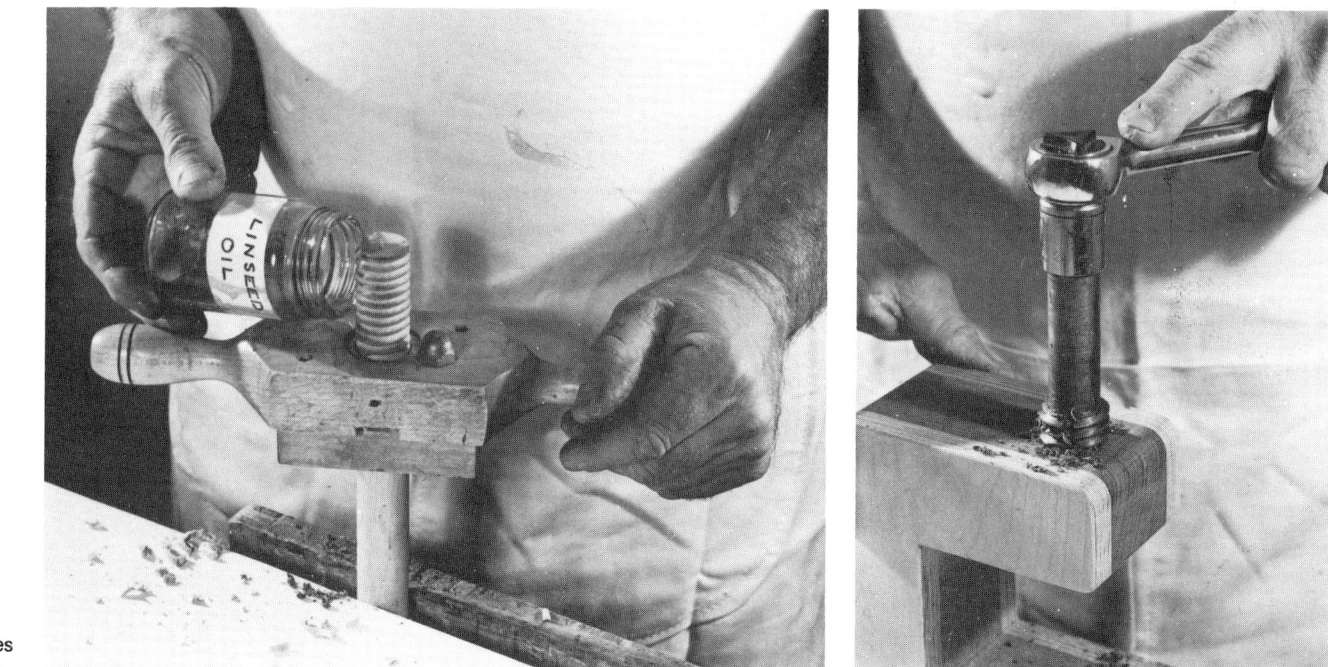

These photographs tell their own story - of damage and restoration.
TIMBABOND No.688 was mainly used for the difficult task.
The veneer and inlay consisted of Satinwood, Spanish Mahogany, Indian Rosewood, English Lime, etc.
V.S.O.E. Carriage - IBIS.

Laying out for photographing some of the re-conditioned panels of my favourite carriage of the V.S.O.E. - AGATHA, a satisfying moment after many months of hard work.

Woods mainly Satinwood and Ebony.

A happy time having just finished cutting and taping together the veneer of the last one of four new quartered panel replacements for the highly decorative carriage of V.S.O.E. - IBIS (what tales these carriages could tell).

ABSTRACTED SCULPTING FROM TREE BRANCHES

There is a great deal to be learnt from nature - the 'best designer' by far. These two pages have been specially included to give a basic foundation for working hand in hand with the natural formed shapes of tree branches developing abstracted sculpture. This type of sculpting is very interesting and helpful in developing observation skills and 'life' in sketching and shaping. It also gives a practical insight into tree construction and grain formation of wood. Basic work can be done at any age, the tools and skills required are limited and the results can be very stimulating and gratifying. Most types of trees produce suitable materials, e.g. Beech, Ash, Yew, Dogwood, Scotts Pine, Cyprus, Walnut, Chestnut, Willow, Maple, Oak, etc.

ONE METHOD OF APPROACH

1. *Look carefully for sharp angled or interesting twisted branches from suitable trees. It is surprising the wealth of material about and available on request.*
2. *Cut out any interesting areas of branches revolving them in all directions to view all the various structural possibilities.*
3. *After making up your mind on a particular 'raw sculpture' - saw to size.*
4. *Peel off any bark with a knife other than where it may be used as a feature, then develop the shape with files.*
5. *Make and fit any necessary base, clean up with abrasives, leave natural, or apply an appropriate finish.*

Working happily in a windfall tree sawing raw sculptural possibilities. Enjoying every minute in the woods, learning from examining and working in natural shapes has a lot to offer a would-be enthusiast.

Fledgeling

Wood Beech

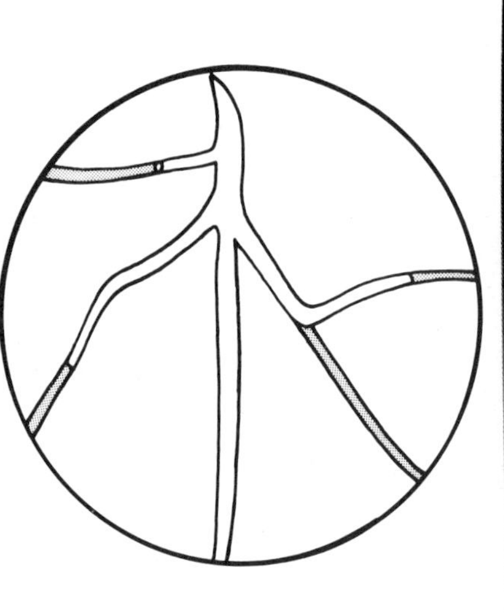

Dachshund

Wood English Yew

King Cockerel **Wood** Beech

Baseball Pitcher

One of the rare finds which occur from time to time. It was a freak formation due to damage during early growth.

SERVICES SECTION

HELPFUL ASSOCIATIONS

National Wood Carvers Association, Edward F. Gallenstein, Editor of 'Chip Chats', 7424 Miami Avenue, Cincinnati, Ohio 45243.

Ducks Unlimited, Inc., National Headquarters, P.O. Box 66300, Chicago, 111. 60666. (Dedicated to the conservation of waterfowl and perpetuation of the sport of duck hunting).

International Wood Collectors Society, Atten : W.G. Cookman, Secretary, 3155 Edsel Dr., Trenton, Mich. 48183.

Guild of Master Craftsman Publications Ltd., Parklands House, Keymer Road, Burgess Hill. Sussex. Tel : 0444645267.

INTERNATIONAL EXHIBITIONS

U.S.A.
International Wood Carvers Congress - A division of the International Folk Art Show held in conjunction with the Great Mississippi Valley Fair, 2815 West Locust Street, Davenport, Iowa 52804. First Thursday in August for ten days.

CANADA
Canadian Agricultural International Wood Carving Exhibition - Toronto. Exhibition Place, Toronto, Ontario M6K 3C3, Canada.

MAGAZINES

Wood Carvers Special Magazine, Chip Chats - Editor Edward F. Gallenstein, 7424 Miami Avenue, Cincinnati, Ohio 45243.

Craft Design and Technology News - Elliott Publications Ltd., 9 Queen Victoria Street, Reading RG1 1SY.

Practical Wood Working, Editorial Department, Kings Reach Tower, Stamford Street, London SE19 LS.

Do It Yourself, Link House, Dingwall Avenue, Croydon CR9 2TA.

Working Wood - Editor Tony Talbot, Five Poplars, Pankridge Street, Crondall, Farnham, Surrey.

Crafts Magazine - Editor Martina Margetts, Crafts Advisory Committee, 12 Waterloo Place, London SW 1Y.

Popular Mechanics, Box 646, New York, N.Y. 10019.

Workbench, P.O. Box 5966, Kansas City, Mo. 64111, U.S.A.

National Wildlife, 1212 Sixteenth St., N.W. Washington, U.S.A.

North American Decoys, Box 242, Heber City, Utah 84031, U.S.A.

MISCELLANEOUS

International Sculpture Center Bulletin, The University of Kansas, Lawrence, Kansas 66045. 743 Alexander Road, Pinceton, N.J. 08540.

Winston Churchill Memorial Trust, 15 Queen's Gate Terrace, London SW7 5PR.

FILM MATERIAL ON SCULPTING

Victor F. Kayfetz, Visual Instruction Productions, 295 West Fourth Street, New York, N.Y. 10014, U.S.A.

POLISHES, STAINS, GARNET PAPER, WAXES, ETC.

Fiddes & Son, Trade Street, Cardiff.

TOOLS MANUFACTURES

Carving Tools
Henry Taylor (Tools) Limited, The Forge, Lowther Road, Sheffield S6 2DR, England.

General Woodworking Tools
U.K.
Stanley Tools Ltd., Woodside, Sheffield S3 9PD.
U.S.A.
Stanley Tools Ltd., Division of Stanley Works, New Britain, Connecticut 06050, U.S.A.

Leather Working Tools
Tandy Leather Company, 3 Tandy Center, P.O. Box 2686, Forth Worth, Texas - 76101.

TOOLS SUPPLIERS

U.K.
Alec Tiranti Ltd., 21 Goodge Place, London W.1. and 70 High Street, Theale, Berks.

U.S.A.
Pentalic Corporation, 132 West 22 St., New York, N.Y. 10011.

Brookstone Company, 127 Vose Farm Road, Peterborough, New Hampshire 03458.

Wood Carvers Supply Co., 3056 Excelsior Blvd., Minneapolis, Minnesota 55416.

CANADA
Heinz Jordan, & Co. Ltd., 900 Magnetic Drive, Downsview, Toronto, Ontario M3J 2C4.

Benoi Deschenes, C.P. 563, St. Jean-Port-Joli, Quebec, Canada.

WOODS

Fitchett and Woollacott Ltd., Willow Road, Lenton Lane, Nottingham NG7 2PR, England.

U.S.A.
Constantine, 2050 Eastchester Road, Bronx, N.Y. 10461. (Also inlays).

Woodcraft Supply Co., 313 Montvale Ave., Mass. 01801, U.S.A.

Wood Carvers Supply Co., 3112-16 West 28th St., Minneapolis, Minn.55416, U.S.A.

Robert Butler, 341 East Waring Ave., State College, Pa. 16801, U.S.A.

Craft Tool Company, 1 Industrial Road, Word Ridge, New Jersey 07075, U.S.A.

E.J. Shiroda, 17910 Wood, Melvindale, Mich. 48122, U.S.A.

JEWELLERS FINDINGS

U.K.
Dryad, P.O. Box 38, Northgates, Leicester LE1 9BU.
U.S.A.
Rock Haven Art Metal Co., Box 8, Whitefield, N.H. 03598.
Grieger's Inc., 900 S. Arroyo Pky., Pasadene, Calif. 91109, U.S.A.
AUSTRALIA
Superior Gemstones Pty. Ltd., 42-44 Treacy Street, Hurstville, N.S.W. P.O. Box 266, Hurstville, N.S.W. 2220, Australia.

OTHER SELF PUBLISHING BOOKS BY THE AUTHOR

(All available direct from P.O. Box No. 13, Sutton-in-Ashfield, Notts, England).
The Stanley Book of Do It Yourself Furniture.
The American Bi-Centenary Book of Do It Yourself Natural Wood Sculpture.

RECOMMENDED BOOKS BY OTHER AUTHORS

Contemporary Carving and Whittling by W. Ben Hunt, (The Bruce Publishing Company, 866 Third Avenue, New York, N.Y. 10022, U.S.A.).

Carving Animal Caricatures by Elma Waltner, (Dover Publications, Inc 180 Varick Street, N.Y. 10014, U.S.A.).

The Craft and Creation of Wood Sculpture by Cecil C. Carstenson. (Publishers Charles Scribners & Sons, New York, U.S.A.).

The Art of Bird Carving by Wendell Gilley, (Published by North American Decoys, A. Division of Hillcrest Publications Inc). (P.O. Box 242 Heber City, Utah 84032, U.S.A.).

Let's Carve Wooden Placques and *How to Carve Faces in Driftwood*. (Harold L. Enlow, P.O. Box 18, Dogpatch, Ark. 72648, U.S.A.).

Books About Wood, RR3 Owen Sound, Ont., Canada.

Contemporary Costume Jewellery, Elyse Summer and *The Frame Book*, Thelman Newman, Jay Harltey Newman, and Lee Scott Newman. Crown Publishers Inc., One Park Ave., South, New York, N.Y. 10016.

Contemporary Art with Wood, Dona Z. Meilach, Crown Publishers Inc., 419 Park Ave., South, New York, N.Y. 10016.

Manual of Wood Carving and Wood Sculpture, Frederick A. Brunner, 369 High St., Westwood, Mass. 02090, U.S.A.

Creating Modern Furniture, Dona Z. Meilach, Crown Publishers Inc., One Park Ave., New York, N.Y. 10016.

Game Bird Carving, Bruce Burk, Winchester Press, 460 Park Ave., New York, N.Y. 10002 or an autographed copy from Bruce, 461 Brewer Road, Grass Valley, Calif. 95945, U.S.A.

Wood for Wood-Carvers and Craftsmen, Robert L. Butler, 341 East Waring Ave., State College, Pa. 16801, U.S.A.

How to Carve Totem Poles, Paul N. Luvera Sr., 2102 9th St., Anacortes, Washington 98221, U.S.A.

ACKNOWLEDGMENTS

This book has been sponsored by Tretobond Limited and inspired by the enthusiasm of W. Stefan Koprowski, their Managing Director.

I am also indebted to :

Her Majesty, Queen Elizabeth II.
The Duke and Duchess of Devonshire, Chatsworth House, Derbyshire.
The United States of America Embassy, Grosvenor Square, London W.1.
The Southwell Minster Authorities, Southwell, Nottinghamshire.
Bob Hope - Entertainer Elite.
J.B. Sherwood, President of Sea Containers, and Captain behind the Venice Simplon Orient Express.
Mr. William Devitt, Alain de la Motte, Malcolm Peakman, Thelma Stevenson, Maggie Gibbs, Bob Timmings, Charlie Watts, and the rest of the excellent staff of Sea Containers.
Designers John Sleep and David Miles.
Edward F. Gallenstein, President of N.W.C.A.
Chester D. Salter, Secretary of the Great Mississippi Valley Fair.
Stanley Tools, Woodside, Sheffield, and Stanley Tools, New Britain, Connecticut, U.S.A.
British Airways, Nottingham, London and Rome.
Nottinghamshire County Council.
Henry Taylor Tools, The Forge, Sheffield.
Dennis Abdy and David Rogers.
Fitchett and Woollacott Limited, Nottingham.
Celcon Limited of London.
Lervad, U.K. Ltd.
Lotus Cars Limited, Norwich, Norfolk.
Derek Wroughton of Dryad, Leicester.
Black and Decker Ltd., Maidenhead, Surrey.
Simon Chapman, Kingsway Public Relations, Doughty Street, London.
Elliott Productions Limited, Reading.
The Canadian National Exhibition, Toronto, Canada.
Mr. Herbert Siegel, Director of Industrial Arts, New York City, New York, U.S.A.
Victor F. Kayfetz, Visual Instruction Productions, New York City, New York, U.S.A.
Royal Doulton Tableware Limited, Stoke-on-Trent, Staffordshire, England.
A.V. Instruction Systems, Somers, Connecticut, U.S.A.
Josiah Wedgwood and Sons Limited, Barlaston, Staffordshire.
The Charles Dorin Partnership, Harrow on the Hill, Middlesex.
R. and J. Roberts, Alfreton, Derbyshire.
The Mettoy Co. Ltd., Northampton, NN5 7XA.
J. Denys Britton, Woodthorpe, Nottingham.
Rod Shirley, Ad-Print Services.
The lovely young ladies who acted as models for the jewellery.
The numerous children who helped in testing the toys and making some excellent suggestions in re-vamping original test models.
My grateful thanks go to my wife Marian for typing the MS, for a limitless supply of hot coffee and other help and, above all, for encouragement and patience.

PHOTOGRAPHERS

Brian Cocker ARPS, Director, Barmouth Studios, Sheffield.
Tom W. Brynes of Chicago, Illinois, U.S.A.
John Wilkinson of New Market, Ontario, Canada.
Aeronews Int., Fiumicino Aeroporio, Italy.
Eric J. Wala, Davenport, Iowa, U.S.A.
Victor F. Kayfetz of Visual Instruction Productions, New York City, U.S.A.
Geoff Bell of Gotham, Nottinghamshire, England.
Neil Lancashire of Kirkby-in-Ashfield, Nottinghamshire, England.
David Hague of Sheffield, Yorkshire, England.
Grid Studios, Sheffield, Yorkshire, England.
Wedgwood P.R. Department, Barlaston, Staffordshire, England.
J. Walters and Associates Ltd., Mexborough, Yorks.
Dryad, Northgates, Leicester.

Footnote :
We all depend on each other in doing anything worthwhile and all those above did a great deal in many aspects of developing this book.

My sincere appreciation.

JOHN MATTHEWS